Undoing Time

ADVISOR IN CRIMINAL JUSTICE TO
NORTHEASTERN UNIVERSITY PRESS
GIL GEIS

Undoing Time

American Prisoners in Their Own Words

Edited and with an Introduction by Jeff Evans

Foreword by Jimmy Santiago Baca

Afterword by Craig Haney

(2001)

Northeastern University Press
Boston

Northeastern University Press

Library of Congress Cataloging-in-Publication Data

Undoing time : American prisoners in their own words / edited and with
    an introduction by Jeff Evans ; foreword by Jimmy Santiago Baca ;
    afterword by Craig Haney.
        p. cm.
    ISBN 1–55553–459–7 (cloth : alk. paper)—ISBN 1–55553–458–9-
(pbk. : alk. paper)
    1. Prisoners—United States—Biography. 2. Prisons—United States.
3. Prisoners' writings, American.   I. Evans, Jeff, 1961–

    HV9468.U53   2000
    365'.6'092273—dc21
    [B]   00–034875

Designed by Janis Owens

Composed in Caledonia by Coghill Composition Company in Richmond,
Virginia. Printed and bound by Edwards Brothers, Inc., in Ann Arbor,
Michigan. The paper is EB Natural, an acid-free sheet.

MANUFACTURED IN THE UNITED STATES OF AMERICA
04   03   02   01   00   5   4   3   2   1

To the endless memory of my father,
Dr. William T. Evans

Contents

Foreword by Jimmy Santiago Baca   *ix*

Acknowledgments   *xiii*

Introduction   *3*

Back in the Dayz

1937   Richard Hinger   **15**

The Mystery of Aunt Lilly   Lou Torok   **19**

The Chicken   Charles C. Mallos   **23**

110ᵗʰ Street   Darlene Nall   **26**

Where I Come From   William Skeans, Jr.   **29**

Invisible   C. Kaye Ferguson   **37**

I Killed My Wife   Oscar Chandler   **39**

Turned Out   Lamont Bolder   **47**

A Shot in the Dark   Christopher Lynn Garner   **55**

Back in the Dayz   Lalo Gomez   **63**

Martha   Ronald Gearles   **73**

End of the Game   Kevin Lee   **76**

Years without Days

Revolving Door   Robert L. Johnson   **87**

From **From the Inside Out**   Jeff Parnell (with Mike McLane)   **95**

Danny   Steven King Ainsworth   **102**

Another Day   Michael Wayne Hunter   **107**

Reflections from Death Row   Michael Ross   **112**

**What It's Like Being a Drag Queen in the Illinois
   Department of Corrections**   Tonya Star Jones   **118**

Prison Break Memoirs   Nemo Valentine   **122**

Grief behind Bars   Phillip Santiago   **127**

Christmas: Present   Robert Chambers   **135**

What Happened to Your Message?   Barry Conn   **138**

Upon Completing Twenty Years   Easy Waters   **146**

Salvation

Notes from Life and Death   Benjamin La Guer   **163**

The Ice Man Speaks   Cheyenne Valentino Yakima   **168**

One Hundred Soldiers   D. Michael Martin   **179**

A Part of Me Set Free   Kevin James   **185**

The Prison Pump   Jon Marc Taylor   **194**

Freedom from Within   Jennifer Howard   **198**

Hired at the Last Hour   John Beasley   **207**

When Student Teaches Teacher   Larry Bratt   **214**

Prison as Monastery   Ronnie Turner   **216**

Jaye's Story   Jaye Bookhart   **220**

Salvation   Juan Shamsul Alam   **223**

Reunion   Christopher J. Rodriguez   **234**

The Tale of a Kite   Larry Bratt   **242**

Afterword by Craig Haney   245
Editor and Contributors   257

Foreword

When I started reading *Undoing Time*, a con named Vincent came to mind. I'd helped him parole out: got him a job, his book published, paid literary readings, an apartment, and a car. Six months later, he relapsed into heroin and cocaine and went on a robbing spree. He hit everyone who had helped him, taking even our computers with years of our work stored in them, many without backups.

I wondered how many of these writers were like Vincent. Despite being sympathetic (I too served time in a maximum-security facility), I had grown cynical. I expected remorseless renditions blaming others for their situations, querulous ideologies with a revolutionary mission, or self-pitying defiance.

These writers' stories are anything but self-serving, however, and they quickly changed my frame of mind. Perhaps because writing changes both reader and writer and helps one to reflect and understand what happened, I sensed that writing these narratives became a creative way for these prisoners to reenter society. Because society wouldn't let them in, they invited society into their world. By doing so, they've become known men and women. And to become known by others is to have others acknowledge your existence and witness your life as a human being.

Most of these writers lived in dark voids under indescribable abuse. Writing helped shatter the dissociative survival modes of their harrowing lives by breaking the routine pattern of obsessive repetition that their criminal activity represented. The achievement of each story is that the reader is given a memorable opportunity to understand these prisoners in a more benign light. We begin to see them differently. Our first realization is that they are not all the predatory ogres the media and politicians said they were.

I read on, and my comfort zone of stereotypes began to erode as I saw them as strangely familiar people. The apathy that had allowed me to dismiss them was replaced now by my realization of how severely they lacked self-esteem.

For the last fourteen years, I've struggled to recover my own self-esteem. I have had not only hundreds of people helping me, a loving girlfriend and kids, but academic distinctions and literary acclaim as well. Still, with all that, it's been an unimaginably painful journey. I wouldn't have made it without support from many social quarters. Imagine having no support, the barest grounding for elementary socialization cut, and being left at the mercy of degenerate adults.

That's the tale these stories convey. Sweeping aside the glamorous versions of crime that Tinsel Town portrays in movies, they sketch out portraits of grim, powerless lives filled with violence, broken families, and excruciating negligence. For most of these writers, their childhood environment consisted of dope fiends, alcoholics, or thieves who lied, cheated, stole, and raped, plundering their innocence and any chance of a normal life. When this happens to you as a kid, it virtually guarantees you'll end up behind bars.

And the more poor people we have behind bars, the more correctional stocks soar and investments pay off golden dividends. The institutionalization of human beings has become a profitable, multibillion-dollar industry where convicts are marketable commodities on Wall Street. Of course, you can't have this lucrative business destroying lives without the media toying with people's fears. John Doe, the diligent citizen, doesn't have time to check into it and analyze the truth—he's gravy-training on the economic prosperity wagon too. Sure, the media perpetuates the perception that criminals eat children and massacre the innocent. Sure, the street corner kid is a rich dealer with homes in the Bahamas and millions brimming his bank accounts. Sure. We are obliged to lie to ourselves because we know that from President Clinton on down to the lowliest county jail turnkey, it's all about money and connections—the food chain—not justice. Buying a new boat or a new truck is far more conducive to the general good and a more peaceful society than having treatment facilities or community involvement.

Over two million people in the United States are locked up behind bars. From that pool of mostly nonviolent offenders comes a handful in *Undoing Time*, to break the silence and chisel at our blind bias. We are all connected to a national madness that absurdly expects prisoners to change for the better as we deep-freeze them in six-by-nine cells and torture them in inhumane environments. We seek to reduce crime while we do everything in our power to create it. We pay lip service to compassion and demand unmitigated punishment. We want to empower those with the least power in society and yet violently oppress the voices that speak up for the poor. Crime has become primetime entertainment—you purchase an *America's Most Wanted* subscription and get a baseball cap for free. We numb our discerning faculties as we indulge in the sensationalized spectacles of famous people in limos and tuxedos that have demoralized our sense of decency.

Against this background of greed and indifference, these writers, through the redemptive act of writing, announce to the world beyond the walls and bars that a spark of life still burns in them. From this vulnerable source, where their words collide with their damaged spirits, they strip away the armor and communicate their humanity. They never expected to find themselves exiled from society and, in some cases, condemned to death. Yet they don't write to avenge themselves or to plead their cases, but to communicate who they are and what went wrong. It's their version, not the legal drivel with which lawyers and court documents or hysterical media assault us. These men and women were not born bad. They simply didn't have the resources mobilized in their behalf. They are the displaced, the disposable, and the dispossessed—the forgotten ones. Their stories are about the dues they paid for making bad decisions—decisions that, largely owing to their own inventiveness, they've survived.

Writing helped these men and women figure out what happened. As one word led to another, the wasteland of their lives came into focus and made terrible sense. Their writing justifies them and the experiences they lived. As writers, they saw things differently because the words they wrote were unlike the words they usually used. When they wrote, they released feelings they had never allowed themselves to feel safe enough to express in any other environment. With their internal ears they heard their own stories being told as they would tell them. At this climactic crossroads, their journey became spiritual—they became meaningful human beings in a society that had branded them as nothing more than worthless criminals.

Here, finally, are voices that represent open doors to hearts that share what life is like behind enemy lines. The words of those facing execution imbue the text with honesty and give the anthology its rigorous reckoning. These stories let us comprehend the moral dilemmas of prisoners and never delude us with patriotic anthems of rehabilitation. These writers explore how they became unknown men and women and, through their stories, invite us on their odyssey of becoming known men and women.

Jimmy Santiago Baca
Albuquerque, New Mexico

Acknowledgments

Many gifted and generous people contributed to the preparation of this book. Terry White at *Inside Journal*; Alice Green and Robin Busch at the Center for Law and Justice, Inc., in Albany, New York; Jenni Gainsborough at the National Prison Project in Washington, D.C.; Sheila Maroney at the Fortune Society in New York; Ellen Friedland at PWA; and Nolan Williams at *Inner Voices* all helped get word out to prisoners across the country about my work at no expense to me. Jimmy Santiago Baca, America's greatest living poet, gave the project his blessing. Reza Asef, Keith Hamilton Cobb, Chris Cozzone, Gordon Eng, Carol Evans, Mark Evans, Craig Haney, Steven Ling, Margarett Loke, Alane Salierno Mason, Oscar Medina, Evangeline Morphos, Saundra Reilly, Karen Rowe, Karine Schaefer, Anthony Serfes, Antonio Soddu, Janice L. Sugarman, Steven Tate, and Andrew Wallenstein lent guidance, comfort, protection, selflessness, and their invaluable opinions. The thirty-five men and women whose words fill this book endured over seventy rejections with me; without them, *Undoing Time* would not be. Bill Frohlich, Emily McKeigue, Sarah Rowley, and Larry Hamberlin at Northeastern University Press provided an oasis for this project. Their care, vision, insightfulness, and expertise are all reflected here. Finally, I must single out Christopher Rodriguez, who inspired this work and read through hundreds of manuscripts with me in 1996 and '97, but who also did a meticulous copyediting job when the original manuscript was completed.

I thank them all.

Undoing Time

Introduction

Shortly before the U.S. Supreme Court struck down the death penalty in *Furman v. Georgia* in 1972, my father brought me to a roadside attraction in western Massachusetts. It consisted of a simple trailer parked outside a busy shopping center. Inside was a mock setting for an impending execution. In one corner, a frightened-looking mannequin stared at me from behind the bars of a makeshift cell. A few feet away was a wooden chair outfitted with electrodes and heavy leather straps. One of the correctional officers hosting the display invited me to sit in the chair, but I was too mesmerized by the figure behind the bars to move. Intended to instill fear and loathing, the spectacle succeeded only in arousing my sympathy.

That experience affected me long after the ghastly peep show was hauled away, never to return. Even after capital punishment was reinstated in 1976, I continued to wonder about the people whose lives had ended so grimly, and others who were caged like animals for years and sometimes decades. I had no idea who they were, only that they must have done something terrible and that they paid dearly for it. I wondered: Were they always bad? What were they like as kids? Did anybody ever love them?

Films and television have significantly affected what we know and how we think about prisoners. TV news programs regularly highlight the misdeeds of the most nefarious offenders. Hollywood, too, has been fascinated by the subject. For the most part, filmmakers have stuck to the stereotypical portrayal of convicts first promulgated in prison films of the 1930s and '40s (*Each Dawn I Die* and *Brute Force*, for instance): the convict as a helpless victim, preyed upon by a ruthless predator who is eventually brought to justice by the movie's hero. The current HBO drama series *Oz*—a sadistic, male version of the 1980s cult TV series *Prisoner: Cellblock H*—attempts to inject realism into its story lines by posing hard-hitting questions about the judicial system. But with its endless scenes of men being eviscerated, raped, or tortured, *Oz* is as much about American justice as *Seinfeld* was about something.

For true-to-life accounts of prisoners, you need to turn to convict writers. In his remarkable 1998 anthology *Prison Writing in 20th Century America*, H. Bruce Franklin traced the rich history of modern American prison writing to the plantations and penitentiaries of the post–Civil War South. Much of the convict writing then was in the form of prison work songs, which had evolved from slave songs, and later became a wellspring for many popular American musical forms, most notably the blues.

In the early 1900s perhaps America's best-known prison writer, Jack London, wrote about his harrowing experience as a prisoner in a New York penitentiary when he was barely eighteen. His crime: "having no fixed abode and no visible means of support." Half a century later, Malcolm X penned his landmark *Autobiography of Malcolm X*, which gave rise to a number of other noted works by prisoners in the decades that followed, including *Attica Diary* by William Coons, *In the Belly of the Beast: Letters from Prison* by Jack Henry Abbott, *Committing Journalism: The Prison Writings of Red Hog* by Dannie Martin, and *Live from Death Row* by Mumia Abu-Jamal.

Although the United States now imprisons more of its citizens than any other country in the world, prison writers remain relatively few and far between. Obviously, writing is not the number one career choice among convicts, and illiteracy in the prison population is high. But what few works they have produced have additional significance.

In the preface to his 1994 collection of offbeat prison vignettes, *Iron House: Stories from the Yard,* Jerome Washington wrote: "In prison . . . authority is capricious, thoughts are contraband and writing is a deadly, serious business." What was he referring to? While Washington was serving time at Attica during the post-riot 1970s, officials confiscated his

4

typewriter, manuscripts, and years of research before he sued the state for violating his First Amendment rights—and won.

Correction officials also tried to suppress Dannie Martin's writing. Martin was placed in solitary confinement for having his essays published in the *San Francisco Chronicle* in the mid-1980s. His subject: the brutal conditions he observed in the federal penitentiary in California where he was serving time for bank robbery. (And as several writers whose work appears in this book would inform me, over the years they too had their cells ransacked and their writings seized by prison officials.)

Although these prison writers offered stark glimpses of their world within prison walls, I still wondered about who they were. I was interested in their personal histories, in the people who mattered to them, in how they viewed their crimes and the people who put them behind bars, and in what they expected once they were freed. Most of all, I wanted to know what they thought of themselves, and if any of them ever took responsibility for their actions or sought forgiveness or made a conscious choice to end their criminal thinking and behavior.

As a survivor of several encounters with criminal violence, including having my throat slashed during a robbery by a gang of teenagers wielding meat cleavers in a New York City subway, I had to set aside my prejudices—and my fears—to begin this task, which, ironically, I began with the assistance of a prisoner convicted of a violent crime.

In 1993 I met Christopher Rodriguez, a streetwise and well-read young man serving time at a maximum-security facility in upstate New York. Chris had been published in national and local magazines, and I was impressed by his literary skills. I asked him if he might be interested in helping me with a prison writing anthology I was putting together, by reading manuscripts and giving me his thoughts. He agreed to help.

In 1996 I began soliciting autobiographical writings from prisoners nationwide by placing ads in magazines, newspapers, and prison newsletters. I received hundreds of submissions. Some of the envelopes bore postmarks from familiar-sounding places like Attica, San Quentin, and Soledad. But most were mailed from backcountry towns with names like Eight Mile, Alabama; Stringtown, Oklahoma; Humble, Texas; and Swanton, Vermont. A few towns had names that seemed incongruous with prison: Freeland, Michigan, and West Liberty, Kentucky, for example. Men and women from their late teens to late seventies submitted work. Whites, blacks, Latinos, and prisoners of Native American ancestry all contributed manuscripts (although I received none from prisoners of Asian descent).

I was astonished at the range of occupations the writers represented. They included cops, firemen, physicians, lawyers, gangsters, computer programmers, war veterans, dope peddlers, pizza shop owners, truck drivers, graduate students, grandfathers, grandmothers, musicians, slackers, executives, the homeless—even a Catholic priest and a playwright nominated for the Pulitzer Prize.

A reflection of the American prison population, submissions by men far outnumbered those by women. Many writers indicated that they were high school dropouts. Some had obtained their general equivalency diplomas while in prison. A small number had attended college or received advanced degrees. Their crimes ranged from check forgery to armed robbery to rape and serial murder. Many had drug-related convictions. A few cases had gotten national attention.

Oscar Chandler's "I Killed My Wife" was one of the first pieces I received. This eighty-two-year-old retired truck driver from Illinois explains why, at age seventy-seven, he had used a dog leash to strangle the woman he calls "my love, my life, my companion and co-pilot." Chandler begins his shocking tale: "I took a life that I revered tremendously. After considerable soul searching, I am content that I did this."

Several former gang members submitted work, but Lalo Gomez's saga "Back in the Dayz," detailing his violent odyssey through various Chicago neighborhoods in the 1960s and '70s, was the most riveting. Here he recounts with disturbing bluntness an event that followed a beating by rival gang members:

> The next day, we caught the . . . Greasers who'd beaten us down as they were chillin' at a theater near their hood. As they were sitting there enjoying a Bruce Lee flick, me and Romero walked up behind them and slit their throats. One of them choked on his blood and ended up joining his leader. The other one lived but will never talk again.

A few writers used the opportunity to write about the abuse they had suffered as children. Some of their disclosures are shattering. In

"Where I Come From" William Skeans recalls how a timely visit by a social worker saved him from certain death at the hands of his enraged foster father:

> The woman in red had arrived at the house as Richard was swing-ing my limp body by the ankles, slamming me against the walls and floors. The woman in red had reached into her purse and withdrew a small-caliber pistol she carried for protection. She had to shoot Richard three times before he stopped.

I received a number of submissions from prisoners serving life sen-tences. C. Kaye Ferguson, a lifer in Tucson, Arizona, recalls in ominous detail the moments before she left for school on the day her father, an army officer, shot himself in the head:

> He was overtired and understandably quiet through breakfast. During the few minutes before I had to leave for school, I showed him a project that was due that day. The exceptionally long time he studied it made me uneasy.
>
> A gun belt and holster containing my dad's army-issue .45 pistol were draped over the back of the chair my schoolbooks were sit-ting on.

In contrast, Larry Bratt, a literacy tutor serving two life sentences in Maryland, describes the overflowing joy one of his students, a grown man, experienced when he realized he could read by himself for the first time. In "When Student Teaches Teacher" Bratt recounts:

> One day . . . magic occurred. Kevin read an entire three pages . . . before he asked me to help him with the word *fledgling*. Before I could respond, that beautiful lightning bolt struck. His face illumi-nated with joy. Then, just as suddenly, he was wiping his eyes, but he couldn't stop the flood.

Several men under sentence of death also contributed their writings. In "Another Day" Michael Hunter, an inmate on San Quentin's death row, describes a surreal moment in one of the prison's exercise yards:

> As I watch the condemned men sweating in the sunlight, I begin to imagine the marbled headstones bearing the chiseled names of

their murdered victims scattered about the yard. Suddenly, the exercise yard becomes more crowded as we are joined by the ghosts of the victims of the violence that led to death row.

I see one man followed by more than a dozen crying and sobbing boys, asking why he had to take their lives.

The loss of loved ones, particularly fathers, was a recurring theme. Having lost my own father without warning when I was in my twenties, I could empathize with the many prisoners who wrote about their loss—through death, divorce, or abandonment. Some chose to remember the good times they had with their fathers. Richard Hinger, who is serving four life sentences in a Nevada prison, remembers his dad as "an Oldsmobile man" who "always had a baseball game on the radio." Benjamin La Guer's father, on the other hand, was a shadowy figure who never took his son to a baseball game. In "Notes from Life and Death" La Guer writes about how he came to know his father only after his incarceration in a Massachusetts penitentiary:

> In the prison's visiting room, my father and I became friends. We told each other our secrets. Curious about who I was, I began asking my father who he was. I asked him about our fathers, and if they had been noble or scandalous. My father said, in words I ought never to forget, "All men have more scandal than nobility in their hearts. That's what makes us human. Don't trust a man who says he is noble." My father had never spoken like that before; he spoke as if he had surprised even himself. . . . In the end, I realized that I admired the old brown man.

While some prisoners chose to write evocative memoirs, others considered their present circumstances, many questioning the system that holds them captive. In Jeff Parnell's journal, "From the Inside Out," a fellow prisoner, Mike McLane, writes:

> I question the efficacy of a system of punishment in which the offender, already having serious character defects, is put into a giant pressure cooker with many other unbalanced and disturbed people for years at a time and left to stew in his own juices without ever being required or encouraged to deal with the character flaws and methods of thinking that got him there in the first place.

RACHEL JAKOFF

Prison is where many inmates first turn to God or encounter religion. Following a chosen spiritual path is one of the few freedoms inmates have. Indeed, religion was once integral to American incarceration. In his essay "Prison as Monastery," Ronnie Turner from Nashville, Tennessee, explains:

> The word *penitentiary* comes from the idea that a prisoner would be penitent while incarcerated. In the beginning, a prisoner was placed in a solitary cell to be alone with the Bible and his thoughts, much like a monk. The notion of a solitary cell was not based on punitive desires. The purpose of solitary confinement was not only reflection and penitence but also to protect against the mutually polluting influence of other offenders. The system was scrapped not because it did not work but because it was expensive and interfered with prison industry.

While a number of writers openly discussed their crimes, and sometimes their motives, only a handful referred to their victims or to their victims' families in a conciliatory way. Some alluded to their offenses but avoided discussing specifics. When I asked one contributor to illustrate his piece by briefly touching on some of the details of his crime, he declined, explaining, "I am not comfortable discussing the violence I have inflicted on others. On some level, I feel like talking about those things is glorifying them."

While reading the submissions, I had the feeling that the authors were looking at themselves in a way they never had before. Though many recalled childhoods savaged by violence and neglect, nearly all refused to bow to self-pity or to remain shackled to the past. Several prisoners wrote me, including those whose work I chose not to include, thanking me for taking an interest in their lives and for giving them an opportunity to express themselves in a way they were unaccustomed to—freely and without prejudice. One man described the experience as "cathartic." Another wrote, "This is a way of rehabilitation for us—and an atonement."

In all, Chris and I considered over four hundred submissions, from which I selected thirty-six for this anthology. I chose a wide range of themes and styles and tried to remain gentle in my editing. With the writers' assistance, I have included a few footnotes to clarify street and prison argot that might be confusing to some readers.

It is important to remember that while these selections represent a broad spectrum of experiences and opinions, their authors do not form a true cross-section of the nation's prison population. Absent are the voices of juveniles, the illiterate, those in county jails, foreign nationals detained in American prisons, those classified as "criminally insane," and military prisoners.

How these writers' stories will end remains to be seen. What is certain is that all of these "souls on ice" face daunting challenges ahead. Some have already been buried alive and will never again see the light of a free day. Some will beat the odds and begin new lives on the outside. Those who have families awaiting them will find themselves thrust back into the role of husband, wife, or parent again. But for others, perhaps as many as two-thirds of those released, freedom will be unforgiving. After a few wavering attempts to get their lives back on track, they will be reabsorbed into the ever-expanding "belly of the beast" that now holds some two million Americans and for which this nation spends over $30 billion annually to maintain. Certainly, many will remain criminals for the rest of their lives.

While working on this project, I constantly questioned what it meant to give these men and women—some of whom have committed monstrous crimes—a forum in which to talk about themselves. Was I being too charitable? Was I dishonoring crime victims everywhere by allowing them to have their say? Was I dishonoring myself?

The authors whose work constitutes this book have reached deep down and, in their own way, reached out. For me, their stories reveal that, as Melville observed, "a thousand fibers connect us with our fellow beings"—no matter who they are or what they've done. Many of the experiences detailed in this book parallel our own. These prison writers yearn for some of the same things we do, including, in most cases, forgiveness. It may be too late for many of them to undo the harm they have done, but it is never too late to show mercy to those who need it most. It is my hope that *Undoing Time: American Prisoners in Their Own Words* lends a new and much-needed perspective on the shadow world of prisoners by humanizing this mostly dehumanized segment of American society.

Jeff Evans
New York

Such is the remorseless progression of human society, shedding lives and souls as it goes on its way. It is an ocean into which men sink who have been cast out by the law and consigned, with help most cruelly withheld, to moral death. The sea is the pitiless social darkness into which the penal system casts those it has condemned, an unfathomable waste of misery. The human soul, lost in those depths, may become a corpse. Who shall revive it?

—*Victor Hugo*
Les Misérables, *1862*

Back in the Dayz

1937

Richard Hinger

Ely, Nevada

I was born in 1937 in Pittsburgh. People had iceboxes then, not re-frigerators. The iceman used to carry those big, cold crystal blocks of ice held in big iron tongs. We kids would hang around, sucking on the chips he'd break off for us.

Organ grinders would cause a panic of laughter with their little capu-chin monkeys that came up to you on their little chains, their big, fearful eyes watching you closely. They'd take a penny and pop it in the little pouch around their waists, but for anything silver, they would politely tip their hats.

Carnivals were big time, and the freaks were a real attraction. For a dime, you could get a glimpse of the weirdest stuff, like the world's largest rat (which I later learned was a capybara from South America), the ten-thousand-year-old petrified woman—we were terrified of seeing her, but curious enough to push each other in laughing and screaming.

Downtown Pittsburgh at Christmastime was a wonder to behold. The big department stores competed with one another with mechanized window displays of Santa and his elves. Crowds would gather in the falling snow as carols played on loudspeakers.

Coal was delivered through the long, sooty chutes running down into the basement, the big, black chunks of bituminous shooting and rum-bling into the bin next to the many-armed, big, fat furnace. On cold winter afternoons, we would stand on the small grates in the floor and get so hooked on the updraft of hot air that we couldn't leave the spot.

Our wet shoes and gloves we placed around the edges of the grates, and they would get stiff and twisted, drying into parodies of their former shapes.

I would walk to school with wet, combed hair that froze in the icy wind, and then, as I sat in class, it would melt, sending rivulets of water down my face, soaking my neck and shirt collar.

I would get called to the blackboard, where I would desperately try to hide the evidence of a youthful erection. After wetting the bed while staying overnight at my aunt and uncle's, I would wake up, embarrassed, then spend the rest of the night trying to dry the sheets quietly before everyone else woke up.

Our Aunt Flora came to live with us. She was wonderful and we all loved her. Sadly, we watched as she became senile. Soon, she just wanted to rock in her rocking chair and eat chocolate-covered cherries, and then she didn't know who we were anymore.

Rumors spread around our school of the Blue Hood. Now, this was scary stuff. There was a tunnel that the train passed over. Everyone said the Blue Hood hung around that tunnel. We avoided it like crazy, although we never quite knew exactly what the Blue Hood did. The name alone was enough!

We used to chase crayfish in a creek near the tunnel. Some of the kids said sewers emptied into it, but nobody knew for sure and it didn't keep us out.

The train whistles in the night brought adventure to our young ears, as did the radio shows. There will never be anything like those radio shows.

On weekends, we rode streetcars with passes to places like the zoo, the planetarium, the Museum of Natural History, and we sang songs like "Found a Peanut" the whole time.

Roller coasters were something we had to grow into. The red line above your shoulder meant you couldn't go. So we stood on tiptoes. We had horrendous rock fights. Sometimes they got a little wild. Everywhere we went, we ran.

The movies featured lots of monsters—Frankenstein, the Wolf Man, the Mummy, Dracula. I don't think there was anything scarier than Frankenstein, except maybe the Wolf Man. Frankenstein, although absolutely terrifying, moved slowly and you had a chance to escape him.

The Mummy just kept coming after you relentlessly. And Dracula was only after girls, so we boys were safe. But the Wolf Man moved fast and watched you like a hawk. He really had me worried. He was waiting around every bush.

We all swam at the chlorinated public pool in the park. Those were infantile paralysis days, and nobody was taking any chances. Often the pool was closed because someone had gone to the bathroom in it, and there would be a "floater." My big brother, Bo, taught me how to swim. He threw me in the deep end and I had to make it out by myself. He also taught me how to high-dive. "Put your toes at the end of the board and dive out as far as you can," he said. I did it that way all my life.

My dad was an Oldsmobile man. He liked light blue and white. When I was little, he took me everywhere. He always had a baseball game on the radio.

I'm glad my dad died before I came to prison because he wouldn't have liked that. Prison was something we saw in those old James Cagney movies. I never thought I would end up in one, especially with four life sentences.

I wasn't a troublesome kid. I graduated high school and joined the Marine Corps, got an honorable discharge, and embarked on life. It was fine until now.

Prison, particularly a maximum-security one, where I am, is a world of its own. Lots of unfriendly faces. Freedom, like my youth, is gone. It's something I remember but can't have anymore. In some ways, prison is like an insane asylum.

Once incarcerated you had better be prepared for bad food, bad company, and many times, even bad dreams. The monotony could kill you. What's worse, you wish it would. But it doesn't. Day after day, the time amounts to lost years. Watching birthdays, Christmases, births, and deaths pass you by. Most people on the outside don't care. This doesn't affect them.

I think what keeps you going in prison, if you have a life sentence, or multiple life sentences, is not the good times—because there aren't any—but rather the times when it's not too bad. When you are tired enough to sleep, or when some endeavor or distraction occupies your mind for a time. When where you are for the moment doesn't really matter. There are certainly those anxious times when it greatly matters.

That is the "hard time" when you want out so bad it's hard to breathe and your heart beats fast and your temperature rises. Then you have to get hold of yourself and calm down and try to put your mind at ease. You have to pretty much forget what is out there, and what your place in it was. And what it would be, or could be, if you weren't in here. Or what your friends, your family, and maybe someone you love intimately are all doing. Even though it may be abhorrent to you, where you are is all you've got right now, and that's the real world you live in for the present, the near future, and maybe even forever, for as long as you last. That's something else you can't dwell on. You hang on to those times when you were free, and times when it isn't too bad. That's what keeps you going. That, and maybe a little faith in something.

The Mystery of Aunt Lilly

Lou Torok

West Liberty, Kentucky

In northwestern Ohio, the asphalt roads stretch for miles between cornfields and dairy farms that never seem to end. The farmers are strong, honest family folk who are as good at raising children as they are at raising crops and herding livestock.

As an eight-year-old Hungarian immigrant orphan, I was welcomed into the family of Frank and Mary Buckenmeyer, who were feeling the pangs of empty-nesters since all of their children were grown and had left the land for life in the big city of Toledo.

I was always welcome at the home of any nearby Buckenmeyer who had children my own age. It didn't take me long to expand my territory to the nearby farm of Bob Buckenmeyer, Frank's brother, whose wife had died giving birth to their fourth child. Bob struggled to raise his four children as best he could, but there never seemed to be enough money from farming to keep his family together. Never one to shirk responsibility, Bob took a job in a store in nearby Swanton to put food on the table for his remaining family.

I soon discovered that life was grand at Bob's, where there were so many joyous hours of play in the fields and barns and in the otherwise empty house. Dorothy, Irene, Bruce, and Bob, Jr., were ideal play-mates, and our life of unsupervised playtime might have gone on forever except for a mysterious event that took place one day.

One morning, shortly after school ended for the summer, Aunt Lilly showed up to take charge of the children. Since I spent so much time with the Buckenmeyers, Aunt Lilly must have assumed that I belonged there, too, and simply herded me with the rest of the energetic brood.

How could I ever forget the odor of coal oil mixed with burning logs of apple wood, pine, or cottonwood that always stuffed the big, black potbellied stove in the living room and took the chill off the late evenings and early mornings? Aunt Lilly filled the air with other more delicious odors of fresh baked breads, pies, roasts, and endless provender as she baked and cooked then cleaned and fussed over our appearance. She sometimes seemed like a pest to us, but Mr. Buckenmeyer, who left early each morning for his job in Swanton, confident that his children and their hanger-on friend would be well supervised and provided for, regarded her as a saint from heaven.

Aunt Lilly seemed to slip into the rhythm of daily life on the farm. Instinctively, she governed the performance of daily chores of all the children and shooed me off to perform my own responsibility of taking Frank and Mary's cows to pasture after they had been milked each morning, then back to the milking barn in the evening. Milking, however, was left to the adults because I seemed to get more milk on the ground than into the stainless steel pail. I was quite good, however, at directing a stream of milk into the mouths of the eager, meowing kittens that swarmed the barn, waiting for the warm gift. The cows preferred the firm and gentle grasp of Frank and Mary and showed their displeasure at my playfulness by kicking the milk bucket, which usually was a sign for me to go out and play.

If I arrived too early at the other Buckenmeyers, Aunt Lilly would seat me in the kitchen and let me help her shell peas or peel potatoes until my playmates had finished their own chores.

It is hard to believe how much of a mother figure Aunt Lilly was and how much we all came to depend on her. No matter how early the children rose, Aunt Lilly would have breakfast waiting on the table. Aunt Lilly's surrogate mother role extended far from the farmhouse. She made sure that all four Buckenmeyers were ready for church on Sunday morning when Frank, Mary, and I picked them up. Our playtime in the 1935 Plymouth sedan would be cut short when Frank and Mary placed Aunt Lilly in the back with us children. But that didn't keep us from private jokes and giggles—all of which Aunt Lilly pointedly ignored—although we thought we occasionally detected a subtle grin. Aunt Lilly was good at hiding her emotions. She maintained her authority by never allowing us to penetrate her ironbound expression. And it was extremely effective. Although I never saw Aunt Lilly lift a finger to punish any of us, she never had trouble handling us.

After church on Sunday, the whole day belonged to us children. We found games and other interesting things to do on one farm or another, with endless acres of fields, streams, groves of trees, and abandoned barns in which to romp and find adventure. Always at mealtime we would hear the big iron bell on the porch ring out as Aunt Lilly signaled that food was on the table. She didn't have to ring long to bring us all on the run.

Aunt Lilly ruled with love, care, and attention, and I never heard her raise her voice no matter how unsettling our behavior might have been. She always wanted to know why we did what we did and seemed satisfied with the answer no matter how childish it might have seemed to someone else. Aunt Lilly always seemed to be in tune with us.

If any of us made a mess, Aunt Lilly simply got a rag or a broom or a mop and handed it to us. It was always explicit that since we made the mess, we were expected to clean it up. Aunt Lilly was a good housekeeper and took care of other dirt and grime wherever she found it. But our mess was our own responsibility. She expected all of the children to make their own beds, and although there never seemed to be any punishment for not making beds, there never were any unmade beds while she was around.

Our summer idyll ended early in September when school started. Aunt Lilly made sure the four Buckenmeyer children and I were cleaned and dressed. With our lunch bags in our hands, we were marched down the half-mile dirt lane to Angola Road, right in front of Frank and Mary's, where the school bus would pick us up. Aunt Lilly always accompanied us to the bus stop and was waiting for us when the bus returned in the afternoon.

It soon became a custom for me to do my homework around the big kitchen table with Aunt Lilly in command. Aunt Lilly never read our books or our homework. We did all the work. She was there to make sure we did it. Years later, it dawned on me that Aunt Lilly was probably illiterate but did not want us to be.

After we finished our homework in the evening, Aunt Lilly would have a baked treat waiting for us. Later, we all gathered in the living room around the potbellied stove for games and talk. At the right time, she would shoo me off down the dirt lane back to my own foster home.

One of the joys of childhood is its timelessness. I never counted the days or weeks or months or years, but nature kept count, and one day— I'm not even sure how many years later—Aunt Lilly died in her sleep.

As funeral arrangements were being made, Bob Buckenmeyer called his wife's family to tell them that Aunt Lilly had died. "Who is Aunt Lilly?" they asked. Bob had always assumed that since Aunt Lilly was not from his side of the family, she must have been from his deceased wife's family, sent by them to help him raise the children.

But no one knew who Aunt Lilly was or where she came from. No-body even knew her last name. She arrived with no possessions and died without anything to indicate who she was or where she was from.

Somewhere in a small country graveyard in northwestern Ohio, Aunt Lilly is buried. Her gravestone bears no last name. It doesn't have to. Aunt Lilly's name is forever engraved on my heart and on the hearts and minds of four lucky Buckenmeyer children.

The Chicken

Charles C. Mallos

Starke, Florida

Years ago, after my parents split up, my old man took me to Long Beach, California, with him, where we lived in an apartment over a bar. He had gotten out of jail and discovered my mom had been seeing another guy. So he took us kids. My older brother and sister were eventually sent to live with my dad's brother in Michigan, but I stayed with my father. I didn't mind. I loved my father very much.

Dad was a bull of a man but very intelligent and loving. He was also an alcoholic. Cirrhosis killed him at forty-three, but that's not what this story is about.

I was ten or eleven at the time and began to roam the streets a little at night. Me and my buddies would throw eggs at cars, shoot out porch lights with sling shots, or steal cans of whipped cream from grocery stores and gorge ourselves.

When I'd get home from school, my dad would usually be at the bar downstairs, and there'd be two or three dollars on the table for me to buy my supper with. Sometimes I'd go down to the bar and eat Slim Jims and play the electronic shuffleboard or bowling game. All the barflies would pinch my cheek and tell Dad how awfully cute I was. But more often than not, I'd go down to the Pike.

The Pike was a strip of beachfront that had a carnival-like atmosphere seven nights a week. There were rides like the double Ferris wheel, the Tilt-a-Whirl and "the world's largest roller coaster." For the faint-hearted, there were various games of skill, like the balloon shoot with darts and the .50-caliber machine gun that shot BBs. Or you could try to knock down a stack of leaden milk bottles with a suspiciously light softball. If you succeeded, you'd win an expensive stuffed animal.

For kids, there was a penny arcade. For a penny, you could test your degree of masculinity by squeezing together two metal handles. The tighter you squeezed, the stronger the shock you received. A meter gauged your status: "He-man," "Weakling," or in some cases, "Wimp."

The most fascinating attraction of the arcade was the chicken that played the piano. You'd put in a nickel, and the chicken, after receiving a shock from the wire grid floor, would tap out a halting rendition of "Mary Had a Little Lamb" on a toy piano. For this remarkable feat, it was rewarded with a food pellet that dropped magically into a small feeding bowl. I was unfamiliar with terms like "operant conditioning," "stimulus-response," and "positive reinforcement," so at first I didn't realize the bird received a shock each time a nickel dropped into the slot. There was just the dual satisfaction of hearing the chicken play the piano and the feeling of benevolence each time it gobbled up the food pellet.

I thought the chicken was living the life of Riley. It sat in a sparkling glass box right on the busiest and flashiest corner of the Pike, with nickels coming in faster than you could count. What a life! But as the days and weeks passed, I noticed the bird began to ignore the food pellets. Standing among a crowd of children surrounding the cage, I looked into the chicken's round eyes and saw torment and hysteria—real or imagined. The trapped bird was being pushed to the point of insanity, if chickens can go insane. Occasionally, a kid would put in a nickel before the song was over and the shock made the bird jump and begin the tune again. Having realized the true nature of the game, I winced each time this happened.

It dawned on me that the chicken's life was not so grand after all, and I wondered how long it would be until it was released or retired. Or was it condemned to spend the rest of its life in the cage despite having committed no crime, other than being born a chicken?

Early one Saturday morning, as I wandered among the deserted rides and closed arcades, watching maintenance men scrub the sidewalks and empty trash cans, I saw a panel truck parked by the chicken cage. I walked over just in time to see a man wearing rubber gloves snatch the now dead chicken out of the rear door of its enclosure. Holding it by the head, its lifeless body swinging limply, he tossed it into the back of the truck. To my surprise, he put a live chicken back into the glass box. I felt as if I were observing a dark, secret ritual.

When the truck had gone, I walked closer to inspect the new recruit. It was identical to the last one, and had I not witnessed the replacement, I would never have known the difference. I wondered how many chickens had died inside that box, how many just since I'd started visiting the Pike? Something was terribly wrong with this conspiracy, I thought. It hinted at something bigger, something evil and menacing. For a long time, the death of that chicken bothered me. I never could quite put my finger on it.

110th Street

Darlene Nall

Marysville, Ohio

In 1958, across the United States, five million workers were unemployed, Explorer 1 was placed in orbit, and I was born the fifth of five children. My southern, Christian parents migrated to Cleveland, Ohio, for opportunities that they imagined only a large city would present. To an Alabama coal miner and his West Virginia bride, this was the first step in a dream that would enrich their lives. Among their relatives, they had shown perseverance. Several of them later followed. But these loving individuals would eventually become alcoholics, drug addicts, convicts, and young corpses.

Three generations would be drawn to the homes on 110th Street, located on Cleveland's East Side. The street would eventually attract dope dealers, prostitutes, junkies, and burglars and would be transformed from a suburban, predominantly white neighborhood to an overcrowded ghetto. One Hundred and Tenth Street was lined with trees, fire hydrants, small businesses, and apartments. Under roofs that leaked, we all sought refuge and stability. But on that one street many lives were turned upside down.

It wasn't long before the men found work. They obtained city and factory jobs. Their titles ranged from trash collector to welder. These were some of the highest-paying jobs at the time.

For recreation, there were bars, after-hours joints, pool halls, strip joints, brothels, and transient motels. The women and children went to church, Bible studies, street club meetings, Boy and Girl Scout meetings, and to the YWCA.

We never got too close to strangers, but made an exception with our neighbors. They were also from the South. Together, we ate plenty of Cajun and soul food. There was plenty of liquor and harsh, sometimes violent, disagreements. My uncle George was shot six times by his stepson for allegedly beating his wife, my aunt Vivian. Another time, a fellow drinker killed my father after an argument. My older brother was stabbed repeatedly by my uncle Brad, and my other brother was shot in the head with a .357 Magnum while attempting to steal an automobile. Aunt Frances, who always had a beer in one hand and a cigarette in the other, survived lung cancer. Aunt Mary, who always said, "You must have a little wine with your supper," became crippled with arthritis. We would suffer tremendously from the guilt placed on us. Our parents accused us of killing my mother's mother. She was eighty-three when she reluctantly moved to Cleveland. The change proved too much for her. We may have smoked, cursed, and been abusive to one another, but we loved Grandma.

My mother retired early so she could care for her illegitimate grandchildren. My brother who survived the stabbing joined the armed forces. My oldest sister introduced me to beer and marijuana and my other sister started beating me.

Neighbors paved the way for me. Soon, the older, married males started telling me how cute and built I was. I began to wear revealing clothes and too much makeup, and began cutting school, popping pills, sipping beer and wine, snorting cocaine, and shooting heroin. This kept alive my dream of wanting to be someone special.

After cutting school one nice autumn day, I got the shock of my life. All of a sudden, I knew I was not alone. Two of the ugliest men I had ever seen grabbed me. A gun was placed to my head, and moments later I was raped of my virginity and my dream. I didn't tell anyone at the time because I was, after all, guilty of being in the wrong place at the wrong time.

I was no longer part of anyone's dream—my parents' or my own. Reality was upon me. I realized that my mother's brother, who used to always sit me on his lap, was a deviant. My oldest brother returned home from the service one day, full of acid, and later, as he went through withdrawal, started having convulsions and thought that bugs were crawling all over him. I remember, as a child, holding my other brother's arm so he could get a fix, then getting a chill as I kissed his cold lips at his funeral. My oldest sister would take me to private drinking clubs, introduce me to smelly drunks, and later, give me marijuana and beer to help me sleep.

Then there were the continuous beatings I suffered at the hands of my other sister. They started when I was about ten and never ended. As my mom recited the Twenty-third Psalm, I was taken to jail, while my sister lay in the hospital recovering from the multiple stab wounds I had inflicted on her for beating me.

One summer day, a fight broke out at the 110th Street Annual Festival. Gang unit officers had their guns raised, and one of them had his foot on the back of my son's neck, as he lay there sprawled on the ground alongside his cousins and other kids from the neighborhood. I watched them sentence him to prison, where he presently resides and is my pen pal.

My mother, who never smoked, drank, swore, or experimented with drugs and never harmed or abused anyone, suffered more than anyone did. She was the initiator of a dream that would rapidly deteriorate through the course of her life. How could God allow her all this pain?

In 1995 thousands of black men and women marched to Washington in search of yet another dream. I am in prison among thousands of dreamers. My only consolation is that some of us who migrated to 110th Street are still alive. Although we have gone through some vicious times, we still pray the Twenty-third Psalm. Today, my family still resides on 110th Street, where flowers grow and my two grandchildren attend elementary school. Through them, my mother's dream has become a reality.

Where I Come From

William Skeans, Jr.

Attica, New York

After five years in prison, I lie in my bed in solitary confinement and tell my story.

My name is William James Skeans, Jr., and I am twenty-six years old. I served two sentences prior to this one and have spent a total of seven and a half years in prison. I do not say this with pride or with shame. I committed crimes for money because I was lazy, self-destructive, and felt rules were for other people. I have been paying for those crimes and will continue to do so until my debt is paid in the eyes of the courts and society.

I do regret the pain I have caused the victims of my crimes. I have changed. I am more educated. I no longer have a nonexistent self-esteem level. I have looked into my heart to see why I so hated myself. By accepting my previous life, I have given it less control over my actions and have finally come to like who I am.

I was born the fourth child in a family that would grow to have ten children. My family was what people harsher than I would term "white trash." We had no money. We lived on food stamps, welfare, and handouts. As a young boy, I knew very little about the financial goings-on in my home. Not until I entered school did I realize not everyone lived the way we did.

My mother, Geraldine, was firmly ensconced in her second marriage at the time of my birth. She would go on to marry four more times by the time of this writing. My eldest sister, Cynthia, was a product of rape when my mother was fifteen years old. My older brother, John, was the product of her first marriage. That marriage ended in the death of her husband before my brother was born. My older sister, Jean Marie, was the love child of an affair my mother had with a married man who, instead of leaving his wife for my mother, died of a heart attack. My father then married my mother and gave Jean Marie his last name. As I was growing up, she was the only sibling who shared my last name. At twenty-one, I would learn that I have eight other half siblings who share my name.

I came into the world on November 29, 1970. Although I had yet to meet my father, who left my mother shortly after my birth, I would constantly be told throughout my childhood that I was just like him. I daresay that his absence played a larger role in my life than his presence ever could have.

My earliest recollections from childhood are of my stepfather, Edgar, my mother's third husband, lying with me on the floor of our Far Rockaway, Queens, New York, home and teaching me how to read. I was four years old. He was patient with me and taught me how to sound out words. I proved a quick study. One fond memory of my budding reading skills was a day in the summer of 1975. My family had spent the day at a state park in upstate New York. We were there for an annual party of CB radio talkers. My mother and stepfather were both CB aficionados. My mother's CB handle was "Pink Panther." I cannot recall Edgar's. On the way home, I started to read aloud the street and highway signs as we passed them. One sign read "Union Turnpike—Next Exit One Mile." I said out loud, "Onion Turnpike—Next Exit One Mile," and my mother and stepfather laughed as if it were the funniest thing they had ever heard. I was glad to have pleased them. Edgar then explained to me about long and short sounds.

While we may have appeared to a casual observer to be a happy family, truly we were not. Edgar was physically and sexually abusive to all of my mother's children.

I remember a game he used to play when we were home alone. He would blindfold me and make me guess what it was he put in my mouth. He used his "fingers" quite a bit. My sister, Jean, got the worst of it. I later learned that my mother had some knowledge of these goings-on, and she coped by drinking. Heavily.

She was also pregnant from the time I was six until I was nine. Edgar Fernando was born first, when I was six. Philip Joseph was the second child, born eleven months later. Anthony Vincent was born thirteen months after Philip. Anthony, or Tony as we called him, was born with spinal meningitis, and no one believed he would ever make it home. Finally, after six months in the hospital, Anthony came home. My brothers and sisters and I scoured the house for change and bought four packs of Bubble Yum bubble gum. We put them on a tray, stuck toothpicks in them, and waited for baby Tony to arrive. As kids, we were close and sought consolation from one another for our abused lives.

Luckily, my mother had developed some spine and threw Edgar out soon after Tony's arrival. The ensuing times were hectic days of threats, beatings, and police involvement, until one day my mother took a couple of shots at Edgar with a .357 Magnum from an upstairs window. He didn't come around after that.

Shortly afterward, my mother married a man named Lamont. In the eyes of her Italian family, this was the worst sin she could have committed. Although Lamont claimed to be 100 percent Apache Indian, he looked like your average black man. He was a truck driver who would be gone for weeks at a time. Then he would show up with gifts abundant, stay for a few days, and be gone again. My mother later discovered that Lamont was a bigamist. His other wife lived in New Jersey with their twelve children. We found this out when his oldest daughter tried to torch our house. She poured gasoline all over the porch and in front of the house. As she lit her torch—a stick wrapped at one end with gasoline-soaked rags—Lamont tackled her to the ground.

That ended the relationship between my mother and her fourth husband. But he would haunt my mother and our family until his death in 1992 from an overdose. Lamont's impact on my life could be summed up in one compound word: pothead. He turned me on, when I was ten, to marijuana—an addiction I still have today.

We were eventually evicted from that house. My mother had nowhere to go with six children, so she decided to place my three younger brothers and me in foster care through the Department of Child Welfare. The day she did that was, without a doubt, the most horrible day of my life.

My mother took us to the twenty-fourth floor of a high-rise building.

A woman in a red suit greeted her, and they talked while we played in a room full of toys—more toys than any of us had ever seen, except for on television. I was eleven years old. Eddie, Philip, and Anthony were five, four, and three respectively, and were known affectionately as "the boys."

After a while, my mom called us over. She hugged each of us and said to me, "Billy, I'm going to get you and the boys some lunch. Wait here." She then pulled me close and whispered fiercely in my ear, "Take care of your brothers." Then she got up and walked out of the office.

Five-year-old Eddie, who was so emotionally sensitive, somehow knew that Mom was not coming back. He screamed a piercing scream that still haunts me to this day and took off, running at top speed down the hallway. Philip and Anthony, thinking this a grand game, were hot on his heels. The woman in the red suit was close behind, and I brought up the rear, my mother's words still fierce in my ears.

I bolted past the woman in red, then Anthony and Philip, who were whooping and hollering like Indians charging a cowboy outpost. I turned a corner and saw my mother in an elevator. As the doors started to close, Eddie, running full speed, screamed, "Mommy, take me with you!!!" When my mother saw him, she sank to her knees and started sobbing uncontrollably, her body shaking with her sobs. I caught up with Eddie, tears streaming down my face, and tackled him to the ground and held him as tight as I could. Just before those doors closed all the way, my mother's eyes met mine. That moment seemed to last forever. The woman in red knelt on the floor and wrapped her arms around Eddie and me as my two youngest brothers circled us, whooping their Indian war cries.

Hours later, the woman in red drove us to a house in Howard Beach, Queens. I would nearly die in this house four months later, my mother's abandonment being truly complete. The foster "mother's" name was Linda; her husband, Richard, a police officer, was not home yet. Linda led my brothers and me and the woman in red to a downstairs bedroom that was part of a beautifully finished basement apartment with an attached garage. This was to be our room. There were three beds. Philip and Anthony got the large bed, and Eddie and I got the twins.

After the woman in red had gone, Linda, using a much sterner tone, told us to stay downstairs and to not ever, under any circumstance, come upstairs. Richard arrived home later that night and came down-stairs. We all stood to greet him and were all smacked senseless as soon as he walked into our room.

"You fuckin' kids better listen to my every word." He punctuated every word with open-hand and backhand smacks. "Don't *ever* come out of this room. I have a big, mean dog that lives down here and he'll bite your fuckin' little dicks off!" He beat us some more, then left. We weren't fed until dinner the next day. Linda and her six-year-old daugh-ter, Judy, brought our food. Neither of them spoke to us. Behind Judy was the dog Richard had mentioned—a very large German shepherd. I later found out he was as mean as Richard said he was. Richard made it a point to come downstairs and beat us regularly to show us he meant business.

We were fed every couple of days. I used to climb out of a window in our room and slip across the street to a restaurant. There, I would sneak food from a window of the restaurant's kitchen and bring it back to our room.

Whenever the woman in the red suit came to check on us, which was usually every couple of weeks, Linda would lead us to a bathroom, order us to shower, then give us clean clothes to dress in. She and Richard would then warn us that we would all surely die if we said anything about our treatment. Richard told us what to say, and we did what we were told.

After four months of this, I realized that there was a good chance that one of us *would* die. I got the worst of the beatings for trying to protect the boys, who were getting hit hard. But I knew that if Richard were to kill one of us, he couldn't hide it from the woman in red. So I did something I think I'll always feel some guilt about, but not a lot. I killed the dog.

I waited for the day when the woman in red was to come. Richard always came home early for these visits. I lured the dog into the garage using food from dinner the night before. Earlier, I had found some rope in the garage. I made a noose, and when I got the dog's head in it, I tightened it. I got the other end of the rope over a rafter. Then I pulled and hanged the dog. I instructed my brothers to hide under the big bed. When I made a loud noise in the garage, Richard came downstairs. He saw his beloved dog hanging there dead, with the rope in my hands. I said, "I killed your fucking dog, Rich. What are you going to do about it?"

His answer was a scream of rage. I saw his fist coming, and when it hit, I saw no more. I woke up in the hospital and was told I had been in and out of consciousness for a whole week. When I woke up, I woke up alone. A nurse later came in and talked to me. She said my uncle Joe had called and that he would be there later. Uncle Joe came and told me that the woman in red had arrived at the house as Richard was swinging my limp body by the ankles, slamming me against the walls and floors. The woman in red had reached into her purse and withdrawn a small-caliber pistol she carried for protection. She had to shoot Richard three times before he stopped. Richard was, in fact, in the same hospital as I was, under arrest and handcuffed to his bed. Uncle Joe told me that my mother had picked up my brothers and that they were at home with her. I asked how long it would be until I got home. "Not long," he said. But he lied.

I stayed in the hospital for three more weeks. The woman in red came for me. When I thanked her for saving me, she cried. When we pulled up in front of that same house in Howard Beach, I cried. Linda was there crying her apologies and saying how Richard beat her, too. I stayed there for another six months without once hearing from my mother. I never felt so totally abandoned. I was near death in the hospital, and she never visited one time. I was at Linda's for six months, through my birthday and Christmas, and my mother never called or came to visit.

One day, she came for me. We left and that was it. She never mentioned it again. I brought it up thirteen years later, when she came on her only visit to me in prison. She said she didn't know what I was talking about. I guess it was too painful for her to remember, so she shut the memory out. She did it well, and I still haven't forgiven her. I've tried, but I always see her on her knees in that elevator.

Shortly after I turned eleven, I witnessed my mother kill a man. It was on a Sunday. We all were at my great-grandmother's house for dinner. It was summertime. Nana, our great-grandmother, asked if we could spend the night. My mother said OK, but she would go home. I asked my mother if I could go with her. She saw something in my eyes that made her say yes. I wasn't the only one who didn't want her to leave again. Eddie started to cry. My mother let him come too.

We were very tired by the time we got home. I was holding my brother's hand in one hand and my mother's back pocket in the other. She led us to the door of our small welfare house on Thirty-ninth Street in Rockaway Beach. I heard her say, "Son of a bitch!" And then I heard *Boom! Boom! Boom! Boom!* The next thing I knew, my mother was pushing Eddie and me into the room right off the door. Looking into the living room, I saw a black man lying on the floor, his eyes boring into mine. There was blood everywhere. Those sightless, staring eyes still plague my sleep. Then I was past the doorframe and into the side room. I had been squeezing Eddie's hand so hard I broke two of his fingers. The man turned out to be a burglar.

As I mentioned earlier, I am twenty-six years old now. I've spent a great deal of time in prison. I did my first bid at seventeen for assault, robbery, and burglary in the first degree. I got out at nineteen. I was back four months later. I got out again at twenty-one. Just before my release, Billie Jo Skeans contacted me. I had never heard of her, but she turned out to be the sixteen-year-old daughter of my father, whom I'd never seen. She told me of seven more children from as many women that my father had sired. She also told me that my father wanted to speak to me and gave me his phone number.

All my life I had envisioned meeting up with my father. Because of my love of reading, I had read many books, my favorite being stories of knights and wizards that fought creatures like orcs and trolls, dragons and goblins. To me, my father was one of those knights. His journey—all knights have journeys—is what had kept him away for so long. When I called him, he even sounded like I thought a knight should sound. I forgave his absence totally and agreed when he asked me to parole to his home and live with him and my brother Patrick William Skeans, who was the same age as my sister Jean Marie.

But when I was released to his home, I was shocked at the disparity of the image I had of my hero-father and the man who greeted me. I had envisioned a tall warrior. I am six foot four and weigh 220 pounds. My father is five foot five, thick, and stocky.

It soon became clear that we could not get along. After all the time that passed, he tried too hard to be my father and I too hard to be his son. I left his house and have never heard from him since. His absence for most of my life hit home when I realized that I could never truly have a father in the sense of a dad or a pop, someone to guide me, or to be a parent. I found my father, only to lose him to the distance of twenty-one years.

I've been in prison for five years now and I believe I'll be here for at least three more. My crime was robbery. I know now after all this time that I will never commit another crime. I am different in so many ways. I guess in some part, I owe that to my parents. Until now, I was that little boy of eleven that was looking into my mother's eyes in the hallway of the child welfare building. I was the young boy who grew up in a household where father figures were absent or abusive. On this bid, I let that boy go and I grew up. I realized that there are no knights and that my mother only did what she had to, to get by.

Another reason for my change was when I realized that as long as I was in prison, I would never be human. In prison, you become attuned to one particular sound: keys. When a convict hears keys, he can't help but remember where he is. Especially in solitary confinement, where I am now serving a year. The sound of keys jangling is the only sound that means anything. When your life seems to revolve around that sound, you know that you are being kept apart from humanity. Another being controls you utterly and completely. I know I'll never come back to prison, because, after all these years, I have found my humanity and discovered that I really like being human.

Invisible

C. Kaye Ferguson

Tucson, Arizona

I was a head taller, fifty pounds heavier, and thirteen that spring. My dad had stopped home to eat and clean up after spending forty-eight sleepless hours in maneuvers in the cold and muddy countryside near our post just outside Crailsheim, Germany. He was to report for duty as officer of the day for another twenty-four-hour stretch without sleep. Already worn down from various health problems, he was overtired and understandably quiet through breakfast. During the few minutes before I had to leave for school, I showed him a project that was due that day. The exceptionally long time he studied it made me uneasy.

A gun belt and holster containing my dad's army-issue .45 pistol were draped over the back of the chair my schoolbooks were sitting on. As I bent to pick up the books, an overwhelming urge to take the gun paralyzed me. Fear of my dad's wrath and the effect such an action would have on his career prevented me from succumbing to the urge. I walked to school with a sense dread I could not explain.

School started as always. We eighth graders were given a math assignment to complete while our teacher, who was also the principal, gave an English lesson to the seventh graders. The school secretary interrupted the class and informed the principal that he had just received an urgent call in his office. As the door closed behind them, a boy in the class looked out the window and saw an ambulance pull up in front of the building where my family lived. An MP jeep was seconds behind. I joked that the men in the white coats were coming to get me. Though there was a grin on my face, my stomach had turned to ice and wrapped itself around my heart. The teacher returned. I was needed at home.

A freezing wind had risen. The mud I walked on began to crystallize and crunched harshly beneath my feet. Chilled breath dropped wetly to curl around my cheeks. Nature seemed determined to slow my already reluctant steps as I walked the half block to the door separating me from the stairs I would have to climb to our apartment. As I rounded the corner of the building, the ambulance drove away. An MP was standing just inside the door. He said nothing as I passed him. My body grew heavier with each step up to the landing. At the top of the stairs, a second MP silently stood guard. A third blocked the closed door to the bathroom off the hall while a fourth stood guard in the kitchen entryway.

Mrs. LaHoya, the dentist's wife and coffee-klatching buddy of my mom's, sat at the kitchen table. Opposite her sat Mom, tears streaming down her face. They told me my dad had shot himself in the temple and had been taken to the post infirmary. We sat in a weeklong silence of three hours. The only movement was our habitual sipping of coffee from cups Mrs. LaHoya would fill to make herself feel useful.

The entry of the provost marshal brought the wait to an end. He informed us my dad had died. As an afterthought, he stated it was best because he probably would have been a vegetable had he lived. Mom didn't seem to hear him. He asked if there was someplace we could stay for a few hours while his men checked things out. The suicide note had not yet been found.

Women who had gathered outside the apartment building formed a phalanx around us as we walked to Mrs. LaHoya's apartment. They led Mom to the living room and set her on the couch. She was like a jointed doll: hollow, the expression frozen on her face. A neighbor filled a basin with warm water and gently washed dad's blood from mom's legs, while I, left standing in the living room arch, wrapped in my cloak of guilt, became invisible.

I Killed My Wife

Oscar Chandler

Vienna, Illinois

I took a life that I revered tremendously. After considerable soul searching, I am content that I did this. I know that my wife is looking down at me with peace in her heart. And I feel, in some way, that she's trying to thank me for relieving her of all the pain and suffering she was burdened with. She is at rest now. Will someone please help me put my mind at ease?

The question I am trying to validate and reconcile is: was it murder, as I was charged, or was it a mercy killing, as people I tell the full details to try to convince me? Or was it an assisted suicide? I will allow others to be my judge, as I try in my own way to put into words what took place on March 1, 1996.

My wife, Hazel, was despondent, depressed, and disturbed because of her physical condition. She had been under a doctor's care for a heart condition for years before we met and fell in love with each other. She was not a terminal case by any standard set by the medical profession. But in her own mind she was. She wasn't suicidal, but she was ready to die and wanted to in the worst way.

May 1, 1971, two weeks before my fifty-third birthday, was a wonderful day. I was a cross-country truck driver for a moving and storage company headquartered in Indianapolis. It was there that I met Hazel, who would later become my wife. About three weeks after our meeting, I had to leave Indianapolis. I asked Hazel to join me. She worked for a dry cleaning firm in Indianapolis, but managed to take a week's vacation to be with me. I promised I'd have her back in time to report for work the following week.

A few days into the trip, Hazel began to experience a nagging pain in the center of her chest. I dropped my trailer at a company agent in Cincinnati and deadheaded back to Indianapolis so Hazel's own doctor could see her. After examining her, her doctor told her to check into the Methodist Hospital in town for a heart catheterization. But because of her weakened condition, the procedure had to be postponed until early the next year.

In 1972 she was admitted for the catheterization. During the procedure, the doctors found two blocked arteries. They scheduled her for double bypass surgery a week later. It was to become the first of two major heart operations.

I was not in Indianapolis at the time, but I kept in daily contact with Hazel. When she informed me that the surgery was scheduled, I promised her I would be there with her. And I kept my promise.

I arrived home the evening before the operation and went to the hospital to see her. Upon seeing me she perked up and said, "Now I am ready." I went back to the hospital the next morning before she went into surgery. Her nephew and his wife were there also. She went into surgery with a big smile, knowing she was not alone.

The surgeon repaired one artery and left the other one for a future operation. He said that Hazel would not have lived another two months without the surgery.

At the time, we were living as husband and wife. It wasn't until thirteen years later that we got married. Hazel seemed to be getting along fine until about 1980, when she began to complain of slight angina attacks, shortness of breath, and blurred vision. Although I tried to convince her to see a cardiologist, she didn't make an appointment until a year later.

In early 1982 she was admitted to Saint Vincent's Hospital for another catheterization. Tests showed her physical condition had worsened owing to the medications she had been taking. Her blood had become so thin that it was doubtful she would have survived the catheterization. Instead of scheduling the surgery, her doctor sent her home to build up her strength. He also took her off all medications except nitroglycerine, for her angina. The doctor's orders were no trying activity, only bed rest. But Hazel was very active and had a difficult time dealing with the orders. I made sure she followed them.

During the last four or five years before I retired in 1980, Hazel would take cross-country trips with me. Often she would tell me that those were the happiest years of her life.

In 1982 it almost ended. Hazel began to have the symptoms of angina again. She returned to the hospital for the catheterization. This time, the news was even worse: the doctors found four blocked arteries, with 30 to 90 percent blockage. Two days later, she was back in surgery for the second bypass operation. She was not optimistic this time. She kept saying, "I'm afraid I won't come out of it." She almost didn't. Around five o'clock that afternoon, the surgeon came into the waiting room to tell us that everything had gone fine, but that they'd almost lost her. He explained that they had spent the last three hours trying to stop her bleeding.

The next morning, I was at Hazel's bedside. She was just beginning to breathe on her own. The nurses told me she'd be able to talk and take soft food that evening. I stayed with Hazel and talked to her and told her everything that had taken place.

The following afternoon, I was at her bedside again. She had been transferred to a semiprivate room. She was perkier than the day before. Her hospital stay lasted about a week. Prior to her discharge, the doctors and nurses showed me how to clean and dress the area of the incision. The doctor told Hazel she could return home only if she were willing to follow his orders of complete bed rest.

Her doctors told me what she could and could not eat, and how to prepare her food. I enjoyed being her nurse, cooking for her, and bathing her. I did for my wife knowing she would do the same for me if the circumstances were reversed. I was never too far from sight or sound, except when I had to leave to do the necessary shopping.

Four days after Hazel came home, she began to have trouble breathing. She asked me about getting an oxygen tank. I called a friend who was an EMT, and he told me to come down so he could show me how to operate the equipment. He had an oxygen tank ready by the time I arrived and told me it would last from twelve to eighteen hours, depending on the pressure. I took what I had just learned back home with me and hooked up everything just as he had shown me. Hazel began to breathe a little more easily and continued to breathe this way throughout the night.

The next morning, however, the tank was empty. I called to see if I could get a replacement. I explained to the EMT on duty what the problem was, and he advised me to get Hazel to a doctor. I called our doctor, who told me to bring her to Bartholomew Hospital in Columbus, Indiana.

At the emergency room, our family doctor rushed Hazel into X-ray, where they found her chest cavity filled with fluid. After draining about a quart of fluid from her chest, the doctor kept her overnight for observation. They released her the next day. A week later, she returned to have more fluid drained. After that, she seemed to be on the road to a full recovery. A year later, her doctor gave her a clean bill of health after finding everything in good order. She was doing great and living life to the fullest. My wife and I picked up where we'd left off years earlier. We began taking short weekend trips, dining out, and spending quiet evenings together again. Oh, how life can be when you're in love and the one you love is in love with you.

Then, in 1986, we sustained another blow. Cataracts began to rob my wife of her vision. Hazel loved to drive and be driven about the countryside. Now, suddenly, even this was being taken from her. After surgery on both eyes, the ophthalmologist informed her that both retinas were damaged beyond repair. The news floored her. She went into a state of depression from which she never fully recovered. Her doctor told her that her sight wouldn't worsen, but it wouldn't improve either.

I became her eyes. She could still see well enough to find her way around, but that was about it. On shopping trips, she could distinguish colors and shapes but was unable to read price tags. She could no longer dial a telephone, write a letter, or sign a check. To get the news, she listened to the radio or the television. In many ways she became lost in her own home. No matter what I did to help, it couldn't replace what had been robbed from her. I took over all the household chores: I cleaned, cooked, did the shopping and the laundry, took out the trash. Even the little things like dusting and washing the dishes were my job. I enjoyed doing most of these things. If I had to, I would have done them standing on my head for Hazel.

Her brother and I became best friends. He used to say the only thing he disliked about me was that I had spoiled his sister. Hazel was my sweetheart, lover, and constant companion. We were close twenty-four hours a day. Things didn't always go smoothly, but there didn't seem to be anything we couldn't resolve by talking it over.

When we moved to New Haven, Illinois, where Hazel was born, her life fell apart. She became even more despondent and depressed and suffered blackouts, vertigo, and spells of wanting nothing more than to be left alone. Once, she checked into a hospital where they ran all sorts of tests. She came home for two or three days, only to return to the hospital for another series of tests. During one of these stays, she underwent a colon examination because they had found some blood in her stool. They didn't find any cancer, but two polyps had to be removed. The surgery was traumatic for Hazel, something she could never put out of her mind. Later, another doctor wanted her to go through the same exam, and the procedure leading up to it completely threw her off balance. Until her death, she never got over it. She would talk about it constantly, asking, "Why do these things happen to me? I just wish I could die and get away from all this pain and misery."

In the mornings, we would always have coffee and toast together, and during our conversation, I would ask Hazel if there was anything special she would like to do. It seemed that during the past couple of years, I would get the same, depressed answer: "Please, just let me die."

I'd always come back with an answer like, "You don't mean that. What would our dog, Mac, and I do without you?"

She'd reply, "I'm tired of taking all this medication just to stay alive for more pain and suffering. It's not worth it."

I was constantly reminding her to take her medicine, both morning and night. Some nights before going to bed she would say, "I hope I'll go to sleep and not wake up." I believe she sometimes deliberately forgot to take her medicine, hoping that very thing would happen. A couple of times she said, "If I was a stronger person, I would commit suicide. But I am just not strong enough."

Then came the morning of Friday, March 1, 1996. Hazel awoke before I did, which was unusual. I usually got up about four o'clock to plug in the coffee maker so the coffee would be ready when we got up. Then I would go back to bed. On this particular morning, around five or five thirty, she woke me up and told me the ceiling light fixture had broken. I got up to check it out. The wiring had indeed shorted out and the fixture needed to be replaced.

Since it was the first of the month, I planned to go to the post office, pick up our Social Security checks, return to the house to make out the deposit slips, then go to the bank. I usually did this alone. While the two of us were having our coffee, Hazel turned to me and said, "I'd like to go to the bank with you." I said, "That's fine. Be ready when I get back from the post office."

When I returned from the post office, she told me she had had a slight angina attack. She said she didn't feel up to going. I poured another cup of coffee, made out the bank deposit slip, and got up to leave. Hazel then stood up, looked directly into my eyes, and said in an unbroken voice, "I wish I could die. There is nothing more to look forward to, nothing but you and Mac to live for. You two would be better off without me. Please, *please* just let me die." She turned her back to me. With no conscious thought or comprehension of my actions, I grabbed the dog's leash that was hanging on the wall by the kitchen door, flung it about her neck, and proceeded to strangle her.

I will always believe that she was begging me to help her in some way, to relieve her of all the misery and suffering she had to contend with. The only thing she said to me was, "Not this way."

There was no struggle to get free, no fight at all. For me, there was no premeditation, no anger whatsoever. Just the feeling that Hazel would suffer no more. By nine thirty that morning, my wife—my life, my companion, and my co-pilot—was dead. Her suffering had ended.

I had to get out of the house. I went to the bank, and on the way there I asked myself, "What have I done? I just killed the one person in my life I truly loved. Someone, please tell me it's not true." But it was true. Then, a foolish and selfish thought entered my mind: maybe I could cover myself and make it look as though an intruder had done it. But at the same time, I knew I could never do such a thing.

I arrived back home around eleven thirty and called Hazel's brother. I told him that something had happened to Hazel. When he arrived, I broke down completely. He knelt down next to her body and checked for a pulse. Not finding one, he looked up at me and said, "She's dead. I wonder who could have done this?" He never suspected I had done it because he knew how much I loved her.

The coroner, the sheriff, and state police officers convened at the house, and an intensive investigation began. At first, no one suspected me of the murder. Then little things began to point to me. One investigator finally asked me if I had anything that I wanted to get off my chest. If I did, now was the time to say so. I told him no. He then asked if I would agree to take a lie detector test. I said I would, and he repeated, "If you have anything to say, say it now because you can't beat it." I continued expressing my innocence.

Today, I am convinced I really wanted someone to prove to me I had taken the life of someone I loved very much. The test proved to me that I had done it.

I broke down and confessed. I told them that I had done it—that I had killed the one and only person I had ever truly loved, but that I did it for her. She had suffered enough. Her failing body, her state of mind, her depression, her wanting to die finally got to me. She got what she'd been asking for—peace.

I was booked into the Saline County Jail that night on a first-degree murder charge. I wasn't allowed to attend my wife's funeral on March 3. On Monday, March 4, I appeared before the county prosecutor, who again read me my rights and asked if I understood them. He explained that, under the new sentencing guidelines, I was facing twenty years to life in prison, and would have to do a minimum of twenty years. However, if I were to plead guilty to a lesser charge of second-degree murder, I would be facing a maximum of ten years. Since I was just three months shy of my seventy-eighth birthday, I couldn't possibly opt for twenty years to life. With that sentence I would, in all probability, never be free again. I pled guilty to second-degree murder.

That same day, I went before a judge who was very considerate. He asked if I understood everything he was saying. I said I did. He sentenced me to ten years, five of which I would have to serve. For good behavior, I would get another three months cut, dropping my time to serve down to four years and nine months. The judge and prosecuting attorney recommended that I serve my sentence in a minimum-security prison. But according to the Illinois Department of Corrections guidelines, I didn't meet the requirements for minimum-security prison status. Upon my arrival, I was sent to Menard Correctional Center for processing. A few months later, I was sent to Big Muddy River Correctional Center, where I am presently confined.

I have not written this looking for sympathy or forgiveness for my actions. I only want to clear my conscience. I believe I did the right thing. Quantity without quality isn't life. It's just an existence. To watch Hazel suffer on a second-by-second basis was a living hell.

As I go to bed each night, I know in my heart that my love, my life, my companion and co-pilot, is now at peace. For me, all that's left is to await the end of my sentence.

Turned Out

Lamont Bolder

Garden City, Georgia

It was always hard for me to get any control of my life. When I was two years old, I was adopted along with my brother and sister. The family that took us in adopted misplaced children for a living. They owned a small contracting business as well, but we were the supplementary income needed to make ends meet.

We weren't the only misplaced children in this venture. There were four other misplaced children, discards from a different demented situation. We all had a small price tag on our heads. And it added up. In those days, it was a normal thing for people to go to an agency and adopt a few kids. There wasn't a whole lot of background checking going on. The more you could get, the better you got paid. Who said you had to invest the benefit money in the kids anyway? As long as you did a little something for them, that was cool. An outfit once a month, maybe. Shoes? Maybe if the soles were gone.

But what put the icing on the cake was that this family already had kids of their own. Now, that's insane. If they were struggling with what they already had, why get more? Simple! No one was giving them money for their own kids.

We lived a subnormal life of the "adopted kids" on the block. Everyone knew it. Although we all were of the same nationality, we were still minorities. Now ain't that something? Deep inside each of us, we were being psychologically damaged to varying degrees. I guess I came out the worst: the black sheep.

I was an average kid by all appearances. But there was something inside of me. Something ominous. And even today, I don't have a name for this entity that's still a part of me. It's been within me as long as I could recognize it and give it a life of its own. I can almost call it something other than myself, but not quite. I will tell you this: it's rational, impulsive, and dishonest in a calculated and sometimes deadly way. Nonviolent and cunning, loving, caring, sensitive, and emotional. Always considerate and modest, dependable and fair, vindictive and remorseful. Most of all, it's insecure and trusting. This description may pose a problem for you, but bear with me. I can see now what I couldn't see or understand then. There was never a real need to reflect on it until now.

 I did all the abnormal things a kid would do during adolescence: I broke windows, stole from stores, and took change from my stepfather and stepmother without asking. At night, I would sneak into my stepfa- ther's bedroom while he took a bath and stick my hands as far as they would go into his old work coveralls. I would always come up with two things: a lot of change, and a handful of concrete dust. No matter how many times I stole some change, I'd always get the concrete dust to go with it. That was the only time I'd be able to hit him; it was my mainstay. Mommy's pocketbook was just a supplement in hard times. But all I took was change. I was scared of the dollar bills. They seemed to scream with accusation. Like if I took a dollar bill and tried to spend it at the store, they would know I wasn't supposed to have it. Kids were only supposed to have change.

All of a sudden, my world shattered. I don't know the exact details or even remember the day anymore. But I was taken out of foster care and placed in a boys and girls home. It was a world of competitive, misplaced, evil, confused, and angry children. Children who knew they needed to pay someone back for something, but didn't know who it was they were supposed to pay back for their misfortune.

No one ever told me why I was taken from foster care. I don't think anyone thought they owed me an explanation. Never mind that I was scared and confused. Never mind that I didn't understand why I was being separated from my brother and sister. It didn't seem to matter to the powers that be that a family was being broken up and that irreparable damage was being done to all of us. No one said anything. They left it to me to figure out. But I had no time to. My main concern was to overcome my fear of being in a new environment.

From age two to eleven, I was in foster care. I was just learning what my family was really about. I was just getting to know them in the intimate way families get to know each other. Then I was taken away and placed in this cold place I called home for the next four years. The coldness of the place was its lack of parental warmth. There was only the steel calculation of rules.

But adjusting wasn't as hard as I thought it would be. I never had it at home like I had it at this place. I had everything a kid could ask for. There was a full array of sports facilities: a basketball court, softball field, football field, archery arena. We had a recreation room filled with arcade games, including pinball machines, shuffleboard, and an electronic bowling machine. We also had pool tables, Ping-Pong tables, board games, and card games of all sorts. There was even a big ol' swimming pool in the middle of this paradise. I learned how to swim and went on to earn a certification to be a junior lifeguard.

In the years I spent in this place I learned to be prideful and egotistical. I became dependent on my peers for support no matter what the endeavor was. Without them, I was nonexistent. I depended on them to be noticed and to be accepted.

I was afraid, too. Afraid of who these strange children were. They seemed so much more dangerous than I was. But from my fear I developed this notion that I could convince a person that I was someone I wasn't, and in turn, they would stop and think twice about who they were dealing with. Over the next four years in this destructive adolescent environment, I taught myself how to be what I wasn't. At first, I would only use these attitudes for confronting others. As time went on, I modified these façades according to a given situation. I could be a fighter, gangster, lover, even a worldly young man. Whatever suited the situation, I became.

But in the end, my multiple façades caught up with me. Not only were my peers caught up in these charades, but the staff was, too. After compiling a dossier of my activities, mostly through snitches and witness accounts, the staff concluded that my presence at the home was counterproductive for those who were model residents.

I was summarily expelled from this paradise I had called home for the last four years. It hurt. But you'd never know it by looking at me. I was still wearing one of the many façades I'd developed during my stay. Deep down inside, though, I was warring. I was crying. I wanted to strike back. I was afraid of those who were in control of my life. Those unknown and mysterious people who made decisions about where I lived and who would take me scared me to death. Even today, I am scared to death of the people who make the decisions I am sometimes not in a position to make.

I was given over to foster care again. This lady and her husband were very amusing to me. I had a general liking toward them because I understood where they were coming from and what their purpose was for having me: more money! They already had two other boys that they had contracted out from the city for a few uncertain years. Then I arrived, and then another boy right behind me.

Let me tell you about this unique mix. Not only did this couple have four adopted boys, but they also had three boarders. These boarders were laborers who got paid, then drank up their money. They did this in varying degrees.

The youngest guy, Dennis, was the coolest. We could see eye to eye about a lot of things. We talked a lot about everything. I enjoyed that with him. He smoked a lot of weed and he loved Earth, Wind and Fire. He turned me on to both and I loved it. I guess I could say I loved him too. He became a big brother figure to me. He was kind and gentle in his conversations, never mean or vicious. Never negative. He always had a positive outlook on life. I'm not sure if he worked or not. Most of the time he was gone. But when he was home, he made time for us, me and my three other brothers of adoption.

Then something took place that caused my world to turn upside down again. I wasn't quite sure what really happened. My life has had so many crises. But I ended up being moved and placed in a boys home again. Then, from that boys home I was adopted one last time. That was when my life took a turn for the worse.

The boys home was just like any other. But what was different was that one of the counselors took a real interest in me. That struck me as odd. Why was he interested in me? I asked him about it, and he told me that his interest was strictly parental. I guess I believed him to a point. But I was at a point in my life where I trusted no one. No matter how much he talked to me, he could never gain my trust. But we talked and he grew closer to me. He said it was because of my vulnerabilities. I guess that could be true, but it still didn't satisfy what I felt.

As I continued to talk to him, I became interested in some of the things he said. He told me he wanted to adopt me. He said I needed to be away from the environment of the boys home in order to grow. Then he spoke of things like my own room with a stereo and tape player and all that good stuff. I liked what I was hearing. But there was to be more to it than just what I wanted. At the time, I never considered that, so I agreed to the adoption.

The preparations for me to move into my new home were being made at the same time the paperwork was being processed for me to belong to someone all over again. I became excited about the idea of having a family setting again. This happiness spilled over into my memories of the family I originally started with. One afternoon, my counselor-stepfather called me to the office building to tell me that everything was final: I was officially his stepson.

Once it was consummated, I moved into my new home, a conservative two-bedroom apartment in a middle-class neighborhood. I was very disappointed. My room was about nine by twelve, give or take a few feet. But I was happy just the same. For a little while, anyway.

If I had any notion that he was going to try and mold me to be what he wanted me to be, I might never have agreed to the adoption. But I wanted out of the boys home, and he was the perfect opportunity. Whatever the circumstances might be, I figured I'd cross that bridge when I got to it.

And I did just that. I was in high school and cutting a lot of classes. I was a loner, a follower, and a coward to boot. I wouldn't do anything dangerous. Still, I wanted to fit in. I'd never fit in anywhere but in an institution. I just couldn't relate to what everyone else was about. They all had family, friends they grew up with, memories of a childhood, and all that normal stuff. I stayed outside the perimeter of that inner social circle. I had nothing to offer them.

Although I became afraid of being too noticeable, I remained steadfast in my efforts to find some peers who equaled my standards, and I found them. Together, we would cut class and hang out by the basketball court. We drank wine and had a good time.

Word got home that I was cutting class regularly. But instead of confronting me with this, my stepfather played it smart. He knew the periods I cut because of a letter he got. He waited until after I left for school the next day. Then he came to the school at the time of my fourth-period class. He found me where me and the fellas would hang out and called out my name. I was deeply embarrassed. I was already ashamed of him. Then he said, "Let's go. We're going home." I was seething. Everybody asked me who he was. They asked me if he was my father. Anyone could see there was no resemblance between us at all. I lived with this embarrassment long after it was over.

What developed in me was a hatred for him and for all the high-class nonsense he stood for. I began to rebel more and more. I wouldn't clean my room or do any of the chores he assigned me. The situation grew worse. At one point, I stopped going to school. He put me out. After some time, he let me back in. But then I'd do something else, and he'd put me out again. And each time it was a little longer. He knew I had nowhere to go. I would call him, and he would play psychological games with me, and I would always end up explaining my inner self to him. He had a Ph.D. in human behavior and thought he knew everything he needed to know about the human psyche. But he was wrong.

It was a regular thing for us to argue. He would yell, and I would sit there and not say a word. And it just got worse. He didn't know what to do with me. One snowy night, he put me out for something again. He was on his way to somewhere and I begged him to let me back into the house. I told him we would talk when he returned. But he knew that wasn't true, because I'd said the same thing many times before. When it came time to talk, I never had anything to say. But he let me in long enough to convince him why he should let me back in.

I had already conceived the idea of taking him out with a steak knife and taking the car and whatever jewelry and money I could find. My heart was in the right place. I had no doubt I was going to do it. So as we spoke, I went into the kitchen to get a glass of water. I knew that there were always dishes drying in the dish rack, and silverware too. As I walked into the kitchen, I was momentarily out of his line of sight, and I took advantage of this opportunity. I turned on the sink faucet and, at the same time, I reached for the steak knife. I purposely knocked over a glass in the dish rack just in case he heard the silverware clang together. I quickly slipped the knife into my pants and pulled my coat closed. I knew he would have his eyes on me. I would completely catch him by surprise by spinning around and stabbing him as I was leaving.

I got my glass of water and came out of the kitchen with the same sorrowful look I had when he first let me into the apartment. I knew he wasn't convinced by anything I said because he started fidgeting. His patience had run out. Finally, he stood up and told me that I had to leave. When he came back, he wanted me to have myself together with what I had to say to him to convince him that I was ready to change my ways.

I walked past him slowly on my way to the door. He said something. But I felt like I was underwater; I couldn't distinguish the sounds I was hearing. My heart was pounding so hard that I imagined he could hear it. It beat so hard it ached. My mouth went completely dry and I couldn't swallow. I was moving in slow motion. My soul was crying out to me not to stab him, but necessity dictated that I had to. I knew that he had no idea that I would conceive of the thing that I was about to do to him. He didn't realize that I was getting ready to take his life because I wasn't satisfied with my own. He didn't realize that I didn't value his life one bit.

Those last few steps to the front door were the longest of my life. Although things seemed to be moving slowly, they were actually moving very fast. Then, in a moment of clarity, I spun around. With the knife in my hand, I lunged for his heart. But he was quicker than I thought he would be. I guess we all are when we see a twelve-inch steak knife coming straight for us and we know our life is in jeopardy. Nevertheless, I followed through with the same conviction I started with. But all I accomplished was a severe laceration to his right wrist. He called out my name when he realized what my intentions were. I told him not to say my name. That scared him.

As all this was taking place, I quickly assessed the situation. I could see he wasn't going to let me kill him without a fight. He was stronger than I was. So I donned one of my façades, dropped the knife, and began to cry. I cried loud and howled about how sorry I was and how I didn't know why I had done it. Then he ran into the kitchen, grabbed a dishtowel, and wrapped it around his wrist. He got his car keys and coat and headed for the door. All the time he kept his eyes on me. I continued to cry as I followed him around the apartment. I tried to help him and, to my surprise, he let me. I even entertained the thought that things might work out after all.

But that wasn't to be. As he drove, he moaned in pain. I got a little concerned in spite of myself. A couple of times, he almost lost control of the car. It was snowing heavily. We finally pulled into the emergency room parking lot. I got out and ran around the car to help him out. I again entertained the thought that everything was going to be all right. But when he got out, he stood hunched over from the pain in his wrist and looked me straight in the eye. He said, "You better leave." Then he turned around and walked slowly toward the emergency room entrance.

I was stunned. I stood very still, then I walked off into the night. I looked back once to see him fading as the distance between us lengthened in the thickness of the snowfall.

A Shot in the Dark

Christopher Lynn Garner

Cuero, Texas

I pull the plunger back and begin filling the syringe with dope. I just scored. My nerves are jumping in anticipation of the fix I'm about to do. I pass the ten-unit mark on the side of the rig, then the twenty. My heart is pounding. I pass the thirty. Sweat beads on my forehead and my hands start to shake. It registers forty now. I pull the rig out of the spoon and hold it in front of my eyes. With eager anticipation, I thump the few air bubbles to the top and push them out. Now I'm ready. I place the rig in my hand and bend my other arm. I find the good vein and place the needle against it.

I pull the plunger back and watch the blood ooze into the rig. I'm ready now and slowly push the plunger, injecting the dope into my vein. I've got ten units in . . . twenty . . . I start to feel the rush. I know I've got to hurry to get the rest in before I lose control. I push the plunger harder to get all the dope into my body. I pull the rig out, but can't let it go. I'm frozen. My mind is rushing, my body is sweating, my legs are shaking. I try to speak, but nothing happens. My heart is pounding. My eyes are wide open. Then, nothing. I go out and hit the floor.

I'm unconscious on the bathroom floor of a fleabag motel room. My spirit is falling through pitch-black emptiness. I reach out, but there is nothing there. I just keep falling and falling and falling.

Time passes and I come to. I feel strange, very strange. I feel as if I've come back from the dead. Everything in the room has an odd air about it. I open the motel room door and the outdoors looks strange, too. I close the door and walk over to the bathroom. I stare at my dope, my spoon, and my syringe. I feel alienated from everything.

Then I pick up the dope and shake out another shot in the spoon. My eyes wobble as I try to draw up some more dope. I can't hold the syringe steady, and the spoon starts to shake. I squint my eyes real hard and try to see how much dope I've got in the rig, but I still can't see. I hold the rig up in front of my eyes, but I can't make anything out. I thump the rig. An air bubble moves around the place where the twenty-unit mark is. I push the air out and return the syringe to the spoon. I can't see the cotton, but I know I'm in the spoon so I pull the plunger back to draw up the dope.

Sweat covers my body. I hear the spoon clang against the countertop, but I can't see if I've spilled any dope or not. I know I drew up some more, so I hold the rig in front of my eyes to see how much, but I can't see anything. I decide I've got enough dope and start to hunt for a vein. I put my finger on the bend in my arm. I know it's there. I place the needle against my skin. I squint my eyes real hard, but still can't make anything out. I know it's there, so I push the needle in. I pull the plunger back. I can't see anything. I push the plunger. I'm in.

My mouth is dry and sweat is pouring off my forehead. I push the plunger in further and start to feel the rush. I taste it in my mouth. I pull the rig out and set it down. My body starts to shake. My mind is rushing. I feel my knees start to give out.

Then I catch a glimpse of myself in the mirror. I see big eyes, full of fear, a body shaking terribly, sweat running down my face. I stand there, gazing in the mirror. I can't move. I'm frozen, staring at myself in the mirror. I feel shock. How did my life get like this?

My mind is working again, so I must be coming down. I reach for the coke and shake some into the spoon. I draw up some water and squirt it on the dope. I place the other end of the rig in the spoon and mix up the dope. I put it in my mouth and taste it. Oh yeah, baby, this is some good dope! I draw up another thirty units or so. I shoot it up and here I go again. Too much! My legs start to give out. I reach out and hold on to the countertop to keep from going down. Sweat is everywhere. My clothes are soaked. I pull off my shirt and my shoes. I'm ready for another one now. I walk to the motel room window, first to make sure that my car is all right and to check everything out. I pull the curtain back.

It's dark outside. I see the cars on the highway with their headlights on. How can that be? It was nine-thirty in the morning when I got here and I know I haven't been here that long. Oh, well, I guess I have, since it's dark. Time for another shot.

I wash my face off with a hand towel and take a few deep breaths. I check everything out on the counter. It looks like I didn't spill any dope. I get the syringe and wash it out a few times and draw up some more water. I shake some dope out into the spoon, but it doesn't want to come out, so I give it a little thump. A rock tumbles into the spoon. It starts dissolving from the dope left in there from the last shot. Too late to take it out. I'll just be careful and everything will be cool. The rock is so big. I'll just have to add more water. There, just right. I drop thirty units and check the air. A bubble at the bottom won't move. I thump it, but still it doesn't move. I shake it again and thump it real hard. It starts to move. But is it? The dope is so thick, I can't tell. Finally, there it goes. I push the needle into my vein and pull the plunger back until it registers. I start to push the dope into my vein, and here comes that taste again! My ears start to ring as I get all the dope in. I pull the plunger out, and here go my knees again. Sweat is streaming off my face. I start to go down again, but I grab the counter just in time. There I am again in the mirror. I just stare at myself. My eyes won't focus; my thoughts are nonexistent. I'm just out there, sweat everywhere.

I turn loose from the counter and start to walk. I make it over to the window and pull the curtain back. The brightness of the sun just about blinds me. I close the curtain and cover my eyes. It was dark just a few minutes ago. How long was I standing there? It's daylight, no question about it. No big deal. Better do another one. I look at the bed. It hasn't even been sat on, so I pull the spread back to make it look used anyway. The phone rings. Who can that be? Nobody knows I'm here. When it stops ringing, I unplug it.

I walk into the bathroom and check my dope supply. Not too bad, still about a half ounce left. That's cool. I shake some dope onto the spoon but it disappears. Oh yeah, that's right, there is a shot left in there from that big rock. I'll just add a little water so I can draw it up. I squirt some water in the spoon and mix it up. I lick the dope off the plunger. Wow! Man, that's strong! I get another piece of cotton, ball it up, and drop it in the dope. I place the point on the cotton and draw up about thirty-five units. I put the rig against my arm and push it in. I check it. The blood is there, so I shoot it up. My knees start shaking again, my heart pounding hard against my chest, sweat pouring out everywhere. My teeth start to grind.

I'm standing halfway out of the bathroom, holding onto the door to keep from falling. My whole body is trembling. I notice the covers on the bed are messed up. Who did it? Somebody was in here! Don't lose it. Be cool. Look around. What was that? Where? Over there! I didn't see anything. Something just moved. I caught it in the mirror. Just cool it man, you're starting to lose it.

Back in the bathroom, I grab a towel and wash my face and body. There, that's better. A shower would sure be nice. Yeah, that's it. I'll take a shower and feel better. Let me draw up another shot so I can do it in the shower. I shake out some dope and draw it up. I get my clothes off and get into the shower. I rinse off real good and grab the syringe. I pop it in my vein and shoot it up. The water gets louder. My body starts to shake. I'm holding onto the showerhead. I can't move. I'm rushing real hard.

Finally, I turn the water off. I pull the shower curtain back and get out. Water is all over the floor. I grab a towel and walk out into the room. Even the carpet is wet! I dry off and get my pants on. I use all the towels to dry up the water.

After I get the mess cleaned up, I decide to go get some ice and a Coke. I grab my glasses and some change and open the door. Man! I can't see anything. I take my glasses off because it's dark now. Nothing I can do about that. I run down to the ice machine and fill my bucket. I stop by the vending machines and grab a couple of cans of soda and a few bags of chips.

On the way back to the room, I remember the bottle of whiskey I have in the car. Back to the room, I fix myself a drink. Boy, does it taste good. Well, I guess it's time for another shot. No, I'm going to wait a few minutes. I turn on the TV and go through the channels, but nothing holds my interest. What's the difference? I might as well do another one.

I shake some more dope into the spoon, draw up some water, and squirt some on the coke until it dissolves. I turn the rig around and stir up the dope. I roll up a ball of cotton and drop it in the dope. I put the needle on the cotton and draw up about thirty-five units. That's how much I did last time. If I want to really get off, I'd better draw up a few more. Yeah, I guess I will.

The syringe registers forty units. I check for air bubbles and get them out. I press the needle into my skin until it goes into my vein. I pull the plunger back and push the dope in.

Out of nowhere, a thought about my wife and kids back home comes to mind. I've already shot the dope, but the thought hangs on. I see myself in the mirror again. I catch a tear falling out of my eye, running down my cheek. My ears start ringing. A scene of my wife and kids at home flashes across the mirror. I remember how much I wanted to be a good man, to be looked up to by my kids, to be respected by my community, to be admired by my wife. I see myself standing in the mirror. I'm standing there in nothing but my pants. My hair is all messed up. I look closer and I see a trail of blood dried up on my arm. Another scene flashes in the mirror of my family, then back to me, then my family, then me. I shake my head and grab a towel to wipe my arm and face off. I know I better go home, but there's still some dope left. I try to pull it together. I tell myself I'll just do one more, then I'll go home.

Since it's my last one, I want to make it a good one. I shake some coke into the spoon and put some water on it. I draw up another thirty-five units but it isn't that thick, so I draw up some more. The syringe registers forty-three units. I push it into my arm and depress the plunger until I get all the dope into my vein. I keel over and bounce off the bathroom wall. I hit the floor with the side of my body. I'm lying on the bathroom floor on my side, trembling all over. The syringe is still in my arm and there's blood running down. The taste of alcohol is strong in my throat; my ears are ringing. My eyes are locked, staring straight out in front of me, but I can't see anything. I can't move.

I hear a morning news show on TV. How long have I been lying here? I manage to get up and find a towel. I scrub the dried blood off my arm. I wash my face off and rub the wet towel over my body. I remember I was going home after that one. Wait a minute. If the morning news is on, she won't be home, so why not just stay here and do another one?

I walk to the window. The sun is blaring down. There is a wreck over on the freeway, and traffic is stopped in both directions. No use trying to leave now. I walk over to my drink. The ice is melted; the whiskey and Coke have separated. The ice in the bucket has melted too. I grab the soda and take a swig. There, that's better. Wow! Man, this is some good dope. Let me see how much I got left. Oh yeah, this will work. I shake it out into the spoon and mix it up. I draw it up and shoot it. I set the syringe down and try to walk out of the bathroom. I'm taking small steps, but I'm moving. I get out of the bathroom and make it a couple of feet into the room. The TV is on, but I can't hear anything. I'm standing, holding on to the wall. My wife flashes in front of my eyes. Places we've been, things we've done. I can't stop it. I start to cry. I'm a drug addict! I don't really believe that, though. I don't know what is wrong, but I am not a drug addict. Yes, you are! No! Damn it, I'm not! Then get it together and leave this stuff alone. No! You can't run my life. I am, you idiot! Damn it, I need another shot. Then get one! I will!

I make it back into the bathroom, my eyes still bouncing all over the place. I get the package of dope in my hand. I hear myself say, "If you're not a drug addict, you can stop right now." Shut up! I'm not playing these mind games anymore. I shake some dope into the spoon. I can't see anything. Dope spills all over the counter. I draw up some water, but I can't tell how much. I stare but still can't see anything. I stir the dope and water up while I hold the spoon with my other hand. I know there is cotton in there, but I can't see it. I hold the spoon with one hand and work the rig with the other. I think I've got some drawn up, but I can't tell. I hold it up but can't even see the numbers on the syringe. There has to be some dope in it! I push the plunger and about twenty units come out, then a squirt of air, then about twenty more of dope. I still can't see anything! I put the needle back in the spoon. I can tell I'm drawing dope, so I just guess by the distance of the plunger from the syringe how much dope I got. I get to where I think I've got about thirty-five units or so, and then stop. I hold it up to the light, but still can't see. I place it on top of my arm, after feeling for the vein, and push the needle in. I think I'm in the vein and since I can't see, I push the plunger. I don't feel any burning and I'm getting the alcohol taste, so I push the plunger on in. About halfway through, I start to fall. I've got to get this dope in. I lean against the wall and push the plunger. I'm sliding down the wall, my body is shaking again, my heart is pounding, my ears are ringing, sweat is pouring. I'm frozen. I can't move. Am I dead? Am I dying? What's going on?

I'm aware of life outside my room. I feel the presence of some kind of spirit beings. I see them! Everywhere. They are moving in circles around me. I sense the atmosphere of Christmas outside my motel room door. People going places, families doing things together, kids smiling and happy. What happened to my life? How did I get hooked on dope? The demons all around me are watching me. I'm frozen on the floor of the bathroom and I can't move!

I hear a late-night talk show on TV. What time is it? It was daylight just a while ago. I've got to get up. I make it over to the curtain and pull it back. It's dark! Cars have their headlights on. I can't go home like this, not this late! I wash my face and body off. I grab some change and walk down to the ice machine. I buy a candy bar and another soda. I fix myself a drink. I take a bite out of the candy bar and set it down. Man, this is good dope! I flip through the TV channels but nothing's on. I decide to do another shot and go home after this one. If I time it right, I can be there before she leaves for work. I walk back to the door and make sure it's locked. I pull the curtain back for another look. Everything is cool. I walk into the bathroom and pick up my dope bag . . .

My spirit is falling again in total darkness, nothingness, emptiness. Then I hear noise. Keys rattling. I hear a door open and sense a presence. Somehow, I come to and get up. I step out of the bathroom door and my motel room door is open! The maid is standing in the doorway. I run her out, shouting at her and slamming the door behind her. I walk back to the bathroom and clean up my mess. The dope is gone. I trash the evidence. I grab my stuff and walk to my car. I start it up and turn on the air while I try to gather my senses and collect my thoughts.

I look at my dashboard clock. It's 3:30 in the afternoon. Good. She won't be home for another hour. I get to the house, but her car is in the driveway. What's going on? She should be at work. I pull into the drive and walk into the house like nobody's business. I ask her why she isn't at work. She tells me because it's Saturday. She wants to talk. I agree to enter a drug program, if it will help her. She is so happy that it makes me think she's glad to be rid of me. I blow it off and enter treatment.

I talk to a few doctors and check the place out. Everyone seems dead around here. Weak! That's what they are—weak! The doc tries his mind games on me, but I ain't like these losers. You can't play with my head, doc. I start to settle in. A couple of people talk about going to the mall. I think, cool, we can leave if we want to. I find out, though, that you have to be there for a certain amount of time and making progress before you can get a pass to leave. Well, nobody is going to put something like that in my face and get away with it. If anyone gets to leave, so do I. Finally, reluctantly, they let me check out. That's cool, because I didn't need it anyway! I call home and tell my wife to come get me. She shows up after a while and we drive home.

It's been three days without a beer, without dope, without anything! I get my keys and start to leave when she hits me with a divorce. I tell her fine, and sign the papers. Now I'm free!

I go to the store to call my connection for a front, but he's out. I walk into the store. The clerk has money all over the counter. Take the money. No, I can't do that! You need a fix, don't you? Man, I can sure use one. Just take the money and go get you some dope. All right, all right! I grab the money and take off. I get away. I make it to a phone and call another connection. He has some, so I go score. I can't wait to make it back to the room, so I pull in a car wash and mix one up. I look around. Nobody is watching. I put it in my arm and shoot it up. My ears start ringing, my heart starts pounding . . .

Finally, I make it to the room. I shoot all that dope up and want some more. I know what I have to do, though, to get money. I can't do it! Yes, you can! It's too late to stop now. What have you got to lose? Shut up, man! I can't throw my life away like this. You want some dope, don't you? Then you know what you have to do. So I rob another store and score some more dope, come back to the room, and shoot it all up. I can't do this anymore! Look, man, if you want some dope, you have to keep this up. Wait a minute. This isn't me. Then who are you?

If I stop now, I've got a chance to salvage my life. If I keep going, there's no chance at all. What do you want? I want to be free from this damned dope! That's what I want! You can't do it! I've hurt everyone. I've thrown my life away. I'm no good. I'm a damn junkie! God, help me—you've got to! I know you're out there. I know you see me. Help me, God! Help me now!

Back in the Dayz

Lalo Gomez

Canton, Illinois

I became a member of one of Chicago's oldest and most violent street gangs at a very early age. I didn't come from a dysfunctional family, a poor family, or anything closely related. Other options were available to me at that age, so I had no real reason to take the destructive path I chose. You could say that I enjoyed the street life so much that I put on the back burner all thoughts of advancing myself in school, being around my family and others who loved me, and heeding the religious values my parents taught me. I couldn't foresee the mess I would eventually get myself into.

My parents did everything they could to keep me off the streets and in check, but I was just too stubborn and naïve to realize that they were doing this for my own good. But sometimes even the best that parents do for their children just isn't good enough. Not because they don't try hard enough. The blame cannot always be placed on them. No parent, no matter how hard he tries, can ever know everything his children are doing. Unfortunately for me, I made a lot of bad decisions, when I could have easily made good ones. The price I've paid for those decisions has been a costly one.

My father moved our family to the West Side of Chicago in the early 1960s at a time when street gangs were just starting to make their mark. We lived in an area that was predominantly African American. Me and my siblings attended a mostly African American school, which didn't sit too well with us. We weren't racist; it was just hard for us to make friends with our fellow students who would mock us because our skin color was lighter than theirs was. That was something I did not fully understand back then.

One day, as I was leaving school, my teacher stopped me and asked me to open my school bag. When I refused, she grabbed me by my arm while one of the other teachers took my school bag. Upon opening it, she discovered that it was filled with toys and lunches. As she began taking them out, most of the kids who were missing things started yelling, "Hey that's mine!" "Yeah, and that's mine!" I was too embarrassed to say anything and just stood there, silent, staring at my teacher. She told me that I was in a lot of trouble and that I should be ashamed of myself.

I didn't want to hear any of that so I lashed out at her with vulgar and threatening remarks, which didn't help my situation any. The teacher then took me to the principal's office. There, the principal attempted to discipline me with an old Catholic school technique called "paddling," which turns a student's ass cheeks blood red after four or five good smacks. I wasn't about to let some principal put a paddle filled with holes to my ass cheeks, and I told him so. He called my parents and told them to come to the school. When they arrived, he informed them that I was being expelled for stealing, using vulgar language toward my teacher, and threatening her. My mother couldn't believe what she was hearing and started to cry. My father took one hard look at me and said, "You really messed up this time, son. How could you do this to us, to *yourself?*" I didn't know what to say.

There were four gangs in the area: the Hell's Stompers, the Latin Disciples, the Spanish Cobras, and the Latin Kings. All four were fighting one another for control of the neighborhood. I got my first real look at a gang fight when the Disciples and the gang I would foolishly one day belong to collided in front of the apartment building I lived in. I may have been only five or six at the time, but I was smart enough to understand, when told by my parents, that this was no ordinary fight. As people watched from their apartment windows, the two warring gangs went at it with bats, chains, clubs, and knives. When the police arrived, both gangs stopped fighting each other and turned on the officers. They overturned police cars and set them on fire, and many officers were seriously injured. The police shot and killed three gang members. I may have been a young buck, but I really got a thrill from seeing those gang members fighting like warriors right in front of my house—and more so, when they all turned on the police. It wouldn't be long before I became part of that same senseless and violent lifestyle.

My parents moved our family to the North Side, where crime wasn't as bad as it was on the West Side. We moved into a high-rise building that was clean and affordable. The neighborhood was also clean and quiet, and schools, churches, stores, and theaters were all nearby. Me and my siblings enrolled in another Catholic school, where I attended the fourth through sixth grades. Two of my brothers and both of my sisters went on to graduate. I, on the other hand, could not adjust to the strict disciplinary code of Catholic school. After the sixth grade, my parents decided again to send me to a public school. That's when the real trouble began for me.

In Chitown, being a member of a gang was like a fad. All the kids my age belonged to one, or wanted to. I became a member of Boricua Power. As time went on, I became more involved with the gang's inner circle. I started doing drive-by and walk-by shootings on our rivals, and selling narcotics. It wasn't long before I started to show true leadership abilities, which earned me the respect and fear of many of my fellow gangmates—especially my rivals. I would "bust a cap" (shoot you) in a hot second, no questions asked. And if you so much as looked at me the wrong way, we'd end up having a serious disagreement. Make no mistake: no matter who you were, you'd end up holding the short end of the stick.

Our crew consisted of me and my four cousins—Reno, Romero, Pete the Burner, and Slick Rick—and my female cousin, Salina, who later became a bona fide member. We were all from families that came to the United States from Puerto Rico back in the early 1950s. This blood bond made us stick together all the years we spent gangbanging and selling drugs. We were inseparable. Salina was gunned down in 1983 by one of our main rivals. May she rest in peace.

I started to have run-ins with the police when I was about thirteen. We were doing a lot of burglaries back then, selling the merch to local pawnshops and people in the neighborhood. We'd use the money to buy ourselves clothes, guns, and drugs and to go to parties or to the movies. We'd also take furniture from the houses we burglarized and give it to the senior brothers from our chapter so they could furnish their apartments. Every time I got arrested, my parents would come and sign me out, since I was a juvenile and not required to post any bail. It wasn't until my freshman year in high school that I started to get into serious trouble.

I was now gangbanging big time, doing drive-bys and walk-bys on my rivals almost every day. Me and my crew were leaving bodies lying all over the place. We had our choice of rivals and would actually sit around a table plotting which rival we'd hit that day. We'd put on our war sweaters, pick out the guns we were going to use, and *boom!* Out we went to shoot us a rival. Our favorite weapons back in the dayz were a .20-gauge sawed-off double-barrel with double triggers, and a snub-nose .38-caliber five-shot. Both weapons could do some serious damage, especially when you shot someone at close range—the only way me and my crew did hits.

At one point, the violence got so bad that our leaders ordered us to chill out because the police was starting to come around the neighborhood, harassing and arresting the senior members. This was something our gang didn't need. So we chilled out—at least for the time being.

One day, while me and my crew were on our way home from school, some senior members from an all-white gang known as the Howard Street Greasers pulled up in a car, jumped out with baseball bats, and started chasing us. Two of them caught up with me and Romero and beat us down with their bats. Both me and Romero ended up in the hospital with serious head, arm, and leg injuries.

During my hospital stay, I plotted revenge. I knew it was going to be sweet—real sweet. Soon after me and Romero were released from the hospital, I got the crew together and off we went to retaliate. We shot the leader of the Greasers fifteen times at close range. He was standing in front of his house with two other Greasers who had helped beat me and Romero down. We shot them too, but they both got lucky and escaped, joining their leader in the graveyard of ignorance. About a month later, we caught those same two Greasers coming out of a liquor store in their neighborhood. We beat them down with baseball bats, the same way they had beaten me and Romero down. Both ended up back in the hospital, this time with severe blunt trauma to their entire bodies.

The next day, we caught the other two Greasers who'd beaten us down as they were chillin' at a theater near their hood. As they were sitting there enjoying a Bruce Lee flick, me and Romero walked up behind them and slit their throats. One of them choked on his blood and ended up joining his leader. The other one lived but will never talk again. The entire Howard Street Greasers gang went underground soon thereafter.

I was now about fifteen and clowning big time. One day me, Reno, and Romero burglarized a house and found two high-powered hunting rifles: a 30-30 Winchester and a 30.06, both with scopes. I smiled deviously when Reno told me, "Yeah, homeboy, now we can really go out and hunt the enemy." We both laughed as I replied, "Yeah, *primo*, hunt them down like dogs!" I wanted to use the rifles to do some burns (hits) on our rivals before I sold them to Luciano, the leader of our gang. I knew that we couldn't take the rifles home with us. Letting Lil Snoop, a fellow gangmate whose father was a gun and knife collector, stash them was our only alternative. In return, Lil Snoop gave me a nickel-plated .22-caliber six-shot and asked me to bring it back when I came to pick up the rifles. The move that the Greasers had given me and my crew prompted us to start carrying guns at all times.

Carrying a gun was like carrying an American Express card—we never left home without one! Unfortunately, two days later, the police raided Lil Snoop's house because of a tip from an old lady who lived next door to him. She told the police that she saw some kids carrying what seemed like guns into Lil Snoop's house. Inside, police officers found an arsenal of rifles, hand pistols, ammunition, and an assortment of exotic swords and knives. Lil Snoop's father didn't have a permit for any of the weapons, so they were all confiscated and he was charged with unlawful possession of illegal firearms and other dangerous weapons. When the police learned that two of the rifles had been reported stolen from a house a couple of blocks away, Lil Snoop's father was also charged with burglary.

That didn't hold up too well with Lil Snoop. He told the police that the burglary of the house and the theft of the rifles were not his father's doing, and that he was only holding them for me and my crew. The police already had it in for us, so they dropped the burglary and theft charges against Lil Snoop's father and arrested me, Reno, and Romero. We were charged with burglary, theft, and unlawful possession of two stolen firearms, although we were never caught with the rifles in our possession, and no one witnessed us burglarizing the house they were stolen from.

The police called our parents and told them to come down to the station to sign us out—again. When I got home, my parents gave me a stern lecture. They told me I'd better chill out or I'd be grounded indefinitely. I did not enjoy upsetting my parents like that. Though I had messed up big time, I still had a lot of respect for them and could only bow my head as they scolded me. The last time my dad had whipped me, I put my hand through the living room window, so he never did me like that again. Grounding me seemed to be the most effective way of getting me to chill out. But even that didn't stop me from going right back to the hood and my crew and our dirty deeds. We were all young bucks who already had a knack for the streets deep in our blood.

Meanwhile, me, Reno, and Romero were disappointed that Lil Snoop ratted us out to the police. So I hollered at Luciano and asked him for his blessing to allow me and my crew to teach Lil Snoop a permanent lesson—one that would make all our fellow gangmates think twice before ratting out one of their own to the police.

A few days later, we caught up with Lil Snoop as he was on his way home from work and shot him six times with the same pistol he'd given me to hold on to. Reno took Lil Snoop's betrayal personally and pinned a note to his forehead that read: "NO SPIC CAN COME INTO ANGLO HOOD AND LEAVE ALIVE!"

He did this to make the police think that the Anglos—an all-white gang that sometimes hung out right around the corner from the store where Lil Snoop worked—were the ones who had shot and killed him. Two known shooters from the Anglos were arrested the following day as suspects in Lil Snoop's murder, but they were released hours later for lack of evidence. Later that week, me and my crew had a shoot-out with the Anglos, whose main chapter was right down the street from our school.

Back in the dayz, the Anglos were all seniors—older gang members. But that didn't faze me and my crew or any of the other peewee Boricua Power members because our organization also had some big bad seniors. If things got too rough for us peewees to handle, we could always count on our senior and junior members to stand up for us. They would not allow any of us to get smashed by the seniors of any of our rivals and would immediately retaliate when we did. None of us Boricua Power members who attended North Side High ever had any run-ins with the Anglos until one day when we were getting ready to leave school.

Me and Badblood, an enforcer from one of our North Side chapters, were walking together. Our crew members were behind us. As we walked past some Anglos who were standing around a car, one of them made a remark loud enough for us to hear. I turned around and asked them if there was a problem. The one who made the remark said, "Yeah, we got a problem! We don't appreciate you spics spray-painting 'Boricua Power' in our hood. Do you have a problem with that?"

"You're the one with the problem, white boy!" I said. "Now, what you wanna do?" The Anglos started opening the trunk of their car to get whatever it was they had in there, but me and Badblood peeped the play and upped our missiles. Our crew members and all the other pee-wees present followed suit. I didn't waste another moment and shot the Anglo who made the remark. Badblood and his crew members shot at the other Anglos, who panicked and started running. Me and Badblood walked up to the Anglo I shot as he lay there bleeding profusely and shot him several more times. We then joined the rest of our crew and the other peewees as they started chasing the Anglos who ran. Me and my crew split up and chased some of them down an alley as Badblood and his crew followed the others into a gangway. Two Anglos they were chasing came out blasting with shotguns they had hidden in the gangway. Unfortunately, Badblood and two of his crew members were sprayed with shotgun pellets and didn't have a chance to shoot back. Badblood was hit in the face and chest, and the two other bro's were shotgunned to death as they tried to crawl away. All three of them died in that gangway.

Meanwhile, me and my crew shot two of the Anglos we chased as they tried to run into a backyard. We had no idea that Badblood and two of his crew members lay dead somewhere else. As we walked back to the hood, the police drove up on us from all directions, jumped out with their guns drawn, and told us to freeze. We were surrounded and didn't have a chance to ditch our guns.

We all ended up in jail, charged with mob action and unlawful possession of firearms, and almost got slapped with attempted murder charges.

Four Anglos wound up in the hospital in critical condition, including the one who started it by making his ignorant remark. One of them died a few days later. The attempted murder charges the police were trying to stick us with almost got enhanced to murder charges, but that never materialized because none of the Anglos were talking and neither were any of the students at the school who witnessed what had happened.

The Anglos who shot and killed Badblood and his crew members were caught and charged with those murders, but were released soon afterward for lack of evidence. The Boricua Power mourned the loss of Badblood, Lil Slick, and Lil Kool. That same week, our leaders sent a crew of bona fide gunners out on a shooting spree. Every Anglo who got caught in their hood, or anywhere else they shouldn't have been, ended up in a coffin. The Anglos soon went into hiding and never resurfaced, at least on the North Side. They did, however, regroup under the name Northsiders in the Illinois State Prison system, where two of their leaders and many of their members remain, even as of this writing.

While at the police station on the day of the shoot-out with the Anglos, the juvenile officer on duty came back with our rap sheets and told us that we were on our way to Juvi Hall. We would have to spend three months there until we went before a judge who would decide our fate. If convicted, we could possibly end up staying in prison until our twenty-first birthdays. Lucky for us, back in the dayz, there was no such thing as trying a juvenile as an adult. But the burglary and possession of stolen guns charges that me, Reno, and Romero had been arrested for just a few months earlier didn't help us none; they only made things worse.

We already had a court date pending in front of the judge and were now back in front of him with yet another serious charge. He told us that we were in a lot of trouble. Unless someone with a lot of input in the community came to say something positive on our behalf, we'd be on our way to St. Charles, a hard-core juvenile detention facility, also known as "gladiator school" because of all the gang fights that occurred there. The judge continued our case for a week. We knew we had to do something fast, so I called Luciano and ran the situation by him. He told me not to worry, because he was going to send us a lawyer he kept on retainer, who would take care of things for us.

The lawyer spoke with the school principal to see if he could get him to speak on our behalf. The principal referred the lawyer to the school cop, who agreed to show up in court and put in a good word for us. The lawyer told us not to get our hopes up, because the judge would have the final word.

A week later, we were back before the judge, who had spoken to the school cop and to our parents. He told us that we were very lucky young men to have people speaking on our behalf and that we should be thankful to them. He decided to give us another chance and placed us on probation for two years. But in the sternest way, he let us know that if we *ever* appeared before him again for anything, he was going to make sure we did prison time, and lots of it.

Boom! Again, we were off the hook and back on the streets. We were taking things for granted, but still too young and naïve to realize it.

When I was gangbanging and drug dealing, I never really got to enjoy true peace or happiness, because I was always looking over my shoulder, never trusting anyone, always wondering if someone was lurking in the shadows waiting to put a bullet in me. No matter how hard I tried to do good, the bad would always surface and prevent me from achieving that. I wanted to have my cake and eat it too. But no gang member can serve two masters. I tried and fell flat on my face, hard.

Before I hung up my colors and walked away from gangbanging and drug dealing, I had it all: money, power, respect. You name it, I had it. One little incident caused me to lose it all. The worst part of losing it all was knowing just how good I'd had it. But I played the game of cat and mouse with 5-0 (police) and I lost. Big time.

I deeply regret that I had to learn my lesson the hard way. Not because I feel sorry for myself, but because of the destruction I caused: the irreversible havoc I created in my community, all the families I destroyed or almost destroyed (including my own), and all the pain and anguish I caused others who didn't have it coming. I've had many recurring nightmares of the life I once lived. But I'm dealing with it.

I have much to look forward to now that I am retired from the gang life and no longer selling poison. I may still be in prison, but I won't be spending the rest of my life in here, as I easily could have. I am thankful that I'm still alive, that I actually lived through the gang life that almost destroyed me. Now that I'm gang and drug free, my goal is to set an example for other gang members who also want out of the gang life. I want to dedicate my time, money, and streetwise skills to help gang members turn their lives around for the better. Especially younger brothers and sisters just now stepping onto the playing field who aren't fully prepared to play the type of deadly game that's played. I want to help them before they make the mistake of getting in too deep. I believe that my newfound faith in God will help me to show those whose lives I've already touched, and will continue to touch, how to remain gang and drug free.

If someone as bad as I was can turn his life around, then I know anyone can. This is my life now, a life that took a wrong turn back in the dayz, but is now back on the straight and narrow. I wouldn't trade it for anything in my past. I wrote this piece to prove that anyone can change. If you are walking down the same destructive path I once walked, you too can change. The choice is yours.

Martha

Ronald Gearles

Concord, New Hampshire

The wind screamed and blasted as I trudged my way through the miserable, black Boston snow, toward the door and the heat of the city shelter. A big, red-faced police officer greeted me there, and to my surprise, gently asked if I was all right. Too cold to talk, I nodded my head that I was OK. He signed me in, and I stepped through the looking glass.

The first thing that hit me was the terrible smell. Vomit, urine, and unwashed bodies all thrown together sent waves of nausea crashing over me. It was all I could do to keep from retching right there in the doorway. Now I knew the foulness of the refugee camp and the hold of the slave ship.

Three hundred of us were packed into a room that could safely and comfortably hold fifty. Men lay on the cold brick floor, end to end and side to side. Once in place, one could scarcely move without touching his neighbor intimately. We were sardines in a can. The scene, almost ghostly in the dim yellow light of the exit signs, showed men moving and writhing to get comfortable on the cold stone floor, not as men, but as some great undulating worm, squirming and struggling to get free of something. Panic began to swell in me, and taking control of myself, I began to step over sleeping bodies and made my way to the bathroom.

The bathrooms were shocking. They were little more than open latrines. Human excrement was everywhere—on the floors and even on the walls, obviously thrown there with great abandon. Blood, old and black and coagulated, stained the broken urinals. And brown water beetles, each the size of a man's thumb, scampered boldly about and feasted on toilet stains, a used condom with blood on it, and on each other. With great revulsion, I urinated and ran fast from the place.

Now I listened. Men snored and coughed and gagged. The cacophony of phlegmatic and tubercular lungs was punctuated here and there by a moan or a scream of someone terrified, thrashing in the throes of a nightmare. My senses were overwrought with the loathsomeness and ugliness of it all. I reached into my back pocket and retrieved my bliss and my agony—a small glassine bag of heroin. I snorted it down in one good blow, and in ten minutes I was ready to take my place in the body of the worm.

I searched for a moment or two until I found a place fairly dry and uninhabited. Then I lay down on the hard brick, resting my head on my arms and wallowing in the glow of the black magic I had just ingested. It was then that I noticed the old man. He was lying there, asleep and dressed in rags—rags layered upon rags, and holes in every rag. He was a bum, a bum with noisy, bad dreams. He kept crying, and snoring, and pleading with someone named Martha. So I lay there watching him dream and listening to him talk to his dreams. Finally, in the wee hours, I grew tired and decided I had better get some sleep, for I would need it if I were to face the morrow and another freezing day wandering the streets, looking and waiting. But try as I might, I could not sleep, for the man was weeping incessantly and calling ever louder in his sleep to Martha. Finally, I seized the old man by the collar and threatened to break his face if he didn't sleep quietly. I didn't hear him again for the rest of the night.

At six o'clock the next morning the lights came on, and the big, red policeman came in and gave everyone ten minutes to be up and out the door. I turned over on the floor, barely awake, rubbing my eyes, yawning and looking around. Suddenly, I noticed a puddle on the floor directly under the old man. He was lying in it, and so was I. I was wet; worse yet, I was pissy wet. The foul smell confirmed it: the old man had pissed himself—and me. I shook him angrily. "Wake up, you old bastard. I'm going to break your head!" But he didn't move. So I shoved him hard, attempting to roll him over. And he was heavy—heavy, I thought, like a dead man. Because that's what he was: as dead as stone, eyes staring off into eternity, mouth open, as if he died protesting his demise, or trying to say one more thing to the world, or to Martha.

Well, I just sat there with him for ten minutes or so, just taking it all in. After all, I'd never slept with a dead man before, and having to go out into the frozen city soaked through in a dead man's urine was a thing that required some small amount of courage and resolve.

Then I began to think about him, about the man, the human being whose life had gone out of him here at the end of the world. Who was Martha, I thought. Obviously, she was someone he cared about very much. And how did he come to this destitution? What was his story? And then I thought about my words to him that night. The last thing this man heard from another human being was a threat to break his face. The last thing he probably felt was fear. Cruel words had ushered him into oblivion, and now I felt like shit. But there was no fixing it now. I took his hat, scarf, and gloves, and headed back out into the cold.

End of the Game

Kevin Lee

Jamestown, California

My name is Kevin. I am thirty-one years old and serving my second prison term. I am in San Quentin State Prison. In California, we have the "three strikes" law, which means on your third serious felony charge, you receive twenty-five years to life in prison. This offense is my second strike. I will be in prison until late 1999. This is my story. If you're expecting a happy ending, you might as well stop reading right now. I'm not going to tell you that I've been saved or reformed, but what I hope to accomplish is that you will understand me. I have just recently become aware of who and what I am. There is no sad story or tragedy to blame. I made myself into the person I am.

I grew up in a middle-class family in the suburbs of San Francisco. I got into drugs and crime at an early age. I never considered myself a bad person. As my crimes grew more serious, so did my excuses for committing them. Shit, nothing was my fault. Everybody was out to fuck me, but I was gonna fuck them first. I found that I liked the reputation I was getting, but hell, I still thought it was only a game. I truly believed that I was just pretending to be this evil person. Nobody else saw it that way.

As the police became aware of me, I grew more and more defiant. I had no fear of cops and I wanted them to know it. I went as far as to find out where certain cops lived. I then went to their homes and took my revenge. This was my first serious arrest. It was for going to one cop's home and busting out his car windows and, shortly after, going to another's and terrorizing his family. I was questioned about several

76

other incidents but not convicted. I could not figure out what the judge was making such a big deal about. After all, it was just a game.

I went to Juvenile Hall, but that didn't even slow me down. I graduated to selling drugs, and with that I discovered guns. I fell in love with the power and the terror I could inflict. I quickly lost all of my friends. No one wanted to be around me for fear of what I might do on the spur of the moment. I chalked this up to them being a bunch of pussies. Soon, my only friends were dealers, thieves, and people even I didn't really like. I still thought, "I'm not really like these people."

My arrest record included assault with a deadly weapon, concealed weapons, theft, fighting, and quite a few other charges, but I managed to escape the system without getting any real time.

But soon things started to get really out of hand. I became deeply involved in drug sales and other serious crimes. I was living in constant paranoia. I never went anywhere without a gun. I knew I was getting in too deep, but still I convinced myself that I wasn't a bad person and it really was just pretend.

I found out where a certain San Francisco cop lived and that he had a lot of weapons in the house. He lived in my old neighborhood. I went down there and hooked up with some old friends who had not seen me in a while. I brought a lot of booze and a bunch of crank* with me. We partied all night, and then I convinced them to take me to the cop's house. I guess they did not think I would really do it because when I went down, I had to make a lot of threats just to keep them under control. I did the job, got the guns, and sold them. Of course, when it all came down, those people snitched me off so fast I didn't have time to think. The cops raided my house and took me away. I can assure you it was not a pleasant trip. They did not care for the fact that I had robbed one of their own. But I had a good lawyer who got my sentence down to two years in a state prison.

I had just turned twenty-two. While I was in prison, I found out that the FBI had me down as a suspect in some commercial hijackings and that several other police agencies were investigating me for other crimes. Around that same time, my father died. It was all getting to be too much. I decided to try and change my life around.

---

* *Crank:* crystal methamphetamine, a highly potent stimulant. Also known on the street as *crystal*, *crystal method*, and *speed*.

Shortly after being released from prison, I met a woman whom I eventually married. She was older than I was and had children. I thought it was just what I needed. I changed my ways, and people were amazed at the person I was becoming. I had a great job and family, a nice house, and just about everything else I could want. This lasted for about four years. Then I began to notice that I was thinking again about crime. I missed the rush. I prayed to God to make this feeling go away. But that helped only as long as I let it. I blamed my feelings on everything and anybody I could. Things quickly became worse. Before long, I began drinking and became abusive to my family and friends. I've always believed that no man should ever hit a woman, but somehow in my mind I convinced myself that what I was doing wasn't really hitting, and if I believed that, then I assumed she would too. I became very self-destructive. I did everything I could to lose all I had. I needed a reason to hate. My wife was afraid to ask me to leave. And in some twisted way, I hated her for that.

One night, I finally snapped and pushed things a little too far. I left the house and went into the city to find some of my old crime partners. Later that night, we went on a rampage. I wound up seriously hurting someone for no reason. The people I was with stared at me in shock and said I was fucking crazy. I remember them leaving me there. How could things have gone so wrong?

I withdrew five hundred dollars from our bank account at the Versatel machine—enough to stay loaded for two days. A couple of mornings later, I woke up in a seedy hotel in a bad part of the city, but I felt totally at peace. Somehow, without realizing it, I had come to a decision. I was going to end my life. It made perfect sense. Since everyone else was to blame for the direction my life had taken, I even played with the idea of taking a few people with me. But in the end, I was just too tired. I went to the corner and bought a bunch of pills from some dope fiend. I wanted to make sure I did it right, so I went to the drug store and asked what the strongest sleeping pills I could buy were. I bought two packs and started for home. My wife let me stay in the family room for the night. I sat looking at the pills and remembered thinking how strange it was that this felt so right.

I decided to take a handful first, so I would be sleepy when I took the rest. I sat and prayed for a while, asking forgiveness for what I was about to do. This was the only aspect of the whole thing that I felt bad about. I ended up falling asleep. At three in the morning, I woke up angry with myself, because I wanted to be dead before morning. So I quickly took the rest of the pills. The last thing I said was, "Let's see what's next."

I woke up in the hospital a few days later. When my head finally cleared enough to think, I was very angry. My wife came to see me and told me she loved me and wanted to try to work things out. She still did not understand what it was all about. After several days in the psych ward, I began to feel better and thought I could try it one more time. The doctor put me on disability for depression. I tried to stop the thoughts that kept getting me into so much trouble. It all worked out for a while, but the descent back was fast and furious.

It all broke one night when my wife and I were drinking. She told me how she really felt and said that everyone in the house hated me and wanted me to leave. She said a lot of things that really hit close to home, and it pissed me off. I walked up to her and pointed my finger at her and said, "Pow, you're dead. You just haven't stopped breathing yet." My mother-in-law was there and she went for the phone to call the police. I grabbed a few things and got out quick. As I was walking down the street, I saw a few cop cars going toward the house. My adrenaline was pumping and it felt good.

It took only a few days to get right back into the swing of things. It had been a while and I felt like a kid in a candy store. I knew some people that wanted me to do some things for them. I decided it was time to try the big leagues.

Within a few weeks, I had already started the process of getting a new name in another state. I went about and burned every bridge I could think of. I talked my sister into giving me a ride, and I remember her not being happy when she found out she was taking me to a gun store. I falsified some forms and got the rifle I wanted. My sister asked me what I needed it for, and I just told her that she didn't want to know.

Back at my mom's house, I worked on the gun, sawing it off as short as I could get it. Then I started making dumdum bullets. At one point, my mom walked in and saw what I was doing. I just looked at her. She didn't say a word. She just turned and left the room. I sat there and thought about how far things had gone. I was a little shocked, but hell, it was a familiar game. I might have walked to the edge of the line, but I hadn't crossed it yet. I could come back whenever I was ready.

What I didn't realize was that I had not only crossed that line but had gone so far past it that I couldn't even see it anymore. My mother and sister and everyone around me were afraid of me. I didn't give a fuck now. There was no turning back. I had finally decided that all my plans were going to work, or I'd be dead. I wasn't planning on going quietly.

A few nights later, I stayed up all night. I had a funny feeling that things were coming to a head. I went out back to smoke some weed. It was real quiet and dark. Something was wrong. I stayed awake and tried to think, but it was hard to because I was so stoned.

Finally, at four thirty in the morning, the phone rang. I knew it wasn't for me because I made all my calls from pay phones and did not give out my number. I went into the front room and listened for the answering machine to pick up. When it did, I knew I was fucked. It was the police and they were looking for me. The cop on the phone mentioned my sister's name. I thought that maybe she was in some sort of trouble, so I picked up the phone. The first thing he asked me was if this was Kevin. I told him no. He asked who I was and I told them that he didn't need to know. Then he asked if everyone in the house was all right. "Yeah," I answered. "Everyone's all right." The cop then told me that they needed me to walk out of the house with everyone in it so a police car could drive by and see if they were all right. He told me that my sister was telling some pretty wild stories about me. I told him again that I wasn't Kevin. Then my mom got on the phone. She was crying. I went around to my room, got dressed, and grabbed my gun. When I turned around, my mom and ten-year-old niece were watching me. My mom asked, "Why do you need the gun?" She said the police told her that I was not in any trouble and that they were not going to arrest me. I laughed and said, "This is all wrong, mom. Something's going on and I don't like it."

I knew they couldn't have a search warrant so soon, so I figured I could talk my way out of it long enough to get away. I took the gun to the backyard just to be safe. When I went outside, it again felt all wrong. I hid the gun then went back inside and told my mom and niece to go ahead and walk out of the house as the police had instructed. My mom pleaded with me not to do anything to provoke them. I told her not to worry. When she got to the end of the driveway, she turned and told me that she didn't see anybody. I walked out and got about halfway down the driveway when all hell broke loose.

Cops in ski masks came out of everywhere. They ran to my mom and niece and pulled them to the ground. I looked down at my chest and saw several red dots from the laser scopes. I went down without a fight. As I was kneeling on the ground with a gun pressed against my head, I looked over and saw my little niece looking at me and crying. I hoped she knew that it was just a game.

The only thing they would tell me was that I was under arrest for felony possession of a firearm. I thought, "Fuck them, they'll never find it." As it turned out, they had evacuated the neighborhood and there were members of two SWAT teams on all the rooftops. They had seen exactly where I'd put the gun. I wouldn't say shit to the cops, and when I got to jail, I found out that my bail was only ten thousand dollars. What a relief. I knew I could make bail. But I figured I'd wait until after my arraignment to pay it. That way, I could buy a little time before my next court date. I did not intend to see that judge again.

When my case was called and I was handed the charges against me, I was in for a shock. They had me for planning to commit murder and several other serious charges. I could barely hear the DA as he spoke. I was stunned. I snapped out of it though, when I heard him ask the judge to hold me without bail. The lawyer I was assigned stood up and reminded the DA that he could not do this without a formal bail hearing. I still felt hope until the judge announced that I would be held on two million dollars bail pending a hearing. I told myself not to trip until I spoke with my lawyer. When I did meet with him, it wasn't good. He told me that he'd had a meeting with the DA and the judge and there was no way in hell that they were going to let me out. He said that they were both in agreement that if I got out, I would go ahead and kill my intended victims and anyone else who got in my way. I still could not believe that people could possibly perceive me in this way. It was just a fucking game! My lawyer went on to tell me that they were going to press for twenty-six years but that with a little time he could get it down to fifteen, thirteen of which I would have to serve. Again, I felt that calm wash over me. I knew what I had to do. The lawyer went on for a while about how it might turn out that they could destroy the credibility of the witnesses and that then it would be a whole new ball game. I had to laugh at his choice of words. I told him to go ahead and do whatever he felt was right. I didn't care.

When I got back to the cellblock, I called my mom and told her not to worry about anything and that I loved her very much. I then spent the day trying to fashion an instrument to end my life. I tried everything I could think of, but nothing was strong enough. Finally, I decided to use a pencil. Since I am not that fond of pain, I was not too happy with this choice. But I figured if I could hit the jugular in the first try, it wouldn't be too bad.

I did a lot of jumping jacks to get my blood racing so I could find the right spot. My cellmate was a trusty, so I was going to wait until he went to work that night before I went ahead with it. By a weird stroke of fate, after my cellie left, the guard dropped off razors to shave. He told me he would pick them up again in about an hour. Shit, I couldn't believe it! I hadn't even thought of trying to get a razor. I sat on my bunk for a little while, staring at the razor in my hand. I knew that once I broke it open to get the blade, there would be no turning back. So, I went ahead and did it.

I did some more jumping jacks to get the blood pumping. Looking in the mirror, I brought the razor to my neck. I held the blade at the very end to get the deepest cut I could. It's weird, but it didn't really hurt. What freaked me out the most was how wide the cut spread open. You could see inside. It wasn't very pretty. It bled a lot, but I knew I had missed any major veins. I made another cut. The same thing happened, so I actually reached into the open wound and made a second cut inside. It hurt like hell, and there was a lot of blood. By then, I figured I wanted to get it done as soon as possible so I did my left wrist first and then my right. I remember there was blood all over the place. Then I got dizzy, so I lay down.

I woke up in the hospital with more anger than I thought possible. They had me strapped to a bed with tubes and wires coming out of me. All kinds of people kept coming in telling me how lucky I was to be alive. My cellie had come back early and found me. If I had been conscious when he did, I would have killed him. After a while, they transferred me to a psych ward at the jail. I was to be on a twenty-four-hour watch for the duration.

Soon after that, my lawyer arrived with great news. The main witnesses recanted their testimony, and he had dug up long dirt on the others. The DA's case was crumbling. This, of course, brought forth even more people and doctors telling me that it was a sign from God that all this was happening. I do believe that God had his hand in this, but I still felt dead inside. I wasn't ungrateful. I thanked the Lord for everything he had done for me, but I just couldn't seem to summon up any emotions.

I made a deal with the DA. I would receive a second strike and serve about four years. The judge reluctantly agreed. He did say that he thought that I was a very scary person and that he felt I deserved a longer sentence.

Now here I sit in prison again. I truly wish to be a better person, but I feel as though I've traveled too far to ever turn back. I look at these youngsters that come in here and think, "Shit, they still think it's all just a game." I try to talk to some of them, but I can tell the way they look at me that they think, *I'll never be like you.* Poor bastards! It's simple. If you play the game, you pay the price.

I wish I could take all those little future gangsters out there and let them see through my eyes and feel what I feel just for a day. It would take all the glamour out of it, that's for damned sure. Maybe someone will read this and come to realize before it's too late that if you keep riding the edge, sooner or later you will fall off. I'm not asking anyone to feel sorry for me. I just would like it if people understood that I did not intend to become this person. After all, it was just a game.

So here I am, at thirty-one. I'll be getting out of prison soon, probably colder and harder than I am now. I'll have a twenty-five-year-to-life sentence hanging over my head. Unless something drastic happens, I don't see a whole lot of good things coming. I hope that I never have to face that situation. Maybe things will change. Realistically, I have to look at my past and the feelings that are with me every day and think about the many situations that will come and force me to make a choice between right and wrong. I really don't know if I have the ability or the will to make the right choice anymore. I know there's no way in hell I'll be doing a twenty-five stretch. Court will be held where I stand. The sentence will be death. I hope that you live your life well, my brothers, 'cause it's a lot easier to get where I am than you could ever imagine.

Years without Days

Revolving Door

Robert L. Johnson

San Quentin, California

The first thing I noticed were the gun towers. They reminded me of a World War II prisoner of war camp from a TV movie I'd once seen. As the gunner looked down at our arriving bus, I realized that the only wars fought in California are the wars on drugs and crime. In that same thought, I wondered exactly how effectively those wars were being waged.

We passed through the manned gates and drove slowly down the outer road that skirted San Quentin's famous yard. The walls surrounding the yard are huge and full of history. They are so old that plants and weeds grow sporadically from cracks in the six-foot-thick monolith. If these walls could talk, they would have stories over a hundred years old to tell.

Inmates walked out of the path of the bus, unconcerned at what, or who, lay within. I saw my fellow males attacking a huge weight yard, muscles glistening on bodies recovering from homelessness, unemployment, economic depression, and the latest reelection tactic—the governmental crackdown on drugs and alcohol. I wondered if certain wealthy celebrities or government officials I had read about in the newspapers had gone through something like this. I wanted to laugh out loud at the thought, but remembered the warning of the guards on the bus: "If we hear one sound from any of you, we'll kick the shit out of every body part with clothes on it (so the bruises don't show)."

We pulled up to R&R—Receiving (us) and Release (the lucky). The bus driver told us to get up and get the hell off his bus. Since we were shackled with belly and ankle chains, the process was just a bit slower than exiting your local Greyhound. My turn finally came and I touched down upon the asphalt of one of the most famous prisons in the world. On the other side of a short chain-link fence, I noticed a group of men in blue—the traditional color of those appointed to remain at San Quentin. They were watching us exit the bus, looking for "homeboys"—men returning on a parole violation. I later learned that these violations occurred quite often for things as trivial as being late when reporting to your parole officer, drinking a beer, or having a bullet in your home. The bullet is considered a weapon.

Once off the bus, we all lined up in our bright orange jumpsuits as a guard with a hand-held metal detector perused body parts for hidden weapons. Inside, we stripped so more guards could look into more body spaces for more weapons. I was given a new jumpsuit, asked several questions about enemies, gang affiliations, and sexual preferences—not exactly a job interview—and assigned to a temporary holding cell with twenty or thirty other prisoners. In each cell, the inmates had grouped themselves by race, county, and gang affiliation. I thought, *Only the strong survive in a place that boasts more deaths than some wars.*

Fingerprints, photos, and a very quick medical check came next. Inmates working for "good time" credits perform most of these procedures. You get five extra days off your sentence for every month you follow the program guidelines. If you screw up, it can all be taken away. If the mistake you make is a serious one, time can be added to your release date.

I wondered for a moment about some of these men. If they worked all day, when did that leave time for the drug and alcohol programs touted by the county judges and lawyers? When did they get the opportunity to improve the mind that placed them here, by taking college classes, for example? When I asked this question aloud, several people around me laughed and said I must be a "cherry"—someone new to the system. One older convict told me his job handing out jumpsuits to inmates was the only training he had ever received. It paid twelve cents an hour. All the programs I asked about had been canceled long ago to save the state money. When I asked how it saved money, the older convict just looked at me and chuckled softly as he shuffled off. I had no more time to ponder this, as our group was herded outside, where we each received a bedroll, one roll of toilet paper, and the most oft-used thing you have while doing time: your identification number. Only the "cherries" received a number; I noticed many of the guys in the group didn't get one.

We were told that we were on our way to West Block. From the groans and curses, I didn't imagine it had the tennis courts or jogging trails that some former stock thief's or political figurehead's had. Boy, if I had only been rich when I committed my crime. Of course, if I had been rich . . .

As we walked up a short inclined roadway, someone pointed out West Block just ahead. Now I understood the groans and curses. It was enormous. Easily several football fields long and six stories high, West Block appeared to have been built just after the ark ran aground. Slime and layers of old paint hung from broken windows and cracked walls. It did not make a good first impression of rehabilitation. This is where they send someone who was drunk in public?

There was a guy who had been sent here a week earlier for stealing diapers for his child. He had been hurt on the job and his disability had run out. The diapers cost about fifteen dollars. The cost of housing the thief would run a little over twenty-seven thousand dollars for the one year he was sentenced to. If the government had continued his disability, his child would have had his daddy and the state would have ultimately saved over six thousand dollars. To make matters worse, the wife lost her husband, and because of that, could now claim General Assistance, costing the state an additional eleven thousand dollars.

We entered the rotunda area of West Block, or "reception housing" as it was also called. There were a few other names floating about that were much more apt. Several guards gave us the welcome speech. It was with some surprise that I heard the guard bashing the system himself: "We all have to work together with what the government gives us." In the coming months, I came to realize that some of our "babysitters" were not bad people. It's just a job. And like any business, some employees are good and some are not. Some felt they were so far above us that they were able to crap roses, and the rest of us were beneath contempt. Seeing them, I remembered being outside, working in the corporate world, stepping on toes without hesitation, while climbing the ladder and seeing everyone below me as cannon fodder.

After being given our cell numbers, we went inside. The first thought I had was that this was what the Colosseum in Rome must have sounded like as the gladiators blooded one another. The noise was incredible. West Block housed over one thousand men in the same area that only several years earlier had held a few hundred.

There were five stories of cells. Each tier had over one hundred cells. Each cell, five feet by twelve, held one toilet, one sink, two bunks, two storage cabinets, and two human lives. I was among the lucky ones housed on the bottom floors, where the air is cool. I felt for my friends who headed up the flights of stairs to the floors above.

I waited by my cell and looked inside. On the bottom bunk was a bearded human with several tattoos who rolled over to check me out. I did the same. It turned out that we would both go on to Old Folsom, also known as "The End of the Earth," and become good friends. His name at San Quentin was Smoke. He was here on a parole violation of absconding—leaving his parole area without permission.

Over the next several weeks, I learned Smoke's story. Again, the government that I had supported for so many years now held my disdain. It is the greatest government on earth, but those who run it oftentimes forget to come out of their glass castles and live with the real people. This is a prime example.

My cellmate fell to the lure of this nation's greatest problem: drugs. First marijuana, then cocaine and heroin. An up-and-comer in a computer corporation, he had lost his job and written a bad check for some merchandise. He then took the "bought" items to another store in the retail chain and returned them for cash. He did this to fuel his drug supply. He never denied his crime, or using drugs. When first arrested, he received time in the county jail. Getting drugs there was almost as easy as getting them on the street. When he got out, his habit continued. The second time he was caught, he asked for help and was offered a program, but only if he could pay 30 percent. The government would pay the rest. But he was unable to pay, so the program was out. The third time he was caught, the county revoked his probation and sentenced him to prison. He did time at another penitentiary and attended some Narcotics Anonymous classes until the instructor found a night-teaching job that paid better.

After being released that time, he got involved with a program called

Jobs Plus. They hire ex-offenders and give them jobs and a chance at a new life. Smoke went to his parole office to discuss working for that program but was turned down because the program was offered only in an adjoining county. He requested a transfer and was initially turned down. After several letters and calls, he was given the transfer paperwork. After he filled it out, he was informed that it would take at least ninety days for the paperwork to be processed. In the meantime, the drugs won again. As his problems became worse—which he admitted were mostly his fault—the habit became worse.

Smoke violated his parole two more times and was here now for violating his third. The ironic thing, he told me, was that when his time was up on this violation, he would reach his "maximum release date" and the Corrections Department would have to release him from their control. He had done a total of five and a half years in prison, and only once did parole or prison help him with his problem. He had two hundred dollars of release money to look forward to, and nothing else. No home, no income, no job. He knows he'll be back. The habit, like a hunger pang, is still growing. The thought of what might lie ahead for me is indeed very sobering.

"Man down, 3-86! Man down, 3-86!"

I awoke with a start. It was still dark outside, though the lights inside made it seem like perpetual noon.

"Man down, 3-86!" was the chant taken up by more and more inmates. Someone in cell 86 on the third floor was down. Whether it was from an illness, a stabbing, or something he did to himself, no one knew. But he was one of us and he was hurt. Soon the building echoed with the cry summoning an officer to that cell. We could hear the keys of a correctional officer slapping against his hip as he slowly walked up the stairs to find out what was wrong this time. Many minutes later, an Asian male was carried down and away on a gurney. It would be days before the grapevine informed us he had been beaten for something he had done on the streets. In here, inmates handle their own justice. Like the Italian *omertà*, or vow of silence, to snitch off the involved parties brings swift retribution.

It was difficult to sleep again, so I listened to the sounds above and around me. Every culture, every type of personality was represented.

Sigmund Freud would have enjoyed it here. I listened as a singing voice of recording quality filled the air. This guy was good. Applause and shouts of requests followed the most recent rendition. Between sets, I could hear the sound of someone preaching the horrors of sin. Perhaps this man would do best to work the miracle of redemption on himself first. I knew in my heart of my good relationship with the Divine. But I was honest enough to know that I was weak. No reception center preacher would change that. But this preacher seemed to think he had the answer to everyone else's problems. I would be happy to forsake all sin—and I mean that—if someone could truly show me how. No one wants to be evil. Some are overshadowed by it. Some need other options. Most are lost or weak. I feel as though I am a combination of all of these.

Now that everyone was beginning to wake up, the West Block flea market opened in full force. The biggest commodities are tobacco and coffee. A pair of eighty-dollar shoes can be auctioned off for a six-dollar can of tobacco. The major currency is envelopes. One thirty-three-cent envelope is equal to one rolled cigarette. Most inmates will begin to stock up on as many envelopes as possible while in the county jail. Food from the bag lunches is also used to buy tobacco or a shot of coffee. Anything from medication to wedding rings can be traded for a smoke. You name it, and it has a price in West Block.

I jumped down and looked out the bars for a minute. I thought for a second that I had seen a girl in here. After my cellie had stopped laughing, he informed me that what I had seen was known as a "he-she"—a man who dresses and acts like a woman. They even have the same mannerisms as women (and use Kool-Aid in the lunches to make lipstick) but are sans the required body parts. I would see quite a few of them during my stay and felt sorry for them, though they are certainly treated well enough.

The weeks passed and I became a "seasoned" con. I learned the proper way to dress, where to sit, and who to talk to. I came to respect my fellow inmates. Some of the minds in here would put Einstein to shame. And I don't mean the doctors, lawyers, and corporate executives who live here. There are alarm system experts who could train the companies that manufacture the alarms. And computer wizards that could break any code known to the modern world.

The most important lesson to be learned here is how to beat the system. So many have tried to follow the rules, only to have them change at the whim of our government. Many prisoners who only need a drug or alcohol program become more institutionalized with each mandatory return. If one is caught having a beer while on parole, he is considered in violation and is usually returned to this same programless environment. No help. No rehabilitation. Only warehousing. You become accustomed to being returned. It is no longer a deterrent but rather a way of life. You begin to look for ways to beat the system instead of cooperating with it.

For example, you may hide your drinking or drug problem from your parole officer by using a chemical under the fingernail that, when mixed with your urine sample, negates the test results. Why tell someone that you need help when all it gets you is another trip here?

This system, like the parent who leaves his family homeless, should be made to account for its wrongs. Don't misunderstand me. I feel that I deserve my sentence. No one forced me to do wrong. And I blame only myself. But I do not deserve to be warehoused. Zoo animals are treated more humanely. I also know I deserve a second chance. I paid for my crime. I've worked hard in here, both at a job and on myself. But how does warehousing men for years keep them from coming back, or help them to beat their addictions?

I complete this story from a minimum-security area within San Quentin. There are about one thousand of us in this unit. Of this thousand, 87 percent of us are here for charges stemming from drugs or alcohol, and nearly all have been returned to custody for parole violations. Instead of attempting to fix the problem, it is being swept further under the rug. With the newly instituted "three strikes" law, judges now have the discretion to sentence an individual to twenty-five years or more for a third felony conviction. *Any* conviction. Under the new law, a judge sentenced a man to twenty-five years to life for stealing a ten-speed bicycle. Another man was also sentenced to twenty-five years to life for stealing a woman's purse to support his lifelong drug habit. In this case, the victim appeared in court on behalf of the defendant to plead that the sentence was both extreme and unjustified, to no avail.

Arguably, the law may have merit in certain cases. However, until the justice system controls the requirements of handing out such life-ending sentences, overcrowding, underfunding, and a complete loss of the future for so many who desperately need the help of rehabilitation programs will continue to plague our prison systems.

While I've been writing this piece, two inmates housed in this unit have died. One overdosed on drugs. He simply fell asleep in his bed and never woke up. Another violator discovered that his wife had left him because he could not beat his habit. He finally beat it. He hung himself.

From the Inside Out

Jeff Parnell (with Mike McLane)

Helena, Oklahoma

April 9, 1996

The visits at Jess Dunn were one of the finest privileges that facility had to offer. Each inmate's family was allowed to bring food and use the picnic tables with outdoor grills during the 8 A.M. to 8 P.M. visits. We were also allowed to take certain items back to the dorm with us when we left.

This is where I first met Andy. As I was signing out from the visiting room, I noticed a tall, lanky youngster, about eighteen or so, with fair skin and big, brown puppy-dog eyes standing by the exit door with a bag of goodies in his hands, reluctant to leave. As I approached him, it was easy to see that his eyes were filled with fear.

"Hey, man, what's the deal?" was my form of introduction to Andy.

"Well, um, see, uh, these black guys are gonna take my candy bars away from me as soon as I leave. They do it every week!" he said, his eyes starting to water.

A sick feeling struck my stomach, the same feeling I got every time I encountered this type of immorality—the strong, or in this case the many, preying on the weak.

"Give me the bag and come on," I said. With Andy close behind, I marched right through the middle of those so-called gangbangers. "Not today, boys!" I broadcast clearly. If looks could kill, I'd have been dead several times over.

If they had given any indication that an altercation was in the wings, I was fully prepared to dish out far more than they were ready to handle. What I couldn't finish, my "Road Dogs"—"Mad Dog" Matlock, "Doc" Coggins, and "Combat" Steve—would have cleaned up with the greatest of ease. Fortunately, all they wanted to do was look hard.

Back at the dorm, and after much investigation, I found out that this poor youngster had been robbed several times. He had lost everything that his family had sent him. He barely owned more than the clothes on his back. That's also when I found out that his nickname was "Snuffy." I learned that he was doing a short sentence, for possession of stolen property.

"Snuffy, who's been robbing you?" I asked.

"Those same guys," he replied.

"Aren't you going to do anything about it?" I questioned.

"Nope. I don't want to hurt anybody and I don't really need any more trouble. So no, I'm not gonna do anything about it," he said softly, with his head down so I couldn't see his eyes.

"Well, then, I guess you're the one who has to live with it," I said.

I felt bad for this boy, but there was nothing I could do. If I had gone around and retrieved all of his property, it wouldn't have lasted. It would have only been a quick fix and not a solution. Besides, I was far too busy to stick with this youngster 24/7. If he wasn't going to stand up for himself, then he was on his own as far as I was concerned.

A week or so later, Snuffy started hanging around with this Mexican dude, Enrico, who had offered his assistance with the problem at hand. I knew it was a mistake, but I didn't say a word. Enrico helped himself to anything and everything that Snuffy had, any time he pleased. A type of protection fee, if you will. Enrico also talked Snuffy into taking him visiting, on the buddy system, whenever Snuffy's parents would come on the weekends. Enrico would then invite all his compadres to share in the wealth, and week after week, they devoured any food brought by Andy's parents.

Finally, I had all I could stand and decided to put a stop to this charade. In my eyes, the "protection" was even worse than being robbed by the gangbangers. Robbery is robbery, no matter how you color it.

"Snuffy, let's talk," I told him. "The time has come for you to be a man. Son, you can't live like this all your life, and it will never end if *you* don't end it. I know you don't like violence, but sometimes there's just no other way. Some people only understand force; therefore, you're going to have to force them to respect you. This whole thing has gone way too far already, so let's put a stop to it. I'll help you and show you exactly what to do, but you'll need to listen carefully and follow my instructions meticulously. Agreed?"

With his head hung low again and in a voice that was barely audible, I heard a single word: "Agreed."

"Snuffy, everyone has fear in them," I continued. "How you use that fear is up to you. Fear can be your worst enemy if you let it eat you up. Or, if harnessed correctly, it can be your best weapon. I'm going to teach you to harness it and then release it at just the right moment. That moment will set you free from this life of terror you've been living. OK?"

"OK," he answered, raising his head.

I looked directly into his eyes and told him first to pray. Pray that the whole ordeal would just dissolve, but if it didn't, that we wouldn't have to hurt anyone. And that if there was no other way than to battle, that we would be protected from harm.

"Snuffy, here's the plan. First, you tell Enrico that he can no longer help himself to your belongings. And also, that he won't be visiting with you any more from here on out."

Reluctantly, he did as I said. I knew that this would stun the Mexican and we would have little time before he retaliated. Sure enough, I saw Enrico on his bunk, working up his anger for a confrontation with Andy.

"Okay, Snuffy, he'll be over here in just a few minutes wanting to fight."

"But I can't fight!" Snuffy said in a squeaky voice.

"Don't worry, I told you that I would show you what to do. First, get your largest drinking cup. Your quart-sized 'Thirst Buster' will do just fine. Fill it three-quarters of the way with hot water. Then add bleach and shampoo—bleach to burn and shampoo to stick."

Looking down, I noticed that his hands had begun to shake. "Can you feel it?" I screamed.

"Feel what?" he screamed back.

"The fear!"

"Yeah, I feel it!" he said.

"Let it build, boy, let it build! I'll let you know when the time is right to pull the trigger and release it."

"OK, OK, OK," he muttered, as his body began to tremble.

Furthering my lesson, I told him, "Now put your stinger* in the cup and bring it to a boil."

"Here he comes, son," I said. "Now, you must do all that you possibly can to talk your way out of this confrontation. You must be absolutely, 100 percent in the right before you use any type of force like this against anyone. Do you understand?"

"Yeah, yeah, I understand," he declared.

In a flash, Enrico was upon Snuffy, backing him against the wall. Spitting in his face, Enrico said, "What's the matter, punk, ain't we friends no more?" Then he head-butted Andy right in the nose with a blow that nearly knocked him out.

"I don't want to hurt you, Enrico," were the only words that came out of Snuffy's mouth.

Enrico then belted Snuffy in the stomach, doubling him over, followed by another head butt.

With blood dripping down his nose into his mouth, Andy shakily repeated his plea, "Please, I don't want to hurt you. I don't want any trouble at all! So please, for the last time, *leave me alone!*"

Enrico's eyes narrowed as he responded, "Why, you weak punk, I ought to run this pencil right through your fuckin' neck!"

With that, Snuffy cut his eyes sharply in my direction, as if to ask, "Now?" I nodded slightly, signaling that it was time to unleash that harnessed fear. With one smooth motion, Snuffy reached for the boiling concoction that had gone unnoticed behind him. *Splash!* Water, bleach, shampoo, stinger, cup and all hit Enrico right square in that mug of his!

"Arghhhhhhhhhh!" screamed Enrico.

The bloodcurdling scream sounded like it had come straight from hell. Instantly, Snuffy grabbed Enrico by his hair. He jerked Enrico's head in a downward motion, while blasting him with uppercuts. The first shot split the aggressor's right eye wide open. Shot number two sliced his cheek clean to the bone. This was followed by a flurry of punches that any boxer would have been proud to deliver. Snuffy beat

---

* *Stinger*: a small electrical device used to heat water for coffee, soup, etc.

Enrico from one end of the dorm to the other, with an audience of one hundred or more. Among these onlookers were the gangbangers that had made prey of Andy so often in the past.

Finally, the po-lice* showed up and broke Andy and Enrico apart. As they were being hauled off to lock-up, I heard a voice say, "Oh, my God, did you see that guy's face? It was bubbling like some kind of experiment!"

After the cops had left the building, I immediately got on the phone and called Andy's parents. I wanted to inform them as to what had transpired.

Andy's father asked, "Did he win?"

"Sure did. Beat him bad!" I replied.

"Parnelli," he continued, "tell my son I'm proud of him!"

A couple of days later, when Andy was let out of lock-up, he made his rounds, collecting all the property that had been stolen from him. It was a funny thing, but none of those bad asses had any objections about returning to Snuffy what was his.

It saddens me that young men like Andy have to suffer that kind of trauma. Unfortunately, sometimes there is just no other way to deal with idiots like Enrico and those gangbangers. Violence is all they understand. I believe that Snuffy received their full attention and respect that day. He was then able to do the rest of his time in peace.

Snuffy is out of prison now and I hope he has learned a valuable lesson—never to return to this madness.

I can picture it now: as that scene was unfolding, there had to be a TV somewhere in the background with ol' "Mr. Legislator" on it, declaring that prisoners have it too easy, while Snuffy was fighting for his life and dignity. Imagine that!

April 25, 1996
(Entry made by Mike McLane)

I am a convicted armed robber. That is the official title bestowed on me by the courts. Like all titles, mine designates where I rank in our social hierarchy and what my responsibilities are. I rank at the bottom—

---

* *Po-lice*: in Oklahoma, convicts' term for correctional officers, pronounced as two distinct syllables.

less than any citizen, as I can never vote or own a firearm. I will likely be legally discriminated against for the rest of my life by anyone who learns what my title is. My responsibility accompanying my title is very clear and easily described: to stay in prison until my sentence is completed.

I don't like my title, but I earned it and deserve it and therefore accept it. I've been in prison for well over a decade now, and I find it rather interesting that I have nearly stopped consciously associating my criminal acts of so long ago with the punishment I am experiencing today. About the only time I consciously associate the act with the consequence is when I'm thinking deeply enough to explain it to someone, which is something we are neither required nor encouraged to do in here.

I question the efficacy of a system of punishment in which the offender, already having serious character defects, is put into a giant pressure cooker with many other unbalanced and disturbed people for years at a time and left to stew in his own juices without ever being required or encouraged to deal with the character flaws and methods of thinking that got him there in the first place. When he is finally released, the statisticians tell us there is an 80 percent likelihood he will return to prison within three years. The media and politicians explain to us that it's because we have it too good in here, and we must like it. After all, we are provided with a bed and three meals a day, and someone to make all our decisions for us. If this sounds good to them, it certainly gives us valuable insight into their aspirations and values.

I propose that our recidivism rate is so high not because we like it in here but because most of us haven't a clue about what choices to make in our lives or how to perceive the world in a manner that will keep us out. What few moral strategies we once had don't work in here and are not valued, so they are forgotten. We learn institutional survival skills based on deception, intimidation, and violence. We become filled with hate and frustration because we know that we are not valued, and our lives seem meaningless. When our lives are valueless to us, so is everyone else's. The cause and effect of the punishment drift further apart with every year endured, and all that's left is an overwhelming feeling of oppression.

This system would make a small amount of sense if the plan were to keep these men forever, or kill them. It makes no sense at all to release them into society after years of conditioning them to live in another world where might is right and hatred is the power fueling existence.

I don't pretend to have all the answers, and it is far easier to point out defects than to propose solutions, but it is clear to me that we must find a way to convince the American people that their lust to seek vengeance and inflict pain on those that injured them only escalates the cycle of violence and solves nothing. We claim to be a Christian nation, but Christianity is based on attitudes of forgiveness and compassion and love for your fellow man—not the desire to see him suffer.

I do not advocate coddling criminals. I only suggest that it could be better handled in a thoughtful and humane way. Either that, or kill us all.

Danny

Steven King Ainsworth

San Quentin, California

March 11, 1996. Somewhere in Merced County, California, this morning, a judge of the Superior Court will wake up, shower, shave, eat breakfast, kiss his wife good-bye, and drive to the county courthouse, where he will dress in black robes, mount an elevated dais, and preside over a gathering of attorneys. He, in concert with the others, will decide the exact date and precise time that the state of California will kill my best friend.

There will not be much bickering at this court hearing. The state, with all its power and money, holds all the cards. My friend of sixteen years holds none. He has no money, no power, nowhere to turn. He won't even be present in the courtroom. His fate will be decided in a remote act far from his death row cell, where he will awaken, wash his face, and eat a breakfast of hard-boiled egg and rehydrated potato.

What won't be said at this hearing—or in the days to follow, which will culminate in my friend being strapped down to a table in cruciform, his arms outstretched and the veins therein punctured by stainless steel hypodermic needles as his live being is filled with a poisonous mixture of drugs until he is declared dead—is that he is a human being and a good friend. Despite how much the state and media try to stigmatize him with the animal label, I will remember Danny for his humanity, his laughter, his pain, his heart, his comforting words, his kindness, and his compassion.

I first met Keith Daniel Williams (Danny) in 1980, when he yelled down the tier to me from his cell on death row, asking me if I needed

102

anything. Did I need some coffee, tobacco, stamps, envelopes, writing paper, or a book to read? Having just gotten up to the Shelf (as death row was called back then) from the adjustment center, nine days after being sentenced to death in Sacramento County, I had nothing and yelled back, "Yes. Who am I talking to?" The voice replied, "This is Danny in cell 28!"

A while later, a guard brought a brown paper bag to my cell with some coffee, tobacco, stamps, envelopes, writing paper, a paperback book, and a note written in shaky handwriting telling me the dynamics of the row and advising me which exercise yard group to ask for. About a week later, I met Danny face to face in the birdcage yard atop the north cellblock where the twenty-seven men condemned to death exercised.

Over the years, Danny and I became close friends. Friendship is a rarity in here. Everyone plays their cards close to their chest, and very seldom do you allow anyone to become privy to your innermost thoughts.

Danny was different. I felt a kinship with him. Hell, we could relate. We both had a lot of time under the gun: he a little more than I, having started his convict career at the age of nine as a ward of the state. Both of us had been through the crucible of gladiator school at the prison for young adults at Deuel Vocational Institution and had progressed through the penal system, ultimately ending up on death row at San Quentin. We would chuckle when we heard the governor talk about career criminals. Shit! We were career *convicts*! Between us, we had over sixty years in custody.

Danny shared my joy at seeing my infant son in 1980. A few years later, in 1984, when my shit hit the fan and I spun out, screaming, yelling, crying, and pleading for the gunrail to shoot me, it was Danny who stepped between the gun and me and pushed me into my cell, warning me that the goon squad was coming. I had allowed my street problems, a wayward wife, no visits with my son, a dying mother, and my frustration with the courts to get to me. Danny tried to calm me down, but I was beyond help and continued to rant and rave. Lighting my cell afire and forcing a confrontation with the guards, I was tasered and forcibly extracted from my burned-out cell and sent to the hole for a year.

Danny kept in touch with me, sending messages to see how I was doing. When my mother died in 1985, he was the first person to console me through my grief. I did the same for him when his daughter was killed by a hit-and-run driver. Yes, even condemned killers lose family members to crime and feel the same emotions as other crime victims.

Now and then, Danny liked to pull a practical joke. One time, there was a tour group of civilians up on the Shelf looking down the death row tier. Danny put a big dust bunny, with broken broom straws hidden in it, down the back of another convict's pants. The convict thought it was a mouse, and when he slapped his backside, he thought the mouse had bitten him! Yelling and jumping about, the guy took off his pants and boxer shorts right there in front of the tour! We all tried our best to cover up our snickers and guffaws.

Later, the guy found out Danny was the culprit and decided to play a joke on Danny. He put some jalapeño juice in the top end of Danny's tube of Preparation H. Well, it didn't work. Some days later, we asked Danny if he used any of it. He said he had, and thought it was real good medicine because it burned so bad!

After seven years, I was able to have my son brought up to San Quentin for a visit. He didn't remember me; he was only three when I'd last seen him. I introduced him to Danny, who was in the visiting room, and they became friends. Danny told my son that I spoke of him often and loved him and that my son should be proud of me.

Later, my son told me what Danny had said. I told him I was happy that he was proud of me, but that he should always keep in mind that there are victims of my crimes that he should also think about. Danny agreed with me, and we talked some more about remorse and restorative justice and how difficult it is for a capital defendant to address these issues publicly.

Over the years, when Danny had the opportunity to talk with younger, noncondemned convicts, I heard him advise them to turn away from crime and to control their antisocial behavior. He would coach these young men no matter what their race. He cautioned that the path they were on would only lead to a life of pain and sorrow. It was as if, by looking at them, he was looking at himself at twenty-five, and he did not want them to repeat the cycle of drugs, alcohol, crime, and imprisonment that he had gone through.

Each time we would receive a bad decision from the court and an execution date would be set, we both would want to give up and die. But I would ask Danny and he would ask me, "What good would it do? What message would we be leaving our children? How would it affect those left behind on the row?"

Danny encouraged me in my art and in other creative endeavors. He enjoyed sending copies of my black-and-white drawings to his friends and family. I enjoyed introducing Danny to my friends and family, and we often arranged our visits so we could have group visits together. Sometimes there would be an at-risk teenager in the group, and Danny would tell him not to look up to us as role models but rather to his parents and teachers, and to stay in school.

Danny knew the value of education. Because of his early contact with the justice system, he had to teach himself to read and write in a prison cell. He read voraciously and found great wonder in words. He felt sad about the decline of public education in California and the nation. He expressed exasperation over society's prison-building boom and the in- carceration of so many young lives at the expense of education and quality schools.

One of the most surprising things to me was that Danny was even able to think. In the late 1960s, after an event similar to the one I described earlier in which I was sent to the hole, Danny was subjected to electroshock therapy at Vacaville. He struggled with speech and memory ever since, and it amazed me that he was even able to put two sentences together.

In the late 1980s, facing execution dates on a seemingly regular basis, I undertook researching my son's genealogy so he might know his ancestry. I told Danny what I was doing and he expressed an interest in doing the same for his grandchildren—yes, he was a doting grandpa— and asked if I would help him. I agreed to. After sending out a few letters, we found a preponderance of evidence indicating that Danny was the descendant of early Saxon, Norman, and Celtic royals. His ancestors emigrated to America in the 1600s and settled in Texas with Stephen Austin's early colonists in the 1830s.

Over the years, Danny and I both lost family members to crime, alcohol, drugs, suicide, incarceration, and death. I could always count on him to help me through the hardest of times. Danny's mother died in 1995, and though I did my best to console him, her passing and a bad court decision moved Danny to publicly express a desire to be executed. He asked me to help him. For the first time I told him no. I would not help him die. The attorney general did not act immediately on Danny's desire, probably because there was a real question of Danny's competence to make such a decision.

But now, all the legal mumbo jumbo and rigamarole are over and Danny is dead. Keith Daniel Williams was executed by lethal injection at San Quentin State Prison and declared dead at 12:08 A.M. on May 3, 1996.

The state raised him from the age of nine, fried his brain at twenty-five, and killed him at forty-eight. I could not say good-bye to him. I did not want to. I told him to send me a sign—not a white feather like John and Julian Lennon's, but a sign nonetheless—letting me know if it is better on the other side. I haven't received it yet.

My friend is dead and I do not think the world is any better for it. His poisoned cadaver joins the rising body count from death row since reinstatement of capital punishment in California in 1977:

> **Four men have been executed.**
> **Two men have been murdered.**
> **Eleven men have committed suicide.**
> **Nine men have died of natural causes.**
> **One man was shot and killed by a guard.**

Another Day

Michael Wayne Hunter

San Quentin, California

It's just another day on a death row exercise yard, another day of pumping iron, exactly like the more than three thousand days I have already spent here at San Quentin State Prison awaiting my execution.

As I stand in line for my turn at the weights, my eyes wander to the nearby cinder block wall that separates me from the rest of the world. The yellow wall contrasts sharply with my blue prison clothing, making me an excellent target for the guards' assault rifles.

My eyes linger on the wall, stopping to note the marks left by bullets that have banged off its imposing surface. I see that no two bullets have hit in precisely the same place. Perhaps to stand in front of a previously scarred spot on the wall will keep me safe from future bullets. I smile and shake my head at such an absurd notion. There is no safe place when a guard pulls a trigger, sending a bullet careening around the yard. If the bullet doesn't immediately hit a prisoner, it will impact and fragment on the wall, ricocheting randomly, often stopping only when it finds the flesh of an inmate. It's almost simultaneous—the crack of the rifle and the moan of the struck man.

My eyes travel up the yellow wall to the blue sky above and join the seabirds wheeling about the sky, surfing in the wind. Their piercing cries mock me as they invite me to join their dance in the freedom of the world beyond the barbed and razor wire that confines me. After a moment, I've had enough and look around the yard at the other condemned men who have chosen to come out today. We are like hamsters running merrily on a wheel, enjoying the illusion that movement is freedom.

As I watch the condemned men sweating in the sunlight, I begin to imagine the marbled headstones bearing the chiseled names of their murdered victims scattered about the yard. Suddenly, the exercise yard becomes more crowded as we are joined by the ghosts of the victims of the violence that led to death row.

I see one man followed by more than a dozen crying and sobbing boys, asking why he had to take their lives after he raped them. The condemned man tries to ignore them, but they crowd around, demanding an answer.

I see another man haunted by his father, his dad screaming that he will beat him bloody when he gets his hands on him. The condemned man answers quietly, "No, you will never touch me again, because you're dead and I killed you." But there is no hint of triumph in the condemned man's voice regarding his Pyrrhic victory over his father, as he turns and walks sadly away from the ghost.

I see a security guard in uniform asking a condemned man, "Why did you kill me? I gave you the money." There is no answer for a moment. Then the condemned man tries to talk about his panic during the robbery and how things just spun out of control. The condemned man tries to find the words that will satisfy the ghostly guard, but fails.

Throughout the yard I see the ghosts of victims screaming, crying, threatening, and imploring condemned men for an explanation of why they had to die. Some prisoners try to walk away, while others try to communicate an answer, only to discover that for some actions, perhaps, there are no explanations, no second chances, no resolutions.

Over in the corner a condemned man stands all alone. No ghosts approach him to ask unanswerable questions. Although a prosecutor persuaded a jury that this man is guilty of murder, he has in fact killed no one. The man will make the final walk to the gas chamber alone in the knowledge of his innocence.

Suddenly, I hear my name called and look up, blinking my eyes as the apparitions disappear. A lieutenant stands looking at me from the far side of a chain-link fence. He has deigned to call my name. I reluctantly approach the fence and say nothing, waiting for him to deliver his orders.

"Place your belongings under your bunk tomorrow. We will be painting your cell."

I deeply resent the idea of green uniforms invading the only place that provides me any sanctuary and barely restrain myself from screaming, "Stay out of my cell, Lieutenant!"

In my years locked in the box that I call home, I've come to know every flaw in the paint, every crevice in the floor and walls. It's familiar to me, no matter the season, how the light filters through the filthy windows of the cellblock. *Don't change my world, Lieutenant.* Because on death row, change is usually for the worse.

As the silence lengthens between us, the lieutenant says sharply, "Do you understand me? What's wrong with you?"

I'm tempted to respond, "What's wrong with *you*? Can't you comprehend that people like me are your job security? Without people like me, people like you couldn't saunter about in ugly uniforms with an aura of baseless superiority." But as these thoughts race through my head, I reply in an outwardly calm manner. "I understand you, and I'm just fine, Lieutenant."

I push away from frustration and sit down, feeling the solidity of the wall at my back. I wonder what an earthquake would do to this wall. Would it fall, allowing me to travel in freedom like the birds above me? I laugh at my thoughts, as I know I wouldn't know what to do with my freedom. After a decade of guards delivering meals to my cell, I'd starve to death in an apartment, waiting for food to arrive. I'd be incapable of opening the door and walking out. I'd just sit there waiting for a guard to search me, place chains on my body, and escort me into the daylight.

I've changed from when I first arrived at San Quentin. Now, when friends want to visit me, I ask them to come one at a time. I find it difficult to converse with more than one person at a time from the outside world unless I know them quite well. To meet more than one person for the first time is almost too much; I feel on edge, panicked.

Looking into the sky, I see the birds have gone; it will soon be time for the guards to lock me into my cell. I worry for a moment that the ghosts will return. But glancing around, I see no sign of them. The ghosts must be off doing whatever ghosts do when they aren't haunting the damned.

My mind drifts to the words of another condemned man. He once told me this story:

"The mother of the man I killed sat with my mom in the courtroom during my trial. It started when she let my mother know that she didn't hold her responsible for the death of her son. My mother cried, and they spent the rest of the time whispering together.

"The next day the prosecutor asked the woman to move. He said it didn't look good to the jury that she was sitting with my mother, and it might hurt his efforts in trying to obtain a death verdict.

"The woman told him that she knew what it was like to bury her own son, and she wasn't going to help the prosecutor kill me so my mother would have to bury her son.

"The jury came back with death. As the deputies escorted me out of the courtroom, I looked back and saw this woman hugging my mother. They were both crying.

"That picture is engraved in my mind. I think about it every day."

He sat in silence for a moment and then added, "I didn't know there were people like that woman in this world. I was so wrapped up in my own rage, in my own pain, I couldn't think about anything except what her son had done to me. Now, it just seems like what he did was really unimportant. I wish I had realized then how much my actions hurt this woman and the other people who loved her son. My actions echoed through so many lives, bringing loss and tremendous pain to everyone I touched. I really didn't understand at the height of my rage the enormity of the simple act of pulling a trigger. I'd do anything to give this woman back her son, but now it's just too late."

I understand this man's emotions. My personal ghosts remind me daily of what a shallow, immature, self-hating boy I was a decade ago when I was arrested for murder.

Sometimes I yearn for the death that the state of California has promised me, but I also wake up in the early morning hours fearing death in the gas chamber. In truth, I fear equally living and dying.

The guards begin to call our names. It's time to return to our cells until tomorrow. I reach out and rub a bullet mark on the wall. It occurs to me that if I attempt to climb over the wall, the guards will shoot me and the wait for my execution will be over. Finally, I will join the ghosts.

But perhaps the bullet will simply paralyze me. Then the guards will roll me into the gas chamber on a gurney. I'll be drooling and unable to control my bodily functions as they prepare me for the cyanide gas. Fear of dying or fear of paralysis—I don't know which, but today I don't climb the wall for the sole purpose of inviting a bullet. Instead, I walk to the gate, the guards place chains on my body, and I trudge toward my cell.

Reflections from Death Row

Michael Ross

Somers, Connecticut

My name is Michael Ross. I am a condemned man on Connecticut's death row. When most people think of death row inmates, I'm the one they think of. I'm the worst of the worst: a serial killer who is responsible for the rape and murder of eight women in three different states, who has assaulted several other women, and who has stalked and frightened many more. I have never denied what I did and have fully confessed to my crimes. The only issue in my case was, and still is, my mental condition.

For years, I have been trying to prove that I am suffering from a mental illness that drove me to rape and kill, and that this mental illness made me physically unable to control my actions. I have met with little success.

So here I sit on death row, waiting for the judicial system to complete the tedious process that, in all likelihood, will result in my eventual execution. And when I am finally executed, many people will celebrate my death. Sometimes, when I close my eyes, I can envision the hundreds of people who will likely gather outside the prison gates on the night of my execution. I can see them waving placards, drinking, and rejoicing. I can hear their cheers as my death is officially announced.

Who is Michael Ross? And what could possibly motivate a clearly intelligent individual, a Cornell University graduate, to commit such horrendous crimes? As you might expect, I have been examined by a multitude of psychiatric experts over the past sixteen years since my arrest in June 1984. All of them, including the state's own expert psychiatric witness, diagnosed me as suffering from a paraphilic mental disorder called "sexual sadism"—a mental illness that in the experts' words resulted in my compulsion "to perpetrate violent sexual activity in a repetitive way." These experts also agreed that my criminal conduct was the direct result of uncontrollable sexual impulses that were caused by my mental illness. The state's only hope of obtaining a conviction and death sentence was to muddy the waters and to inflame the jury's passions and emotions so they would ignore any evidence of psychological impairment. In my particular case, that was easy to do, and the state succeeded in obtaining convictions and multiple death sentences.

What is a paraphilic mental disorder? It is difficult to explain—and even more difficult to fully understand—especially for the layperson (which, unfortunately for me, includes most jury members). I'm not even sure that I fully understand this disease, although I have been trying to make sense of what has been going on in my head for a long time now.

Repetitive thoughts, urges, and fantasies of the degradation, rape, and murder of women plagued me. I couldn't get it out of my mind. These unwanted thoughts and urges filled my mind when I was awake. They were in my dreams when I slept. They were insatiable. I struggled with these urges, day by day, hour by hour. Imagine the self-hatred, loathing, and abhorrence that I developed toward myself when I ultimately failed to overcome them.

The best way for someone who is not plagued with this problem to understand the obsessive and repetitive nature of these thoughts, urges, and fantasies is to remember a time when you had a catchy tune stuck in your mind, playing over and over and over again, driving you crazy. Even if you like the melody, its constant repetition becomes more than merely annoying. When this happens, the harder you try to push the melody out of your mind, the louder and more persistent it becomes, driving you almost to the point of madness. Now replace that sweet, innocent melody with noxious thoughts of physically and mentally degrading a woman, of raping her, and of strangling her. Now you can begin to understand what I had running wild in my head. It is not something that I wanted to be there.

The urge to hurt women could come over me at any time and at any place. Powerful, sometimes irresistible urges would well up for no apparent reason and without warning. Even after my arrest, while facing capital charges, the urges continued.

I remember once being transported back to the county jail from a court appearance just prior to my trial. I was in the back of the sheriff's van in full restraints—handcuffs, leg irons, and a belly chain—when we passed a young woman walking along a wooded stretch of road. I cannot begin to describe adequately the intensity of the urges that enveloped me that day. I wanted—no, I *had* to get out of that van and go after her. The situation was ludicrous. There I was, in the back of the sheriff's van on my way back to jail, and all that I could think about was how badly I wanted to get hold of her. And later, back in my cell, I masturbated to a fantasy of what would have happened had I gotten hold of her.

Even after I was sentenced to death and living on death row, the urges persisted. One day, after a visit to the mental health unit to see my psychiatrist, a young, petite, female correctional officer escorted me back to my cell. I had no restraints on. A small, secluded stairwell leads from the unit back to the main corridor. When I reached the stairwell, I suddenly felt this overwhelming desire to hurt her. I knew that I had to get out of that stairwell, so I ran up the stairs and out into the hallway. I'll never forget how the officer shouted at me and threatened to write me a disciplinary report. She didn't have a clue as to what was going on. She never knew how badly I wanted to hurt her that day, or how close I came to attacking her and possibly even killing her.

You would think that being sentenced to death and living in a maximum-security prison would curb such thoughts and urges. But this illness defies rationality. I am fortunate to have eventually found some relief, however.

Almost three years after I came to death row, I started to receive weekly injections of an antiandrogen medication called Depo-Provera. Three years later, after some trouble with elevated liver function levels, my treatment was switched to monthly Depo-Lupron injections, which I receive to this day. What these drugs did was significantly reduce my body's natural production of the male sex hormone, testosterone. For some reason, whether an abnormal biological hookup in my brain, or some sort of chemical imbalance, testosterone affects my mind differently than it does the average male's. A few months after I started to

114

receive treatment, my blood serum testosterone levels dropped below prepubescent levels (my current blood serum testosterone averages 20 ng/dl, with the normal range being 260–1250 ng/dl). And as this happened, nothing less than a miracle occurred. My obsessive thoughts, urges, and fantasies began to diminish.

Having those thoughts, urges, and fantasies is a lot like living with an obnoxious roommate. You can't get away from them because they are always there. What the Depo-Lupron does for me is to move that roommate down the hall to his own apartment. The problem is still there, but it is easier to deal with because it isn't always in the foreground, intruding on my everyday life. The "monster within" is still present, but the medication has rendered him impotent and has banished him to the back of my mind. And while he can still mock me—he kicks me in the side of the head from time to time, so I don't forget him—he no longer controls me. I control him. I am human again.

You cannot begin to imagine what a milestone this was in my life. A whole new world opened up to me. I had my mind back—a clear mind, free of malevolent thoughts and urges. It was an unbelievable, incredible sense of freedom. It sounds strange for a condemned man to speak of being free on death row, but that is the only word that I can think of that adequately describes the transformation that I have undergone. And there are no words to express the gratitude that I feel toward the man who made this all possible: Dr. Fred Berlin, founder of the Johns Hopkins Sexual Disorder Clinic and present director of the National Institute for the Study, Prevention and Treatment of Sexual Trauma, both located in Baltimore, Maryland. He testified in my behalf at my capital trial; but more importantly, after the trial was over and I was sentenced to death, he continued to help me and was essential in my fight to get the Department of Correction to acknowledge and treat my paraphilic disorder. Without his letters and phone calls, I never would have received treatment, and to this day would still be captive to the monster that resides in my mind.

That's not to say all is well now. One of the results of all this was that I was forced to look at myself. I'm not talking about the cursory manner in which most people look at themselves, but rather a painful, unrelenting search into the depths of my soul.

Many prison inmates are able to lie convincingly to themselves, to see themselves as basically good people who are the innocent victims of a corrupt judicial system or an unfair and uncaring society. Sometimes it is difficult to see ourselves as we truly are. It is much easier to blame others for our actions. I know that's true because for years that is exactly what I did. During this period, I was angry—very angry—with everyone and everything except for the one person that I should have been angry with—myself. It took a very long time—years, in fact—for that to subside and for me to accept who I was and what I had become. It was even longer before I was ready to accept responsibility for my actions.

Now I had to face a whole new set of problems. Not only did the Depo-Lupron free my mind, but it also allowed my moral judgment to awaken, which in turn gave me back something that I thought I had lost forever—my humanity. Now that my mind was clear, for the first time in years, I began to see—really *see*. It was like a spotlight shining down on me, burning away the fog, exposing a shadow of my being. I became aware of things as they really were, as opposed to seeing things through the lens of my mental illness. I started to see things that I didn't like about myself. And many of the things that I now understood brought me great anguish.

I realized how weak and afraid I really was. I had always thought that I was strong and confident. I now understood how I had allowed the monster in my mind to take control of me. I saw what I had become. And for the first time, I became truly aware of the pain that I had brought to so many people—such great and unceasing pain.

After my mind was finally clear and I saw the truth of what I had become and what I had done, I began to feel things, unpleasant, disturbing feelings. I began to feel the terrible agony and distress that I had brought to so many people: my victims, the families and friends of my victims, my own family. I also began to feel the awesome weight of responsibility: for my actions and to the people that I'd harmed. A profound sense of guilt, an intense, overwhelming and pervasive guilt surrounded my very soul with dark, tormented clouds filled with self-hatred, remorse, regret, and sorrow. All of which left me with a deep desire to make amends and achieve reconciliation—something that, under the present circumstances, seems all but impossible.

Yet it is this sense of reconciliation that I yearn for most. Reconciliation with the spirits of my victims. Reconciliation with the families and friends of my victims. And finally, reconciliation with my God and myself. If this happens, it will be the final part of my transformation—and undoubtedly the most difficult part. If only science could create a drug to help me with this problem.

So, what can be learned from this sad story? I'm not really sure because it seems tragic all the way around. One thing is surely true: there are other Michael Rosses out there in various stages of development. They need places where they can go for help. One of the most difficult things for me to deal with today is knowing that had I begun receiving just one little 1 cc injection of Depo-Lupron once a month fifteen years ago, eight women would be alive today. That ignorance, and its resulting guilt, is a burden that I shall carry with me for the rest of my life.

Our society needs to learn from this tragic affair. It needs to act now to recognize Michael Rosses early on, before it is too late. It needs to learn from my case and others like it. It's easy for society to point its finger at me, to call me evil, and to condemn me to death. But if that is all that happens, it will be a terrible waste. For in a sense, society would be condemning itself—to future murders like those I committed. Only if society stops turning its back, stops condemning, and begins to squarely acknowledge and treat the problem, will something constructive come of the events that took the lives of eight women, destroyed the quality of life of their families and friends, resulted in my incarceration and probable execution, and caused untold shame and anguish to my own family.

The past has already happened; it's up to you to change the future.

What It's Like Being a Drag Queen in the Illinois Department of Corrections

Tonya Star Jones

Menard, Illinois

I honestly don't know which is worse: being a drag queen in Chicago's Cook County Jail, which houses 14,000 inmates, most of whom are pretrial detainees, or being a drag queen in the Illinois Department of Corrections (IDOC) maximum-security facilities, each of which houses anywhere from 1,500 to 2,200 convicted felons and all of which are controlled by the mob—Chicago street gangs.

The mob is split into two divisions: "People" and "Folks." People include the El Rukins, the Blackstones, the Vice Lords, the Latin Kings, and the Mickey Cobras. The Folks comprise the G-Ds and the Black Disciples and are the predominant gang. It is impossible not to know this information if you live in the city of Chicago and especially if you go to the Cook County Jail as a pretrial detainee.

By the time an inmate goes to prison in the Illinois Department of Corrections, he will know all about the gangs and much about how they operate. For example, Folks wear their baseball caps cocked to the right; People cock theirs to the left. All gangs have a "P.O. box" to which their members must pay two packs of cigarettes a week.

As for a drag queen entering the system, not only will the gangs rape, gang-rape, and make a sex slave or prostitute out of him, but they will eventually "brand" him as well, which is to tattoo a gang's insignia, and sometimes degrading words, somewhere on his face or body to show that he is "ho" material—fit to be a prostitute.

I was a sex slave and prostitute for the G-Ds. I got branded first in the Cook County Jail, where I got the gang insignia tattooed on my right ass cheek. Later, at the Menard Correctional Center, I had the words "slut" and "bitch" tattooed on my left ass cheek. Menard is a maximum-security facility in Illinois, about an hour's drive south of St. Louis and a stone's throw from the Mississippi River. My function as a sex slave for the G-Ds was to suck any G-D's dick who wanted his dick sucked, and to let any G-D who wanted to fuck me to do so.

At first, I was not a willing participant, and I was most reluctant. But after getting my ass kicked a few times by them, and being told their clever little cliché ultimatums like "Fuck or fight," I got the message that I had no choice but to be a willing participant, and then I cooperated in full.

One of the first times I got gang-raped by the G-Ds was in the Cook County Jail. I was in my cell one evening when seven or eight of them came in on me saying they wanted me to suck their dicks. My first instinct was to run out of the cell. But they caught me and kicked my ass. One of them socked me hard in the eye, then they ripped off my clothes. I was barefoot naked and crying when one of the G-Ds ordered me to bend over and touch my toes. I did as he ordered.

When I got to Menard Correctional Center, the G-Ds once again got me. They gave me some panties, some fishnet panty hose, a makeshift miniskirt and blouse, and some feminine tennis sneakers. Then they told me to "work" the gallery. There were fifty-three or fifty-four cells on the gallery, and any inmate who wanted to have oral or anal sex with me had to give me two packs of cigarettes. Me and another drag queen named Tasha worked the gallery. We were just about the same size— five foot eleven and 164 pounds. Tasha would often take me to her cell on days when the G-Ds would be away at the chapel or yard for big meetings. She would take me in her arms and console me, because she knew I was going through hell. On one occasion, she told me she had a thing for me.

There is no such thing as a secret in the penitentiary, and almost overnight we became known as bull dykes, as well as prostitutes. Tasha fell in love with me and I with her. On certain nights, she would get the gang chief of the gallery to arrange for her and me to sleep in the same cell, where she would screw me all night long. Tasha is an aggressive homosexual and I am a passive homosexual. She was always the "man" of the relationship and I the "woman."

Alas, the love affair ended when I had a nervous breakdown. Being a sex slave and prostitute for the G-Ds for so long was the proverbial straw that broke the camel's back. I was sent to another institution and placed in protective custody, and I have not laid eyes on Tasha since.

When it comes to knowledge of politics and the law, I am the exception to the rule. Most drag queens in the IDOC don't have the slightest inkling of what either is about. What sparked my interest in learning and practicing law were the Clarence Thomas confirmation hearings, during which the entire nation beheld Anita Hill and learned about sexual harassment. No one could understand how she could be a lawyer and yet fail to take notes or lodge complaints about what she felt was improper behavior. I said to myself then and there that I was going to start taking notes and lodging complaints with the proper authorities whenever I felt I was being sexually harassed, and that's what I did. I began spending hours upon hours studying law in the prison law library. I even filed two lawsuits to be allowed to wear panties, dresses, and a training bra while in prison.

Unlike other drag queens, I am totally independent, financially and otherwise. On the flip side, the average drag queen in the IDOC is totally dependent upon having a man financially support her. They refer to their men as their "husbands." We refer to men in general as "trade," and they refer to us as "game." Most drag queens "smoke squares" and "drink mud," and the only way to support their habits is to find a husband. I don't have any habits, except for occasionally sipping lemon tea.

Being a drag queen in the IDOC has its benefits and its pitfalls. Often, the husband-wife relationships that drag queens get involved in are physically and mentally abusive. "Getting up with yo glamour" means punching a drag queen in the face. That happens a lot and is the main reason why I steer clear of a husband-wife relationship. Besides, I'm sexually attracted to the face of a woman and the body of a man, so only another drag queen can truly satisfy my desires. A lot of times, our families have abandoned us and we have no outside support. So we must seek out our own nontraditional family units for financial and emotional support, thus all the husband-wife relationships between queens and trade.

Perhaps the most overlooked facet of being a drag queen in the IDOC, or any other prison, is the sheer courage it takes to be one. I say this because I know there are a lot of undercover homosexuals in here who would rather die than come out of the closet. Furthermore, the average straight man's worst nightmare is to go to prison, where he knows his manhood will be challenged. Yet we drag queens flaunt our gayness in prison without the least bit of fear in our hearts. There is a cliché in the IDOC that an expert lover "bones 'em like he owns 'em." Most drag queens, not all, are expert lovers, and they bone their husbands like they own 'em. And that's what it's like being a drag queen in the Illinois Department of Corrections.

Prison Break Memoirs

Nemo Valentine

East Lake, Michigan

The walls were high. Most of the inmates were serving short thirty-
and ninety-day bits. The joint was filthy; the food, unbelievable. The
officials had this unfunny habit of putting blacks on the yard crew. After
doing a week on it, I was ready to make a blind rush at the wall. Maybe
I could claw up the thirty feet before I got shot. I was desperate.

After the first week, I came out of shock. I started thinking about a
sensible way to escape. I just couldn't get my mind in shape to do the
bit. By the middle of the second week, I had a dozen ideas. But none of
them stood up under second thoughts.

I shared a tiny cell with a young inmate named Dog. He was only
eighteen. He idolized me. Dog had heard about me in the streets of
Kalamazoo. I slept on the top of a double bunk. There were three
counts: one in the morning, one after night lockup, and the third at
midnight. One night, I missed standing up for the count at the cell door.
I was so beat from heaving boxes of supplies that I collapsed on my
bunk. I woke up an hour after the count. It gave me an idea.

Like all good ideas, this one kept growing, crying out for my attention. I thought, I wonder how much of me that pig saw when she
counted me? So I tested her three nights in a row. I'd lie on the bunk
when she came through to count. Each time I'd lie so she saw less of
me. The last time she counted me there was only my back, rear end and
legs visible to her. I got excited. It would be easy to get extra pants and
a shirt. I could stuff them into a possible dummy. I knew my first problem was to find a way to get out of line when filing from the yard. My

second problem was I couldn't leave a dummy in position in the cell during the day. Block porters and pigs would pass through the gallery and discover it.

I decided to solve my outside problem first. At the end of the day, a group of pigs would line us up at the yard gate to be counted. We would then file two hundred yards into the mess hall for supper. After supper, we would file through the hallways to our cell blocks for the evening count. Each of the cell block captains phoned in their tallies to the main office after every count. If all the tallies equaled the number of inmates in the entire joint, then the count was right. A loud whistle blew and the day pigs could go home.

There was no cover between the prison store and the mess hall. A pig with a scoped, high-powered rifle manned a wall that ran parallel to our line of march. It looked impossible. I lost hope.

On my twenty-eighth day in the joint, I noticed something. Earlier that day, I had been on call-out for dental. It was near suppertime. As I passed the dressing station and shower room, I noticed that the door was open. I glanced in and saw a pig hook-locking a wooden door. I stopped and pretended to tie my shoe. The pig then walked up two or three stairs and swung a steel door shut inside the shower room. He started lining up his prisoners for the march to the mess hall.

The shed was maybe thirty feet from the line of march. The door had always been shut. I thought it stayed locked all the time. I'd never had an opportunity to check it with that rifleman on the wall and the pigs marching with me. If my young cell mate was not a rat and handled the dummy end, I'd take a chance. I had written several bullshit letters for him to his girlfriend. So far, they had kept her writing and sending him Bugler tobacco and junk food money. I didn't think he'd rat. I lay down my play to him.

At first, he was leery. I told him he would take the dummy from the floor under his bunk and put it on mine. As soon as the whistle blew, he'd unstuff the shirt and pants and put the blanket stuffing back on my bunk. When the midnight hell broke loose, he'd be clean. No one could prove he had dismantled the dummy. I got his promise to handle the cell end of the plan.

I took packets of Buglers to work the next day. A yard runner got me an extra shirt and pair of pants. I put them on over the ones I wore.

That night in the cell, I made up the dummy. I put it under Dog's bunk and gave him a pep talk until midnight.

I thought the last day would never end. I would be sunk if there were a routine shakedown of our cell. Finally, we lined up for evening count. My knees wobbled as we approached the shed. The pig on the wall walked twenty paces away. Then he about-faced and walked back toward the yard. When he walked away, I made my break for the shed. I hoped it was not locked. The other two pigs were ahead of me. Never in my life were things so tense, so wildly adventuresome. I wasn't even sure that there wasn't a rat in the line. I could hear an excited whispering from the inmate behind me as I slipped out of line and raced for it.

I touched the shed door handle, afraid I'd find it locked. My sweat-hot hands pulled it toward me. It was open! I slipped inside and shut the door. There was a line of rusty bars flush against a grimy window above the door. I leaped up and grabbed two of them. I hung there for what seemed like forever. My arms and legs were in agony. *That whistle is gonna blow any minute*, I kept repeating to myself. Finally, it blew. I swung my paralyzed legs down and released my grip on the bars. The shed was quiet as a tomb. I peeked through a crack in the door, then put my ear to it. The yard was empty. It had been too long already. I had to make my move. Tears flooded my eyes.

Outside the shed, to my left, I could see the silhouetted figure of the wall pig in his cubicle. The cell block roof abutting the wall seemed so far away. But I had to get on top of it. I raced to the side of the mess hall. Using the window bars, I pulled myself up to a standing position on the sill. I reached over and gripped the drainpipe. After shinnying up to the roof, I walked across it to the next building. When I reached the far edge, I looked back at the wall cubicle. The pig was out walking the wall. He had that deadly rifle cradled in his arms. I flung myself flat on my back and lay there panting.

I didn't need anyone to tell me about what the pig manual said about an escaping inmate target. The question in my mind was, if he saw me, would he go for the head, heart, or gut?

Finally, after a smoke, he went back into the cubicle. Luckily for me, the mess hall roof was connected to the chapel building. The connection was a concrete ledge about twelve feet long but less than a foot wide. My heavy state-issue shoes seemed almost as wide. They slipped on the glazed ledge as I made my way across. The wild, late April winds made the walk about as secure as a stroll across a teeter-totter. At the end of the ledge, I looked up. I stretched my right arm up and stood on the tips of my toes. The chapel roof was two feet above my fingertips! I'd have to go back a few yards on that glassy ledge and make a running jump to grab the outside rim of the roof's drain gutter. I had a hundred and ten pounds on my bones. Could the gutter support my weight? I carefully backed up about six feet and stood there trembling, looking up at the rim. I looked back. The pig wasn't on the wall.

I forced myself to forget how narrow the ledge was. I threw a leg out and whipped the other toward it. I pumped them over the gritty glaze. My arms were outstretched to the black sky and I could hear the whispering hiss of the leather soles tromping the ledge. I felt my feet soar off the ledge. I taloned the rim. For a moment, I hung there, dangling in space. My fingernails sent red-hot needles of pain through the tortured flesh at their roots. I chinned up, hurled a leg across the rooftop, and rolled onto its black surface. Gasping, I watched the rifleman walk his beat. He went in.

The edge of the cell block roof was just three feet away. It was even steeper and was coated with squares of slippery shale. It seemed two city blocks away. I dug my brogan tips into the small cracks between the shale squares and started bellying up it. My chest was flaming. When I reached the top, I straddled the six-inch-wide double precipice formed by the two sides of the roof. It seemed as thin as a wire.

It took forever to reach the end of the cell block. If the pig had come out of his cubicle right then, I was dead, because I was in full view. Even from the inside, he could have spotted me.

I stood there shivering for a while. Twenty feet below was the top of a three-foot-wide wall. I couldn't turn back. And I knew I couldn't just stand there. I wasn't sure if I could keep my balance if I hit the wall feet first. Bracing myself, I dropped, legs open wide. I heard my trousers rip. The inside concrete edge of the wall top gouged into my inner thigh. My rear end crashed against the concrete. My body reeled in pain as I sat in the cold, concrete saddle. Freedom was just a few feet away. I swung my gouged left leg from the inner side of the wall and slithered down the edge. I hung by my fingertips for a moment. I felt blood running down my leg into my shoe. Then I let go.

I struck feet first. My butt and back took the rest of the shock. I lay on my back in a fog of exhaustion, pain, and breathless joy. At least ten minutes passed before I could stand. I limped away for a hundred yards. I turned and looked back at the joint. I'd outsmarted them.

Seventeen months later, my aunt down in New Orleans recognized me in a bar and dropped a wire to the law. That blow murdered my trust in people.

Grief behind Bars

Phillip Santiago

Malone, New York

The phone rang.

"Hello."

"Hi, Provi, how are you and Bob doing?"

My sister, Providencia, gave me the same response she had given me for the last three years: "Fine."

I then asked her the same question I had been asking since my twin brother's condition had begun to deteriorate. Luis was infected with HIV and not doing well. "How is Luis doing?" Her answer, as always, was an unenthusiastic "fine."

Three or four months before Luis's death, I sensed that my sister and mother were trying to keep something from me—the truth. I noticed it in their tone of voice and in the responses they gave to my questions regarding my brother's condition. The truth was that he had very little time left.

I would ask my sister if she knew what Luis's T4 cell count was. She told me she would let me know the next time we spoke. I called her once a month, but during the last six months of Luis's life, I called more often. I began to realize through these phone conversations that his hospitalizations were becoming more frequent. It now seemed as if every time I called he was either going in or coming out of the hospital. When my sister would not have an answer for me, I would get angry. She would always have an excuse: the doctor was out or unavailable or the nurse could not give out the information without the doctor's permission.

I knew my sister was intelligent and knew exactly what questions to ask. Maybe she knew what my brother's T4 cell count was all along and wanted to protect me. My sister has always been protective of her twin brothers, although she is two years younger. Or maybe she really did not know or ask—to protect herself.

Our mother, Maria, who is now in her seventies, raised the three of us on her own. When Luis and I were six, our father left us after breaking my mother's nose one night. This led to Luis and me attacking him with a cooking fork and a steak knife, of course to no avail.

We grew up in the Bronx, poor but somewhat happy. My mother always managed to provide for us. She made ends meet with the help of welfare and sewing work she brought home from a local factory and sweatshop. When Luis and I were in our mid-teens, my mother enrolled in night school so she could learn to read, write, and speak English. She learned enough to get by. Eventually, she was able to get off welfare and get a job as a housekeeper at Lincoln Hospital in the Bronx. She has since retired and is living off her retirement funds.

As a child and adolescent, I struggled through school and eventually dropped out of high school in the eleventh grade. Slowly, I started developing antisocial behavior. I attribute this to being raised in a single-parent household, one without the presence of an adult male figure.

Despite having dropped out of Evander Child High School in the eleventh grade, I went on to receive a bachelor of science degree from Marist College, where I graduated with a 3.5 grade point average.

After college, I entered the field of counseling. In 1994 I became a certified HIV and AIDS educator when I began this sentence in a state penitentiary. Except for one year, I obtained my entire higher education while in prison. Although I am in prison for the second time in my life, the college education and degrees I obtained while here have made a major difference. I believe it was a big mistake for the New York State Department of Correctional Services to eliminate its college programs. They do make a difference.

Because of my education, I obtained some very good jobs. Ironically, I've even held jobs as a correctional counselor on Rikers Island in New York City, as a drug counselor in a methadone maintenance clinic in the Bronx, as a supervisor for the Children's Aid Society, and as a case manager with the Salvation Army, which I resigned one month before my arrest.

My brother's education is another story. At forty-five, he died illiterate—totally unable to read or write. He would fool most people, though, because of his articulate manner of speaking. Nevertheless, the last grade he attended was the tenth. How do you reach the tenth grade in the most powerful country in the world and still be illiterate? I will let you fill in the blanks.

As we got older, I began to wonder why he was so slow. Did the open-heart surgery he had when we were twelve have anything to do with it? Or could our school system have been negligent?

The best my brother ever did as far as employment was to work as a janitor for a New York City housing project in the Bronx. The one or two other jobs he held during his lifetime paid the minimum wage and involved hard labor, which was difficult for him because of his heart condition.

Throughout his life, Luis had only one serious relationship. The woman was a loser and a career drug addict with three crumb snatchers. She abused him and took advantage of his good nature and kindness, yet for some crazy reason he worshiped her. The relationship lasted for about a year. After it was over, he returned to live with my mother, with whom he had been living all his life. He returned depressed and brokenhearted.

I can still remember the day I found out about Luis's HIV status. In June 1991 I drove down to the Mott Haven projects in the Bronx with my girlfriend, Beth, to visit my mother. Beth was pregnant with our son, Brandon, and I planned the trip specifically to tell my mother that she would again be a grandmother.

After I gave my mother the good news, she told me, "Tu hermano tiene SIDA!" ("Your brother has AIDS!") I was speechless. I remember that we were talking in her bedroom, while Luis and Beth were in the living room. For a minute or two, I just sat on her bed, not knowing what to say. I finally asked, "How?" knowing damn well that he became infected either from his occasional dabbling with heroin or from one of the many project sluts he had cheap sex with.

I do not believe that I handled my brother's inevitable death very well. I felt that if anyone should have gotten AIDS, it should have been me. After all, I was the junkie of the house. I injected drugs more than he did. I know now that this response is a result of guilt and a part of grieving.

Before my brother passed away in 1996, the only deaths in the family I had experienced were the deaths of my two grandmothers and my favorite uncle. It hurt me to hear of my uncle's death, because I loved him. As I was growing up, a few of my friends died, but none of their deaths moved me to tears or made me grieve.

I spent all of 1970 in the jungles of Vietnam, where I witnessed death practically every day. If witnessing any of the deaths of the hundreds of Vietnamese men, women, children, and friends I made while in the service moved me to the point of grieving, I will never know. During the year I spent in Vietnam, I was stoned out of my mind. For my entire tour there, I ingested, sniffed, and drank: marijuana, heroin, pure black opium, number 10s (a very strong barbiturate in pill form), hashish, liquid speed, and any form of liquor I could get my hands on. Much of the year is a blur because of my drug use and suppression of the horrors I witnessed there.

It is not normal to see people you know torn to pieces or begging you to put them out of their misery and pain. It is also not normal for a nineteen-year-old Puerto Rican from the Bronx to have his friend take pictures of him perched on a pile of dead Viet Congs while puffing on a pipe full of marijuana sprinkled with heroin.

It's ironic, but before finding out about my brother's HIV status, I was content with my life. The extent of my drug use had dwindled to a couple of beers after work. But it was not long after I found out about his condition that I started using hard drugs again. It started out as heavy drinking—beer and scotch—which led to my weakness and downfall. It wasn't long before I was speedballing—mixing heroin and cocaine and injecting the mixture intravenously.

By March 1993 I had developed a terrible habit. I had quit my job as a case manager working with schizophrenics at one of the Salvation Army facilities. I was about to be arrested for a drug sale of forty dollars' worth of heroin, which led to the five and a half to eleven years I am currently serving.

Fortunately, I have been able to come to terms with myself and have learned to take responsibility for my actions. I have done this with the help of a six-month twelve-step program called Alcohol and Substance Abuse Treatment (ASAT). Since graduating from the ASAT program in 1994, I have become an ASAT aide, or peer counselor. As an ASAT aide, I have also had the opportunity to educate men enrolled in a program involving the prevention and treatment of HIV and AIDS.

Several weeks before his death, Luis begged to see me. He told our sister that he was afraid. He knew the end was near. Part of the guilt that I felt was because my mother and sister watched him die a little more each day. I was spared. I felt terribly guilty and my heart was broken.

Near the end, I was given a choice. I could visit him at his deathbed or I could attend his wake. When the New York State Department of Correctional Services policy says "deathbed," that is exactly what they mean: the patient has to virtually be doing the death rattle. This was not the last image of Luis I wanted to have in my mind.

I opted to attend his wake. He passed away on Wednesday, March 27, 1996. By Friday, I was in a correctional facility van for the eight-hour trip to the Bronx.

While I was in the van settling in for the long ride down to the city, the strangest thing happened. There were two other Puerto Rican inmates in the van with me. One of them was being transferred to a facility closer to New York. The other inmate, like me, was going down to attend the wake of a family member. Because we were both experiencing the same feelings, we began talking to each other. To my amazement, I discovered that he also was from the Bronx and was going to the wake of his twin brother. Furthermore, his brother was going to be viewed in the same funeral home that my brother was in! What was even stranger was that his brother's remains were to be placed for viewing in the very same spot my brother had been in, one day later. The only difference was that his brother had been murdered.

I entered the funeral home, handcuffed and wearing the ugliest prison uniform imaginable. I had two corrections officers at my side. I felt like one of the criminals on *America's Most Wanted*. After surveying the funeral home, the officers allowed me, handcuffed, to mingle with my family. There were only a handful of relatives there. My mother was ashamed to tell relatives that Luis had died of AIDS. Most thought he had passed away from heart failure. Perhaps others knew but went along with the charade for the sake of my mother.

The first one to greet me was my sister, Providencia. She was there with her husband of twenty years, Bob. One of my aunts was there, as well as the daughter of one of my cousins. About ten or fifteen minutes before leaving (I was given one and a half hours), another aunt who had just flown in from Puerto Rico arrived from the airport.

Then came the moment when I approached Luis's coffin. That had to be one of the worst experiences of my life. There was my brother, looking a lot thinner than he ever had. But he was not as emaciated as most AIDS victims are at the end of their nightmares. The only signs that indicated that he was a victim of HIV were the pink spots on his lower lip—the remnants of herpes blisters. Apart from that, he looked like his handsome self. My sister had bought him a snappy blue suit.

The first thing I did was to kiss him on the forehead. It had been a little over three years since I'd last seen him. You never would have guessed then that he had just three years to live. Luis was the closest person I lost to death and I loved him very much. For some reason, I kept touching him and kissing him on his face. I guess I was trying to make up for the time I had not seen him. I also knew and found it hard to accept that I would never see him again. If I could have, I would have gotten into the coffin with him and snuggled up next to him.

During the first two months after Luis's death, I was so traumatized and in such denial that I had recurring thoughts of him in his coffin, six feet under the earth. As his twin brother, I felt as if a part of me had been buried along with him. He was banging on the lid of his coffin, trying to get out. They had buried him alive. To help myself cope, I hung on to the belief that his hair, fingernails, and toenails would continue to grow for several weeks after his death. In my heart, he was not dead. Thoughts of his face haunted me. This was guilt. I could not be there for him when he needed me most.

Then, as now, I contemplated the reason for the emptiness I felt inside. I wondered why death was so difficult to deal with. What immediately came to mind were the bullshit euphemisms fed to us as children. Phrases such as "Grandma is going to take a long nap," or "Mommy is going to live with God in heaven." Many times as children, we are not allowed to attend the wakes of relatives. If grownups are speaking of someone in the family who is terminally ill, they will stop talking when a child enters the room. We are "protected" as children only to be traumatized later in life. In some countries, not only are children told the truth about the pet, relative, or loved one that has passed, they are sometimes allowed to participate in the preparation of the deceased for viewing and burial. These traditions are practiced in Eastern and Third World countries. In Western developed countries, we are so frightfully concerned with our deaths that sometimes we forget the real purpose of our lives.

I was raised in a Catholic home. As I grew and became more educated, I strayed from many of the religious beliefs I had been taught. Because of the double standards I have witnessed in my life in certain religions, especially Catholicism, I have truly come to believe in the phrase "Religion is the opium of the people."

As a war veteran, I can attest to the fact that "you will never find an atheist in a foxhole." My brother became somewhat religious during the mid- to late 1980s. He also found out that he was HIV positive at about the same time. Was his newfound interest in religion the result of knowing he was going to die soon? Surely the thought of God or Saint Peter waiting at the pearly gates to hand out judgment is enough to make anyone try to cover his ass and repent in the closing minutes.

My theological beliefs include a God—not a God who doles out punishment and rewards for every good or bad act committed by us, but a "sustaining God," one that has given us life and the means by which to survive.

It would be easy for many people to say that God punished my brother for sleeping around and using drugs. I believe that we alone are responsible for our actions. But I do not believe that my brother is burning in anyone's hell because he contracted AIDS. Although his moral standards may not have lived up to the current politically correct mind-set, it did not make him a bad person. On the contrary, everyone who knew him loved him. I truly miss him and will look forward to joining him.

While standing over my brother's stiff and cold body, I read the following poem to him, in the hope that it would warm his soul. It was very difficult reading and sobbing at the same time:

The End of the Road Is But a Bend in the Road
When we feel we have nothing left to give
And we are sure that the song had ended
When our day seems over and the shadows fall
And the darkness of night has descended,
Where can we go to find the strength
To valiantly keep on fighting?
Where can we find the hand that will dry
The tears that the heart is crying?
There is but one place to go and that is to God,
And, dropping all pretense and pride,
We can pour out our problems without restraint,
And gain strength with Him at our side.
And together we stand at life's crossroads,
And view what we think is the end,
But God has a much bigger vision
And He tells us it's only a bend.
For the road goes on and is smoother,
And the pause in the song is a rest,
And the part that's unsung and unfinished
Is the sweetest and richest and best.
So rest and relax and grow stronger,
Let go and let God share your load.
Your work is not finished or ended,
You've just come to a bend in the road.
                    Helen Steiner Rice**

God be with you, Luis. I will always love you.

---

* Used by permission of the Helen Steiner Rice Foundation, Suite 2100, Atrium Two, 221 East Fourth Street, Cincinnati, Ohio, 45202.

Christmas: Present

Robert Chambers

Stormville, New York

Prison is a world of unending sorrow. It is where reality and illusion bookend the horrific chapters of my life. When the steel gates are slammed closed and the lights are extinguished at the end of yet another day of pain and irrelevancy, the true nightmares begin.

Ten years ago, everything I thought, everything I dreamed, had purpose. Today my memories are sketchy at best and void of direction. When I was a young boy, I could see the greatness of life and the endless possibilities within reach. Now I am just a man who once dreamed he was a child.

Prison has tried to extinguish the fire that burns in my heart, hoping to replace it with the noxious fumes of these haunted walls that surround me. But deep in the midst of this seemingly lifeless heart, buried beneath the ashes of decay, fire still burns. It is the light of this weak but glowing spirit that guides me through the blackness of this pit of inhumanity in which I reside, allowing me to struggle to survive, pushing me to strive for one more day.

I walk around the yard wondering who these people are, these bizarre and troubled men who stare back at me with faces only a defense attorney could love. I walk by the cells in which we live and try to imagine what an outsider would think if he were to see what I now accept as normal. I try to see my comrades through the eyes of the migrating tribes of high school kids that tour the prison as part of the various "scared straight" programs. But I don't seem to be able to do it anymore because I don't remember what it is like to be an "outsider."

I'm a number in a computer in Albany, New York, that marks me as a target for inspection, ridicule, and deceit. As I sit in my little cell at 2:48 A.M., two days before Christmas, I write this daily entry into a log of my adventures as inmate Robert Chambers, #88A3660. This journal is rather large, for it holds the secret of a decade's worth of experiences. This is my life as I have lived it, reduced to scratches on a page. It is a record of the meaningless hope and frightening losses of a person I don't even know. But this journal entry will, like the others before it, be mailed home to collect dust in a desk drawer as its author sits and collects dust in this forgotten world.

Sometimes, though, someone interrupts the sedate routine of slowly dying by sending a letter. Yesterday I received a letter from a girl I dated in high school. She asked me what I would like for Christmas. Since freedom is a bit out of her price range, my wish for this Christmas is to be treated like an average inmate instead of a political poster boy. For ten years, I've read interesting stories of what I've been up to in jail, the life I've led, and why it is more important that I receive more time at parole hearings for the good of society.

Balzac wrote that corruption is powerful in the world and talent is scarce. Corruption has become an instrument of power for the swarming mediocrity. People are taught that to live well, you have to dirty your hands, and that the only thing that matters is to know how to get them clean again, regardless of who must suffer in the process.

Ten years ago, I learned that the courtroom was a battleground for due process and the search for truth. Ten years later, I have learned that people don't want to hear the truth because they don't want their illusions destroyed. To paraphrase Thomas Sowell, it is amazing how many people think that voicing their emotions is the same as making an intelligent argument and that if someone dares to disagree, that person is vilified and said to be wrong. There seems to be nothing as strong in society as the need to believe in something obviously wrong. People are "informed" by a carefully controlled effort to feed deceptive ideas until fiction and reality become one. This is called freedom of the press.

I once believed that someone would recognize the truth and take a stand. However, in a country where our own president confuses the terms *debt* and *deficit,* and Congress trumpets this as a land of democracy when, in fact, the word *democracy* never appears in the Constitution, I must accept the fact that reality is relative to one's bank account.

At night, when the lights are out and the last cigarette is tossed out on the hallway floor, I watch the comforting glow of the orange-red tip and think about the many things I am grateful for, and the aspects within me that can't be taken away. Before going to sleep, lulled to slumber by the agonized cries coming from someone's cell, I always recount the things I've learned to reinforce them in my heart. In these ten years, I've learned never to give up, always to try one more time. I've realized how fast we grow old and how slowly we become wise. And although I will always judge myself on what I do and can do, others will judge me on what I've already done. I've come to the conclusion that responsibility means being accountable not only for my own actions and personal consequences but also for what happens to the community around me as a result of my actions. And perhaps more important, I've learned that to say yes or no requires the most thought.

Prison is tough, dangerous, and lonely. It can kill at will. I am a member of the easiest club to join but the hardest to leave. I live with people who talk about prison sentences that sound like basketball scores. I long for the day when I can make a decision without asking for permission. I only wish I knew how to make it right again. That is what I really want for Christmas tomorrow—a chance to change what is for what should be. That is my Christmas wish from my forgotten world.

What Happened to Your Message?

Barry Conn

Kincheloe, Michigan

Your message says you care deeply about the problem of crime that plagues today's society. Crime alarms you. You worry about peace and security. You foresee the demise of civility from the attack on societal values. Criminals have exceeded the limits of your patience and you demand changes; your calls for lengthier prison terms communicate your intolerance.

Your wrath torments me daily, as twenty-five to fifty years of my life waste in prison. My crime? Burglary. I have a past record of nonviolent offenses and this is my second term in prison. Prison requires inmates to adhere to your rules—they must discipline themselves, acquire skills, and demonstrate respect for your values—or remain incarcerated. You demand that they live by your principles. The long-term allocation of resources toward prisons bespeaks your commitments. But the supplies employed to meet your demands prompt businesslike goals, the nature of which conflict with the ideals of corrections. The message you want sent differs from the one delivered.

The bureaucrats bear your message and, like piglets to a sow's teat, they milk it for all it is worth. "Your ass is our asset," they tell criminals. They promote a businesslike approach to meet your demand with supply, but it provides only illusory satisfaction; the goals of your message remain unfulfilled.

Goals of corrections oppose those of bureaucrats. Correctional systems strive to eliminate the problem; bureaus behave like businesses: elimination of the problem essentially puts them out of business. Unlike

138

the public—the idealists—bureaucrats envision never-ending problems; to them, problems create opportunities. Bureaucrats use every available resource, and unused budgets result in lost revenue. They seek not to eliminate their jobs, as correctional goals idealize, but to further the life and girth of their bureaus.

High recidivism antiquated the philosophies of rehabilitation; the enormity of today's transgressions requires extreme measures. The seemingly logical solution lies in wholesale incarceration. Why, indeed, should the correction of prisoners be paramount when warehousing them seems more apropos?

I recently transferred to one of Michigan's new prisons. Its sight brought about déjà vu, as it cloned the numerous sites I'd visited over the years. It was another warehouse with me its stored product. I had hoped to transfer to a better place, possibly closer to home, or to a warmer climate. But I traveled north, and the green countryside turned to a blanket of dirtying snow, the warmth and bloom of springtime reverted to the dead of winter, and my dreams turned nightmarish.

The prison resembles a high-security military base. Double razor wire fences carve its perimeter into the back acreage of a pig farm somewhere in rural northern Michigan. The strategically placed guard towers, vehicles on patrol, and guards dressed in military-style uniforms assure that its inventory remains within its grasp. Six identical V-shaped buildings store its stock; half of those segregate prisoners in locked-down cells. Its fenced-in walkways guide any movement, and officials brandishing callous demeanors and armed with a plethora of ambiguously written rules maintain the prison's control.

I am allowed only one hour out of my cell each day. I trudge through the recreation yard, knee-deep in snow or, during the thaw, ankle deep in slush. The ground only reluctantly releases its grip on me—one foot pulls free only at the consequence of the other's mire—a quagmire symbolic of the system's hold on me and reminiscent of the mess which has become my life. My breath, a gray cloud overhead, reflects my gloom; it follows me through the cold and callousness, the ugliness, and is a reminder of my discomfort. It appears, as I call upward to a heaven that never answers, and dissipates, as do my hopes, into thin air.

I've given up the early dreams: no longer do I seek relief in court or explain injustice to judges. Nor do I try to reason with officials that I was only a property offender and that twenty-five years' imprisonment is excessive and that I have matured and regret my offenses. The system hears only what fits its agenda. I merely fit the bill as inventory. The years narrow my focus to concerns inside the fences: on guards that scrutinize my every move, the enforcement of misinterpreted concepts, and the threats of greater deprivation.

Deprivation represents the concept on which the business aspect of prison thrives: the greater the need to deprive, the greater the use of resources. Deprivation at the maximum-security level costs thirty-six thousand dollars annually per prisoner and nearly double that in segregated confinement.*

Segregated confinement represents the ultimate in deprivation. There a prisoner remains locked in his cell twenty-three hours a day with an hour of recreation in a small, fenced-in pen. He possesses little or no property, and his contact with the outside world reduces to practically none. Prison shrinks a person's world to its perimeter, much like a fishbowl affects a goldfish. But imprisonment in prolonged segregation is like putting the same fish in a shot glass. A segregated prisoner lives in an inactive world reduced to the eight-by-ten-foot cell that confines him. Anything he receives fits through a small slot in his steel door, and "outside" amounts to what he sees from the six-inch by two-foot slit of his window.

Outside his cage, he is placed in restraints around his waist, which bind his hands; chains clasped to his ankles restrict his stride. A tether, clenched by one of two guards like a dog leash, leads him in tow. He resembles a zombie in chains.

When passing the zombies' segregation unit, you avoid being attentive to the insistent rapping on the windows, knuckles barely audible behind the thick glass. You know their dilemma, but you cannot help them. If you look, you see only their silhouettes, like figures lurking in the shadows, or their unrecognizable faces pressed against darkened glass, fingertips scrawling puzzling messages on the panes. As you shrug your shoulders, a disgruntled occupant dismisses you with an extended finger. You sense that the shadows share a world of which you want no part, but one that hangs ever present over your head. Segregated

---

* *ABC News* report on prisons, February 17, 1997.

confinement occupies half the prison's cell capacity. It represents business to the bureau, and oftentimes prisoners find themselves in a fight just to avoid it.

One day, I paid a visit to the segregation unit. The guard who met me at the door placed me in leg irons and tethered cuffs, despite my supplication. I reported there not for wrongdoing but for a hearing, as officials had claimed concern for my safety. The hearing was to determine whether I should be placed in segregation and thus out of danger. These hearings theoretically determine facts and render reasonable conclusions. I was about to learn a new meaning for the concept of reasonableness.

From the outside, the building appeared the same as all the others. Inside, the change of atmosphere shocked me. After being led to the end of a corridor like an obedient puppy on its new leash, I was let in through an electronically controlled door. Deafening screams—claims of injustice and ongoing arguments of what seemed to be hundreds of men—filled the air. They were competing for the "air waves," bellowing from under the steel doors that confined them. It represented their quandary, their lack of control, their rage. They were arguing as a means to reach outside their confinement, but only their voices escaped. Their message went unheard, as if it were the harangued madness from the mouths of a dozen so-called professional wrestlers in unison. Artificial light, clouded by dust, provided the only illumination, and a veil of dinginess hung over the interior. The walls oozed a coat of nicotine and dirt, and debris lay here and there, indications of neglect and apathy toward the occupants. The stagnant air allowed odors to linger, as cigarette butts rerolled into toilet paper reflect the desperation of those that smoke them. Body odor, like that of a wino after a weekend drunk, told of their physical plight. The sourness of fungus that fouled the shower cages was an odorous reminder that nobody cared. Segregation represents the bowels of the penitentiary.

As I entered the room, the hearing officer paused from his study of the file folder on the desk before him and surveyed me over the top of his glasses. Unlike what you would expect of an attorney, he wore an aged sports jacket and faded jeans. His wild hair and half-frame specs made him appear like an Einstein impersonator. The guard led me to a mushroom-shaped metal stool planted in the floor in front of Einstein's desk where the phrase "take a seat" acquired new meaning. My legs straddled the stool as I stepped forward and the guard shackled my ankles to its base, my knees spread-eagle. He then secured my cuff's tether taut to the floor behind me—like the pull of an archer's bow, it tested my spine's limit—and my face contorted in pain as I attempted to maintain balance. Einstein's blank expression told me he had seen this routine many times before. The watchdog within me became alarmed.

"Officials have reason to believe a danger threatens your life," he said while looking over the file. "Two anonymous notes provide the evidence." Dismissing my attempt to object, he read aloud the notes as if dictating to a stenographer.

The first note, written in a dialect that attempted to imitate ghetto slang, depicted a vague story that alleged some group was out to get me. The second note was incoherent and looked as if written by some-one mentally challenged, its script illegible and back-slanted. Both as-serted the same story and used identical slang and misspellings. Einstein paused, then chuckled heartily, as if he just grasped the punch line of some complex joke, and pointed out the obvious: both were written by a single author using opposite hands—a simple scheme to cause me trouble. My indignation subsided; my imaginary tail wagged with vigor. He recognized the ploy of the unknown author; obviously, his comprehension would resolve the matter. Only my tight leash held back my elation. I wanted to jump on his chest and lick his face with the ardor of the eager puppy I was. However, my mood soon changed.

"Excuse me, sir," I said after several minutes, interrupting his typing of the report. An exaggerated shift of my body provided a reminder of my discomfort. "Please say you find these notes ridiculous. Obviously no danger exists."

He paused and peered at me over the top of his half-frames with a look of smug contempt and said, "We need only establish an existence of something, anything, for the record that could be interpreted to jus-tify our action. These damning notes satisfy that need." His eyes beamed with conceit, like that of an author admiring the irony of his words. He seemed proud. "You'll be confined to segregation," he added with the sedateness of a death-sentencing judge, and turned his atten-tion back to his report.

"Wait, sir." I halted him, as the shock rocked me back on the stool, the watchdog in me sensing trouble. "*I've* done nothing wrong." The cuffs refused to allow my hands to help explain, and the anchor pulled me back and forth as I pled. "How can I defend something so stupid, question someone unknown? No credibility exists in this. You saw it yourself." My head bobbed as I pointed this out with my forehead.

"Anything supporting our action is sufficient, regardless of the rest," he mumbled without glancing at me.

"What do you mean, 'supporting your action'? You're supposed to determine the truth, not take sides," I said. (Lawyers act as hearing officials to ensure impartiality at the hearing, but this lawyer's actions merely assisted the bureau's cause, as if he worked for them. He helped the system devour me.) He ignored my plight. My watchdog turned mad dog.

"Are you a hearing *impaired* officer?" I said, my jaw clenched. "Are you deaf?"

My face contorted as if I were embroiled in a tug-of-war. In my struggle to find logic, my shoulders took turns jerking forward in their futile attempt to reach him. I wanted to implant reasoning, to grab his shoulders and shake the understanding into him, but restraints overwhelmed my limbs and I merely rocked on the metal pivot. Like the anchor beneath me, he refused to yield. The common view I sought was beyond my reach.

"Are you brain dead!" spewed from my beet-red face. My only weapon was logic. "I've done nothing wrong, *nothing!*"

The failure to penetrate his persona showed in his eyes. He looked up from his composition unmoved, as if this mechanical bull-like performance came as just another part of the hearing. His eyes were visible, but like a mannequin's, they reflected no interest; clearly, the battlefield extended beyond this hearing room.

Once in segregated confinement, I continued my quest for reasonableness. But appeals seemed never-ending. Filing official forms and making complaints netted no results. Return mail delivered only official denials; they emphasized the significance of anonymous note writing. Daily I paced my empty abode with arms flailing; my soliloquy merely echoed off deaf walls. I became consumed by the idiocy. They valued nonsense more than common sense.

In a final effort to communicate, in dialect resembling Old West cowboy, I began my own anonymous note to the warden, "Looky heya, Pardna . . ." With idiom like "Thumthur fellers" and "Da frr'l be fly'n," I told of a danger to myself should I remain segregated: proof equal to the incredulousness of the stories they held authentic.

Support from the verbally challenged, like the hearing officer's "evidence," so omnipotent, better emphasized the lunacy. My second note, in words made from upside down and backward letters piled like a scrambled letter puzzle, began, "Dear Warden, Excuse my dyslexic condition," and revealed a similar story. The solution sprang from the page. Easily decipherable words revealed a vague warning that, like theirs, held nothing significant or believable. Only the very gullible would find the story believable; it showed to what extent the concept had been reduced to something meaningless. But while I sent out a message I believed to be bold and demonstrative, one that revealed great error and injustice, it meant nothing to its audience, who had other priorities; it made me no gains.

That the notes went unconsidered proved my point at the time: the "segregation" concept lost its intended purpose. It converted from a tool for prison officials to use against serious security problems to merely another means by which they exhaust prison resources and budgets. They claim the need for super-maximum prisons, more guards, and other resource expenditures. They justify these policies in response to your demands. Your frustration with the criminal element opens the doors for the bureaucrats. Your message acts as their catalyst, but ironically, they work to the detriment of your goals.

Capitalism negatively affects the results of correctional concepts. The capitalistic philosophy—greater demand calls for more product—disregards the concept's inherent principles and misdirects its force. Criminals already understand deprivation without reasoning; they know how to disregard logic or humanism. They have traveled paths where personal agendas override the rights of others. They learn nothing from this treatment; reinforcement of these values produces only more of the same.

Reasonableness represents a fine line: a difference between deprivation for civility or for criminality. To deprive illogically in the interest of business counteracts the very principles of civility. In 1984 Chief Justice Burger of the U.S. Supreme Court in the case of *Hudson v. Palmer* opined, "The way a society treats those who have transgressed against it is evidence of the essential character of that society."* Your message represents the demand of society; it seeks an ideal. But true concern for your values can be gauged by your concern for the clarity and quality of your message. Society's character overwhelms its message. It shows its willingness to compromise benevolent principles for self-satisfaction. It condones greediness and dishonesty. It OKs criminality.

---

* *Hudson v. Palmer*, 468 US 517 (1984).

Upon Completing Twenty Years

Easy Waters

Wallkill, New York

When the year began, my hope was that it would be my last one in prison. I stayed busy and tried to buy into the illusion that time passes quickly when you're occupied. I tried not to keep track of the days, but I was more conscious of time than at any point since the beginning of my imprisonment. I even bought a watch, my first in twenty years. I thought that counting every minute would somehow slow time down. But it didn't. The months passed, neither slowly nor quickly. They just passed, like all the time I had spent in prison had passed. Before I knew it, it was July.

My institutional parole officer could have been cast in a gangster film. He wore gold chains and a pinky ring and had a Brooklyn accent that even I—a born and bred Brooklynite—had a few problems understanding.

"This is an initial parole board appearance you'll be making," the PO said. "You spent a lot of time in maximum security before your security classification was downgraded to medium."

"Yes, fifteen years," I said.

"That's a lot of time." He looked down at a folder, my life according to the Division of Parole. "I have some things in your folder. How's that?"

"I went to an executive clemency parole board hearing in 1994."

"I see." He leafed through the papers. "I'll probably just add to what's here. It's quite extensive."

We went through my criminal history.

"I see you have an assault as a juvenile in 1976."

I had to think about that one. "That was just a fight between me and another teenager. Wasn't that dismissed?"

"Yes."

This guy had smashed my hand through a window of one of those old El trains. I still had visible scars on my left wrist, like I'd been nailed to a cross.

"There was also this robbery in 1976."

"Wasn't that dismissed too?"

"Yes."

I had been falsely accused of a crime. The witness had come to court one day, broken down, and said that I wasn't the person. She just wanted somebody to pay for the crime that had been committed against her.

"There's this juvenile robbery for which you were put on probation."

"Yes." I couldn't say anything about that one. I was guilty.

"You had a pattern of violent behavior leading up to the instant offense."

That was untrue, but I couldn't challenge it. I knew it was not a question of truth. "Doesn't it matter that I didn't kill anyone?"

"The law says you're equally guilty."

"I know that, but the law also says that's a 'fiction of law.' A state of facts that really don't exist."

"Still, that's the law."

"I know, and I accept that. I'd just like to think that the fact that I didn't kill anyone and that I've never been armed with a weapon in my life would mean something. And that I've spent twenty years in prison for the instant offense."

"Well, we could let you go, give you another chance. You've got life on the back. If you screwed up we could pull you back in. Will you screw up? Probably not."

The interview continued for about an hour. When we got through all the stuff I had done, the PO wasn't as harsh. He said I had a fifty-fifty chance of making parole, depending on who the commissioners were. He mentioned the names of a few commissioners he thought would be inclined to let me go, even this black woman whose reputation preceded her. She was one of the most feared commissioners sitting on the panel.

Before the interview concluded, the PO told me that because of all the time I had spent in prison, I would be referred to the Office of Mental Health for evaluation.

The psychologist was standing by her desk when I entered the office. She was about five feet, ten inches tall and slim. She had curly red hair and light blue eyes that practically twinkled. Her skin was very white, almost the color of Ivory soap. And she was young—too young to understand what I had been through and the evil I had seen. She introduced herself and offered me a seat.

"You're going to the parole board?"

"Yes."

"Normally, referrals are made for homicides and sex offenses."

"I have a homicide-related conviction," I said.

"How long have you been imprisoned?"

"This is my twentieth year."

She looked up from the papers in front of her. Twenty years was like a magic number. It got people's attention every time.

"What have you been doing the past twenty years?" she asked. "What programs have you participated in?"

I mentioned my educational achievements. She asked what my degrees were in and I told her.

"It seems like you've made good use of your time."

"I've tried."

"Have you refused any mandatory programs?"

"No."

"Any drug abuse in your life?"

"No."

"Alcohol?"

"No. I never even smoked a cigarette. Drank a couple of cups of coffee in 1977."

"Do you have any family?"

"One sister and a nephew."

"And your parents?"

"They both passed away. My mother in 1978, my father in 1982."

"So you were imprisoned when they passed away?"

"Yes."

"Are you in contact with your sister?"

"I call her once a week."

"That's good." She paused for a moment, wrote some things down on a pad that she kept close to her chest. No reading upside down for me. She looked up. "How do you feel about your crime?"

"What do you mean?"

"How do you feel about it? Do you feel remorse?"

I sighed. "It's not that simple. I'm a nonkilling accomplice in a felony murder—a robbery-murder. I didn't know my codefendant was armed. I had no idea he was going to kill. Don't get me wrong. I'm not deprecating the seriousness of the crime. What happened was tragic and I'm sorry about that. I just want somebody to admit that felony murder isn't murder as people normally envision it, especially when you're a nonkilling accomplice."

"Do you feel that you're not guilty?"

"I'm not guilty of murder. I didn't know that the law made no distinction between the actual killer and a nonkilling accomplice. I would have pleaded the affirmative defense or—"

"Excuse me, what's the affirmative defense?"

"It's a defense to felony murder, for nonkilling accomplices. In a nutshell, a nonkilling accomplice shows that he wasn't armed, didn't know his codefendant was armed, didn't solicit or command the killing, and didn't think serious physical harm would result from the commission of the felony. In short, if a nonkilling accomplice can prove these things, he escapes punishment for the homicide and will be punished only for the underlying felony, whatever that might be. Robbery, in my case. Had I known and really believed that no distinction was made between the actual killer and a nonkilling accomplice, I would have copped a plea."

"Were you offered a plea?"

"Yes, eight and one-third to twenty-five years for manslaughter."

"Why didn't you take it?"

"I didn't kill anyone."

"What would you have pleaded guilty to?"

"Robbery. That's all I was guilty of."

149

"How much time could you have received for that?"

"Eight and one-third to twenty-five. The same as for manslaughter. Both are Class B felonies and carry the same sentence."

"How much time did the actual killer receive?"

"Eighteen months. He was a juvenile under the existing law. Today he could get nine years to life, with the changes in juvenile offender laws."

"Have you ever heard anything from him?"

"Yes. In 1980, after he went home and came back to prison for another homicide. He wrote me and said—excuse me, but this is a direct quote—'Gene, I'm sorry for fucking up your life.' The end."

"Are you angry?"

"I try not to be."

"Are you bitter?"

"I try not to be."

"Do you have problems sleeping?"

"No."

"Do you experience depression?"

"I've been locked up for twenty years. Sometimes I'm depressed. That's natural, I think. But I'm not depressed in the clinical sense."

"No, you're not clinically depressed. Would you like to add anything?"

"Yes. When I think of my upcoming parole board appearance, I think about who I was and who I am. I would like to be seen in the present, not in the past. I don't want the thirty-five-year-old to be judged again for what the sixteen-year-old did. I don't want the man to be punished for what the teenager did. They're two different people."

She nodded her head—in agreement, I hoped.

"If you could ask for one thing, besides parole, what would it be?"

Was that a shrink question? "Certainty," I answered. "I'd like some certainty in my life. I'd like to know exactly when I'm getting out of prison. I've done twenty years. Still, I don't know if the parole commissioners will consider that enough time. When is enough, enough? This hearing is for them to decide whether I should do more time. I don't think I can do more time. Maybe if I knew exactly how much more time I had to do, I could deal with it better."

"Anything else?"

150

"A million things. But I think I've covered everything that needs to be said."

"It was . . . educational, talking with you," she said. "Thank you—and good luck."

"Thank you."

It was hard to believe that twenty years had passed and that I had been in prison for all of them. As prisoners, we talked about how quickly time has passed, after it's gone. But in the moment, it never passes quickly. In two weeks, I was going to my parole hearing. I was never more nervous in my life, not even when I was going to trial. I had always enjoyed perfect health, but suddenly I felt ill. I couldn't sleep. I got headaches. I broke out in hives. I caught a bout of diarrhea. I was scared shitless! Scared because I knew what could happen, what would probably happen. I didn't think I could do any more time. Doing twenty years was something I never prepared myself for, but I really did do twenty years, one day at a time. I definitely wasn't prepared to do two more years, the maximum time the parole commissioners could hold any prisoner before a reappearance before the parole board.

Before I knew it, I was sitting in a waiting room, waiting to see the parole commissioners. My whole body was tense.

"Eugene Washington!"

When my name was called, I thought I would just break up. I walked the short distance to the room, but for me it was like a mile, that "last mile" condemned prisoners walk to their execution.

I entered the room. There were three commissioners sitting behind a long desk, a stenographer to the left of them, and the institutional parole officer to their right. The chair I was to sit in was a couple of feet in front of the table.

I sat down and looked at the commissioners: a black man, a black woman, a white woman. The black woman was the commissioner my PO had said would be inclined to give someone like me another chance.

She introduced herself and the other commissioners. I focused on her. It was her show. Usually, when I look at older black women, I see my mother. But this black woman looked different. My mother was slim. This woman was enormous, like she could carry the weight of the world on her shoulders—and had. I was wondering if she had an ax to grind for that reason. She wasn't looking at me like a black woman would look at a man young enough to be her son. I knew I was in deep shit.

"Mr. Washington," she said. "Do you know why you're here today?"

No, I've waited twenty years for this moment and don't know why I'm here. "Yes. To be considered for release on parole."

She then cited the facts of my crime. All I could say was yes. The facts were not in dispute.

"You went to trial?" she asked.

"Yes."

"Why?"

"I didn't think I was guilty of murder."

"But you were there?"

"Yes, but I didn't kill the victim. I didn't even know my codefendant was armed."

"Under the law that doesn't make a difference."

"I know."

"You had a lawyer?"

"Yes."

"What did he advise you to do?"

"To plead guilty to manslaughter."

"Why didn't you?"

"Because I didn't kill anyone."

"But you were there?"

"Yes."

She then went on to my educational achievements, briefly noting them. She also read a reference letter from one of my professors, who had praised me as the brightest guy in the class.

"You applied for executive clemency?"

"Four times."

"Why were you denied?"

"I was told that executive clemency is an extraordinary form of relief and that the governor did not see the need to intervene in the normal judicial process."

"That's true. There are no extraordinary circumstances in your case that would warrant executive clemency. Why did you apply?"

"I believed I was a worthy candidate, that in light of who I am and who I have become, the twenty-year sentence was no longer appropriate."

"You know, you committed a couple of crimes as a juvenile."

"Yes."

"Why did you commit those crimes?"

"I was young. I was foolish. I was susceptible to peer pressure. How can I explain who I was then? Like most teenagers, there was the arrogance of youth and the contempt in which I held my elders, meaning anybody over twenty-one."

"Did you think about the consequences?" the black man asked.

"No."

"You didn't care?"

"I was fifteen. When I committed my crime, I was sixteen. I didn't think about consequences, how people would be affected, how I would be affected. I had no sense of my own mortality. I didn't think I'd end up in prison for twenty years. I wish I could undo what I did."

"If you're released," the black woman asked, "you're going to live with your sister, Jasmine Washington?"

"Yes."

"What does she do for a living?"

"She's an insurance agent."

"Does she live alone?"

"No, my nephew lives with her."

"Her son?"

"No."

"Whose son is this?"

I didn't want to talk about Cam with these fucking people. "My younger sister's."

"Where is she?"

"She's deceased."

There was a moment of silence, though I knew it wasn't for Cam. Fucking people!

"How many bedrooms are there in this apartment?" the black woman commissioner continued.

"Jasmine recently moved to a three-bedroom apartment, thinking that I'm coming home."

"Any pets in the home?"

"A cat."

The black woman commissioner asked the white woman commissioner if she had any questions. I looked in her direction. She shook her head.

"Do you think we've covered everything?" the black woman asked.

I paused for a long time. I wanted to summon up the speech of my life. Actually, I wanted to give her a piece of my mind. I didn't like the tone of this interview. My stomach was in knots. Finally, I said, "Yes."

"Do you have anything you'd like to add?"

"Yes. I really do wish I could undo what happened. It was a tragedy and I'm sorry." I paused, paying respects to the victim. "I know that I can remain at liberty without violating the law. I would like to be given another chance."

"We will discuss this among ourselves and reach a decision," the black woman said. "Have a good day."

"Thank you."

I was surprised I could walk. I felt like I had been sucker punched. I opened the door and let myself out. In the waiting area, other prisoners were gesturing to me, asking me nonverbally how it had gone. I shrugged my shoulders, although I expected the worst. Talk about anticlimactic. I had waited twenty years for this.

I didn't sleep that night, or the next. In Friday's mail call, I got the decision. I felt the envelope. It was thick, which meant that there was a Notice of Appeal form inside: I'd been denied parole. I opened it up anyway and read:

PAROLE DECISION: DENIED. HOLD FOR 24 MONTHS.
NEXT APPEARANCE: 09/98.
BASED ON THE NATURE AND CIRCUMSTANCES OF THE INSTANT OF-
FENSE INVOLVING THE IN CONCERT PLANNED ROBBERY OF THE
VICTIM WHEREIN ONE OF YOUR CODEFENDANTS SHOT THE VICTIM
CAUSING HIS DEATH. YOU WERE CONVICTED AT TRIAL. WE NOTE
PRIOR JUVENILE COURT DELINQUENCY WITH PROBATION SUPERVI-
SION AT THE TIME OF THE INSTANT OFFENSE. WE NOTE YOUR
ACADEMIC ACCOMPLISHMENTS AND PROGRAM PARTICIPATION.
HOWEVER, THE PATTERN OF ARMED ROBBERY CULMINATING IN
THE INSTANT OFFENSE PRECLUDES DISCRETIONARY RELEASE.

Two more years.

That night, I called my sister, Jazz.

"What happened?" she said without even saying hello, her enthusiasm coming across the line.

"They denied me."

"What?"

I read the decision to her.

"I can't believe this shit!"

"I can't believe it either."

"What do they want from you?"

"I don't know."

"How many people did you see?"

"Three."

"Were they white?"

"Two Negroes—a man and a woman—and a white woman."

"Blacks are worse!" Jazz said.

"There's one thing the earth cannot bear: a slave when she becomes queen."

"What?"

"That's from the Bible." Like the devil, I could quote Scriptures when I had to.

"Amen."

We were silent for a moment.

"I'm going to appeal," I said.

"How long does that take?"

"About four months."

"Four months!" She paused. "Do you want me to get you a lawyer?"

"That'd just be a waste of money. I'm the best lawyer I know."

"Do you need anything?" Jazz asked.

"No."

"We'll come see you next weekend."

"OK. Bye."

"Love you, Little Brother."

"Love you too, Jazz."

Two more years.

When the lights went out, I buried my head in the pillow and cried. I hadn't really cried since Camilla's death. When I stopped, I heard the voices in my head, louder and clearer than ever before. They were telling me to be a villain. *Shut the fuck up!*

The following day, I walked around in deep pain. It hurt most because two black people had been involved in the process. Couldn't they see that I had done everything humanly possible not to be broken and to triumph? Couldn't they see that I had my act together, that I wasn't that sixteen-year-old that had broken the law, but rather a man who'd spent more than half his life in prison for a homicide he hadn't committed? Couldn't they see me in the present and not in the past?

Two weeks later, I turned thirty-six. I celebrated my twentieth birthday in prison in the law library, putting the finishing touches on my appeal.

The main reason I could never be a Christian was that I was unforgiving. I couldn't forgive the people who I had thought were my friends, who had hung me out to dry. I couldn't forgive myself for being so stupid, for being a stand-up guy, for not copping a plea. All these years I tried not to indulge in self-pity. I was sinking so low I felt like I was going to fall through the earth into a body of water and drown. Only my anger, like a life preserver, kept me above water.

I had been in prison long enough to know how to get things done. I rarely asked for favors, but I now cashed one in: I spoke to a counselor and had him look up my codefendant, Clarence, in the state computer. I learned that Clarence had been released earlier in the year. Because of the other two homicides he had been involved in as a juvenile, he was denied parole repeatedly and forced to do all his time minus good time. He never should have been released, but he had to be. The peculiar logic of the law said it was "necessary" to keep me imprisoned while letting the actual killer roam the streets in search of new victims.

Two days later I called Jazz again.

"I called Parole," Jazz said. "I talked to this woman named Constance. She was nice. She said what had happened to you was unfortunate, but that the commissioners are human—they have bad days, they wake up on the wrong side of the bed."

"Jazz, *I'm* human, and I've had seven thousand bad days. Every day I wake up in the wrong *bed!* But I try not to let that dictate how I'm going to deal with people that day."

"Yes, but that's how it works. That's the fucking system."

I wrote a number of people I had met over the years—my professors, people throughout the prison system, and my appellate lawyers—and had them all write the chairman of the Division of Parole. They all came through. Jazz, in her inimitable way, followed my instructions to the letter and took them a step further. Every day she wrote a letter to the chairman. She also had everyone in our family write letters, and many of her friends, too. On her own, she went to Albany and met with the Parole chairman. She traveled there every day, in the morning and the afternoon, until, on the third day, the chairman decided to see her.

"I was going to march on his office with about a hundred people," she told me. "He must have thought I was a crazy woman, until I started explaining your case. I said all I wanted—all your supporters wanted—was a careful review of your case."

"How did he take it?"

"He was making promises like a politician."

"Yeah."

For three years I had been monitoring parole board activity. There was seemingly no rhyme or reason to parole board determinations. For example, Abdullah, a first-time felon who had so brutally beaten a homosexual to death with a two-by-four that the man had to have a closed-casket funeral, made parole his first time up after twenty years. Lamont was granted parole after his first appearance, even though he was participating in a work release program when he was arrested and imprisoned for selling drugs for the third time. He wasn't home sixty days when he wrote somebody bemoaning the fact that there were fewer crackheads on the streets now than there were four years ago. Harvey, at fifty, had a criminal history dating back to 1968. He had served seven years for a homicide and was back in prison for his fourth bid, this time for selling drugs. During his latest term, which also spanned seven years, he received fifty disciplinary tickets. He had a mental health history. He had no marketable skills beyond selling drugs. Even the institutional parole officer, who compiled his parole summary for the parole panel, told him not to expect to be paroled. Harvey complained to me how he had never been given a break, although he had been granted parole three times already. He was granted parole a fourth time this past November. The day after he learned that he had made parole, he was talking about "holding court in the streets," that he wasn't coming back to prison, that they'd have to kill him. I believed him. He had one of those wild, beaten looks, with a stitched scar that resembled a zipper across his forehead, probably from being pistol-whipped. It looked like you could unzip his forehead, reach in, and pull his brains out. He had spots of missing hair on his dented dome, like a wild dog with mange. If I were a parole commissioner, one look at him and I would have almost certainly denied him parole.

It seemed if you were convicted of a drug-related offense, no matter how extensive your criminal history was, and even if you were a certified 730 (loony toon) case, you received a get-out-of-jail-free card. Conversely, if you were of sound mind—something hard to maintain after twenty years in prison—had availed yourself of educational and vocational programs, and had marketable skills, you were denied parole. I could not understand being denied parole while some of these characters were granted parole. Maybe, if you were educated, parole commissioners saw you as dangerous. You would not spin through the revolving door. They would never see you again. But wasn't that supposed to be the whole idea?

In November, when my minimum period of imprisonment was up, when I had exactly twenty years in, the two-year hit came down on me like a collapsed building, brick by brick. On that day, I could have walked out of prison. I had visualized the moment, had thought about it so hard and so long that my head ached, trying to make it become a reality. Clarence was already home for the second time. I had thought I would be home for Thanksgiving.

I filed my appeal. It was the most powerful legal stuff I'd ever written. I raised a number of issues: that the parole board did not consider all the factors mandated under the executive law to determine whether I should be granted parole; that the parole board had illegally applied a new parole policy to me because I had a homicide-related offense, and that the determination was predetermined; that the parole board improperly denied me parole in part because I had exercised my constitutional right to a trial; that the parole board should not have focused on my juvenile robbery petition, more than twenty years old; and finally, that the twenty-four-month hold was excessive and unnecessary. Still, there were no guarantees.

Six months later the Appeals Unit denied my administrative appeal. Later I would learn that nearly every prisoner received the same response, with slight variations. I filed a motion in court challenging my parole denial. It too was denied in a cursory manner. I then appealed to the appellate court and in the twenty-second month of my twenty-four-month parole hold I received a paradoxical decision. It stated that the board had improperly denied me parole because I had exercised my constitutional right to a trial and that usually the court would reverse and order a new hearing, but would not in my case because the board had not denied me parole for exercising this right. Two months later I made my second parole board appearance and again was denied parole for the maximum twenty-four months. I appealed again and the Appeals Unit and two courts gave me virtually the same decisions they had during my first round of appeals. I make my third parole board appearance in a couple of months.

This merry-go-round of crime and punishment and more punishment is spinning out of control. I just want to get off before it is too late. The whole prison system is out of control. If it ever had a purpose, it was forgotten long ago. Now the system runs on a perceived need. From this perception it has come to life, it runs on its own mythology, on its own fictions of law that are etched in stone.

Salvation

Notes from Life and Death

Benjamin La Guer

Norfolk, Massachusetts

After resting for more than a third of my life in prison, quarantined behind concrete and steel, encircled by silhouettes of faceless men in uniform and armed guard towers, not only has life for me been a physical roller coaster, but emotionally I have felt suspended in state. I have tried to convince myself, in a multitude of disguises, that although I am physically on this side of the stones, in spirit I must be free.

At night, long after the voices have fallen silent and the imprisoned garrison is asleep in either its dreams or its nightmares, I lie in bed still awake, wondering what has become of me. It's that ultimate question one asks in search of self-truth: that question which arises in the night, when the human heart pounds its loudest.

For most of the morning and part of this afternoon, I have turned and paced between these four stone, beige-colored walls. I've been asking myself in that way one demands answers from the gods, "How is it possible that four thousand one hundred and ninety-nine days could have been stolen from my life's calendar?" I remember when the god, a mortal with human features dressed in a black robe, ordered my days forfeit. He had spoken with the ease of Pontius Pilate, upholding the letter of the law and the verdict of the crowd. It was not the function of this mortal god to deliver justice, he may have thought, only to carry out the letter of the law. These black-robed mortals are referred to as guardians, in modern terms, of criminal justice.

My day had not been different earlier this year, in February, when the uniformed man walked upstairs, stood in front of my cell, and said, in words a child could have understood, "Your father died." The blue uniform then disappeared from sight. I arose from bed, removed a single piece of white paper from the desk's steel drawer, folded it, and covered the window, in need of even greater solitude than that found in a prison dungeon.

Only in prison did I really come to understand my father. He was not one to share his inner life with others. I don't believe there were ever more than a handful of people, including all seven of my sisters and brothers, who asked my father what he thought. My father and I never went to a baseball game. Except for the knowledge that he would leave for work before the streetlights turned off and never returned home before the lights were lit again, I had no idea who my father was. Until the last seven years of his life, for me, my father had been a thing who, by some cosmic order, just happened to inherit me.

For many years, I did not understand why he prayed to his God. Perhaps it was my father's hope, when no other option was available to him, that in the afterlife he could walk across streets of gold. I couldn't understand what he meant.

After many conversations, held in weekly intervals of two hours across a vast row of metal chairs in the prison's visiting room, my father and I became friends. We told each other our secrets. Curious about who I was, I began asking my father who he was. I asked him about our fathers, and if they had been noble or scandalous. My father said, in words I ought never to forget, "All men have more scandal than nobility in their hearts. That's what makes us human. Don't trust a man who says he is noble." My father had never spoken like that before; he spoke as if he had surprised even himself, perhaps having never thought of answering such a question. In the end, I realized that I admired the old brown man. He was human like me.

Earlier that week, in February, because I had known for some months that my father's health was deteriorating, I asked the prison's unit counselor if, upon my father's death, I could be favorably considered for an escorted furlough to attend the funeral. Within hours, I was told I would be granted such permission. And so I waited in anticipation for that moment when my father had waited for his father. I waited for that moment when I, the son of a La Guer, would no longer be connected to the La Guers of the past, for that hour when I would stand alone, linked only to a future.

The lexicon betrays me, of this I am certain, when I say our fathers are the basis of our manhood. When our fathers are alive, we, as sons, are physically linked to all our fathers; in strength, we are linked to that long chain of life. But when he stands no more, only then do we become men, standing only for the history of our future.

No matter how much I have, in the past, spoken of my belief that twelve years in solitude has left me unaffected, truth now told, I am a creature inextricably tied, in both failures and accomplishments, to what has happened to me in prison. It is here, in solitude, that a man attains what is nearest to his nature, where he battles to deliver himself either to his God or his devil. In whatever mold, a man emerges from his battles with scars of honor or wounds of disgrace.

When I finally was to step outside the prison for that trip that would take me in front of my father in his final coffined image—despite all the hours I had spent wandering about, walking across the lawns beyond the stones, in spite of all my efforts to prove I should be worthy—I felt afraid. I no longer had concrete sights or sounds of what was beyond the stones. Why was I afraid?

I can only figure that whatever had paralyzed me in fright had something to do with how twelve years in solitude can transform even the strongest of human beings. It is my understanding that our lower primate brothers and sisters in captivity are often so traumatized that they suffer extreme physical and cognitive impairment. And while I claim no unique insight into the natural science that explains such a phenomenon, I suspect that I am not so different in composite. If one were asked to remove one's spacesuit while standing on the moon, surely the impact would be immediate and profound. That probably is the nearest analogy to bringing a human outside, after a third of his life has been spent in solitude. My emotional paralysis doesn't seem so profound to me now. Yet I can't dispel the feeling that almost half of those who leave prison return. My question out of this feeling is simple: Are these people returning to prison because they are actual deviants, or are they simply unable to adjust?

Often in flashbacks I remember that summer morning when I was taken outside the prison for a court appearance in Worcester County Superior Court. Usually prisoners are brought in from across the state through an underground shaft under the courthouse building, then elevatored up to the courtrooms. For some reason, however, that particular day was different. The men in uniform parked the transport almost two hundred yards from the granite edifice. I say all this to make a point: I have no recollection, except in flashbacks, of the soles of my shoes striking the pavement across those two hundred yards, or of the façade downtown, or of the many faces that I must have seen that morning. It is still a surreal experience. I remember the events, but only as if I were outside myself, as though I know what happened from watching it through an angelic distance.

I still think of that morning. And while I have described that experience to myself inwardly, with mystical metaphors, I should remind myself that I had merely been amongst ordinary mortals.

Perhaps it started happening the instant when I was arrested, that moment when I stood accused, or perhaps later that evening when the steel door slammed behind me and I was left alone in a jail cell. It seems as though I can't suppress those first sights and sounds from all those many years ago. There is no unconscious memory of that instant when all the voices, images, and aromas dawned and faded. Daily I remind myself of that day when life seemed to have darkened. I started to live in a new reality, warped and twisted in on itself. It was isolated and dark, and what wasn't concrete was steel.

The indifference in the hearts of gods is something captured in myths. I say this to preface my attack on the gods. In the courtroom they form their own trinity: prosecutor, judge, and defense counsel. No matter how much I have tried to show these gods that I am a human in their image, that I understand their language, their culture, their Western tradition, nothing I seem to do pleases them. They reside as gods in their own invincible, infallible zone of reality while ordinary, mortal men anguish from their indifference.

En route to my father's funeral, riding in the rear seat along the state's freeway system, I said to myself, "You mustn't be afraid." It wasn't that I was scared of having emerged from the abyss. I suddenly had awakened. Not only had I awakened in a metaphysical sense, stroked by systems of physical oppression and perceptive freedom, but a new reality had exploded within me and there I stood, naked, transient, between two zones. Although I was overwhelmed by the sudden glitter of new images, sounds, and aromas, I was not afraid.

Perhaps that awakening was necessary. I came closest, nearer than ever before, to understanding how easily life can be negated. I had lived not only physically as a prisoner but also trapped in perception. The voice of solitude speaks a human truth greater than that of all the gods in black robes.

Now I stand in front of the window faintly watching the world from afar. I am in exile. I am in peace. I thought I could be like the gods, mimic them in their ways. But I cannot be a god, not even the smallest of saints, for I am merely a man. I am the son of the dust.

As I knelt before my father's coffin, I said, as if in conversation with his spirit, "I have brought uniformed men who carry steel to this sacred place, Dad. I hope that I am forgiven. I will not forgive the gods. I hope to be a son and a father, like you, of Honor."

In his death I became a man, and this is the torch he left me with to battle the gods. From the other side, my father still has the voice of a wizard. He still speaks from the inner fence of my conscience. WAR AGAINST THE GODS.

The Ice Man Speaks

Cheyenne Valentino Yakima

Pelham, Georgia

Before I begin, let me tell you exactly how I came to be called the Ice Man. In 1967, after one of the most violent riots Detroit ever experienced, my parents, Rubin and Rose, packed up all their treasures as well as their six sons and daughters. A seventh child, Randy, would be born in Atlanta, where my family took up residence.

I turned sixteen in 1971. At that age I was already a veteran of the night life, hanging out with the vampires of the midnight stars: hustlers, con men, dope peddlers, pimps, thieves, and every other kind of criminal you can imagine. By the time I turned thirteen, I had already been in trouble with the law: playing hooky from school, carrying a gun, shoplifting, and running around with a street gang called the Young Warriors. Father used to tell me, "If your brain was as big as your courage, you would become a genius."

One night in June 1971, my sister Brenda came home crying and terrified, her face dirty with blood, sweat, and tears, her favorite red dress torn to pieces. When I saw her standing there in the doorway of our apartment building, a burning rage shot through me like a bolt of lightning. I was always protective of my family members, to the point of giving up my own life if I had to.

My father reached out and put his big arms around her, and they sat down on the sofa. The rest of us stood spellbound, staring in disbelief and confusion, as Brenda told us that someone had just raped and brutalized her.

Mother had died a year earlier and was no longer around to give her sweet, loving comfort to her daughter. So father did what he thought was best and called the police. They came and did their usual investigating. But it wasn't enough for my brother Jack and me, so we did some investigating of our own.

Jack, Brenda, and I found the rapist two months later, before the cops did. Jack recognized the guy after Brenda pointed him out. He was known as Big John. He was a short, fat, sloppy-looking individual, dark-skinned with a patch of uncombed hair on his head. Jack said that he had attended Howard High, the same high school that we had attended before I was kicked out. We didn't do anything to him that day, as there were hundreds of people gathered in the park where we found him. Since we knew who he was, it wouldn't be difficult to find him again.

A week later, Jack went into our father's bedroom and took his .375 Magnum that he kept under the pillow. I armed myself with a meat cleaver from our kitchen cabinet. Then we went searching for Big John.

When we finally caught up with him, he was right where we expected him to be—on the corner of Boulevard, right across from the Georgia Baptist Hospital. He was chatting with four or five of his buddies, so we waited. That anger began to burn inside me again as I pictured the hurt and pain on Brenda's face that night.

Finally, Big John was alone. Jack walked up to him while I lingered in the shadows of the dark street. After about ten minutes, they started walking in my direction. As they neared, I noticed that Jack had Father's pistol pressed against Big John's spine. We led the big, cowardly rapist through a dark alley to an abandoned apartment building. The only things inside were dead rats, a lot of trash and a big old icebox.

You could sense the discomfort starting to mount in the pit of Big John's stomach as he began to cop pleas: "What's up, Bro'? What y'all want with me? I ain't done nothing." Jack didn't utter a word. But I was so angry that the words exploded from my lips like an atomic bomb. Screaming mercilessly in his face, I said, "You have made the biggest mistake of your entire life!" I didn't explain to him what he had done, because he already knew. Then, taking my meat cleaver from my back pocket, I hit him across his face. He fell to the floor, grabbing his face with both hands. I ripped his pants off, reached between his legs and grabbed a handful of his jewels. I swung the meat cleaver down and—

169

well, what I did to him is too gruesome to explain. But I can still hear him screaming like a wild panther through it all.

Afterward, Jack and I picked up Big John's limp body and put it in that big old icebox. Before we left, I went out and stole four bags of ice from the Jim Wallace service station, about a block away from where we were. We poured the ice all over Big John's fat body. Then we left.

How he crawled out of that icebox we'll never know, but he did. Somewhere on this earth there's a rapist who might be still walking around, but he won't be raping any more young girls because he's lost the necessary tools. So that's how I obtained the nickname "Ice Man," given to me by my brother Jack.

That was the beginning of my destructive and violent career as a criminal. After that date with Big John, my own life took a drastic turn for the worse, though years would pass before I'd realize it.

I started hanging around an older group of criminals who took great pride in their activities. Those veteran players could convince you that the world was flat, that the sun rose in the west, that there was nothing wrong with stealing, peddling drugs, pimping women, robbing, and just taking what you wanted. To them, you didn't have to answer to anybody for your wrongdoing, because in their eyes it wasn't wrong. Those hustlers taught me that people who worked for a living were weak because no real hustler would work for the Man, sweating on a nine-to-five slave job. Weak people had no place in a world where the strong ruled—it was also like that in the animal kingdom.

Those proud old criminals painted the prettiest pictures, and I was so blinded and excited by it all that I couldn't see the forest for the trees. They took to me, too, and discovered firsthand that I had more heart than brains. They never explained to me what the results would be; I had to find that out for myself. I guess all criminals try to block that part of reality from their minds. "I'll never get caught," they think. "I'm much too smart for that."

In 1975 I went on my first bank job with two old comrades, Sonny and Chief. We called him Chief because, like my father, he was half Indian and stood six feet, four inches and weighed about 240 pounds. Sonny was our driver, so he stayed in the car. With a sawed-off shotgun and an AK-47 rifle, Chief and I entered the bank. When we emerged, we were eighty-five thousand dollars richer. It was more money than I had seen in my entire life. My eyes lit up. I was like a baby with a new toy. My cut was twenty thousand dollars. No, I didn't complain because, after all, Sonny and Chief were teaching me the ropes.

I thought I was rich, and from then on, banks became my targets. Nineteen seventy-five was also the year that my father passed away. I had been put in jail for carrying a gun without a permit. Father came up to the jail and saw me one morning in October. A week later, he was dead. His house had caught fire and he had suffocated from smoke inhalation. Two of the deputy sheriffs at the Fulton County Jail were considerate enough to let me pay my last respects to my father. When the patrol car pulled up in front of the funeral home, I tried to fight back tears that began to flow. I quickly wiped them away, not wanting those deputies to see a tough guy like me cry.

But when the deputies allowed me to visit my father's lifeless body alone, I could no longer hold back the tears, which fell like pouring rain down my face. He looked so unlike the father that I knew, lying there in that golden casket with his dark suit and white shirt. I had never seen him in a suit before. Where once he was healthy, strong, and full of life, now he looked all dried up, like he had been sleeping a long time without waking up to eat.

My own world turned ever so dimmer after my father died. I felt I had no one in this world. We had become the best of friends over the years and now, like a fading sunset, he was gone. By the time they released me from jail, his funeral was over. They wouldn't let me attend. I guess they were afraid that I wouldn't return, and they were right. I then turned to the only people I knew—my criminal associates.

My brother Jack had turned to a life of pimping and drugs. Brenda was never the same after being raped. As my brothers and sisters began to drift their own separate ways, I drifted more deeply into the darkness of crime and violence. When I wasn't out robbing and stealing, I was burglarizing pawnshops or gun stores, transporting the goods up to my cousin in Michigan who, in turn, would sell the guns to the highest bidder.

I was a young, rebellious individual from the very beginning. I never paid much attention to the things my parents said. We were raised as Baptists, but I would usually fall asleep when the preacher spoke of evildoers and demons, only to feel mother's elbow nudging me to wake up.

Mom would always pick at least one night out of the week to read to us from the Bible, and it was mandatory that all the kids be present at that particular time. I will be the first to admit that those old Bible stories were mighty exciting to me, although I tried not to show it. Especially Job. To this day, I still find myself reading about him. When Mom would read those stories, you would have thought she was an actor preparing for a part in a movie. But there was no acting as far as she was concerned.

We were poor people and never owned a house. Father never cared much for big, fancy things. He was a simple man, drawn to simple pleasures of life, and told us often that honesty, dignity, and pride ruled supreme over earthly possessions. But I saw things differently. When I would drive through those wealthy neighborhoods, seeing people dressed up all fancy, wearing those fine, expensive clothes, I figured I could have those same things, too. The only difference was I would get them faster—by stealing and robbing.

The mentality I had developed was "If you weren't brave enough to hold on to your possessions, then people like me would take them from you." Of course, I had come to live by another philosophy as well: like Robin Hood, I would never rob the poor.

I always enjoyed reading, but the only books I would read were those about players, hustlers, pimps, and gangsters—people like John Dillinger, Al Capone, Pretty Boy Floyd, Jessie James, Billy the Kid—anything to do with outlaws and gangsters.

Criminal activity had become a big part of my life. At the time it seemed logical to me. It was better than going to the Boys Club or sitting in church listening to some boring preacher talk about pie in the sky. I enjoyed school, at least when I wasn't getting into trouble with the teachers for beating up some kid or going to the principal's office for playing too roughly with the girls.

One day I took my rude behavior too far. It happened at Howard High School in 1969. I was out in the hallway at my locker, talking with some of my gang members, the Young Warriors. Everyone else was in class. I was the only one still out in the hallway, playing with something in my locker. Suddenly I heard a loud, heavy voice behind me say,

"What are you doing out here in this hallway? Didn't you hear the bell ring to get your ass to your classroom?"

Even before I turned around to match the voice with the face, I knew who it belonged to. I had been to his office on many occasions. It was the school's principal, Mr. Jones. Should I live a thousand years, I will never forget his heavy, deep voice. When I turned to face him, I felt that burning anger swell up inside me like a boiling volcano. We stood there in that hallway, face to face, staring into each other's eyes. As he shouted, saliva from his mouth came flying into my face. When I could no longer control my anger, I hit him. I hit his jaw so hard, he fell to the floor. After he had fallen, I began kicking him in the face, back, anywhere my feet landed. I would have continued to kick him if it hadn't been for the teachers and students who had heard all the commotion.

When I looked up, there was a hallway full of teachers and teenagers staring at me in disbelief and fear. I took off. That was my final day at Howard High School. Years passed by the time the law caught up with me, so they didn't prosecute me.

When my parents found out about that incident, they were feral. Father pulled his belt out one last time. After that, he realized I was too big for belts and too hardheaded to listen, and that I would have to learn my lessons the hard way.

In 1972 I received my GED and learned a few other trades as well: barbering, cooking, baking, and welding. I was even offered a football scholarship to Tennessee State, but I turned it down. I was still too immature to recognize a good opportunity. This all took place while serving a two-year bid in Alto Industrial Institution, a reformatory school for uncontrollable teenagers. I had gotten busted for destroying a service station.

My father had bought me my first set of barbells and dumbbells a few years earlier. I was drawn to bodybuilding from watching the legendary bodybuilder Steve Reeves portraying Hercules at the theater. Bodybuilding and martial arts came naturally to me.

In the mid-1970s I found a martial arts teacher by the name of Sensei Green. He was half black and half Chinese and had been studying the arts for twenty years. His discipline was hapkido and a form of art called the Black Cobra, which he had designed and perfected. Sensei Green worked with me for two years. I then met Sensei Brooks, a Vietnam vet and master of tae kudo kwan. From him I would earn the rank of second *dan* black belt. Finally, I met a fifty-two-year-old Jamaican brother whose Shaolin Five Animals kung fu fighting style was exceptional. He had been into the art for thirty years, two of them training with the Shaolin monks of China. His training was hard and ritualistic. But it was Master Shuhai Liu who took my mind and spirit—not my body—to a higher level of the art.

Through the art you try to find within yourself a mature adult by seeing yourself in very strict and honest terms. According to Master Liu, the point is to make your spirit strong and solid.

There was a time when I used my martial arts skills ruthlessly and recklessly, challenging other students to fights and brawls out in the streets. My knife and bullet wounds are evidence of my misuse of the art. People would pull guns or knives on me, and I would attack them. Looking back, I sometimes smile at how foolish I was.

I understand now the true essence of the arts, that they were intended to be used for the complete development of a person—emotional, mental, physical, and spiritual—so he can become a true warrior and face himself without being weak. "The true warrior must always walk in beauty," Friedrich Nietzsche once said. "All great things must first wear a terrifying and monstrous mask in order to inscribe themselves on the hearts of humanity." I once wore that mask, wore it for much too long. Martial arts gave me a higher level of self-discipline and self-esteem, a sense of belonging, direction, and clearer knowledge of myself.

Today when a prison guard or one of my kinsmen gets in my face, shouting and acting irrationally, I can stand at ease, with no thoughts of striking out violently, because that self-discipline and self-control are mine. When you know who you are, you don't have to go around trying to prove yourself by bullyragging on someone else.

The criminal world had attracted me like a giant magnet, with many colors that glittered like diamonds and gold, but it was nothing more than zirconium diamond and fool's gold. I wanted to associate with a bad crowd of people, people that had no regard for human life. Violence had become just as comfortable to me as a cold Budweiser and a football game are to a guy sitting at home watching TV.

I used to think that none of the poor African Americans or white people would ever rise out of their ghetto environment and amount to anything. So, in order to get my own share of the American pie, I thought I had to rob and steal, taking from those who had already achieved their dreams. As an African American teenager, I felt that I would never accomplish anything without violence and blood. I never took the time to pick up a book and read about people like me, who never had anything but who somehow overcame their tribulations and rose to the top—without crime, violence, or peddling drugs. Only later did I read about people like George Washington Carver, Frederick Douglass, Martin Luther King, Jr., and Andrew Carnegie—people born into poverty but who still possessed an undying will and determination to excel in their individual calling.

I also read about men who put their criminal lifestyles behind them and rose from the prison pit to fame. Men like the Apostle Paul, who converted from a persecutor who approved the murder of Christians to a faithful servant of God; Fyodor Dostoevsky, who spent years in prison, only to emerge as a literary giant; and Malcolm X, who used his prison term to change his life and became a great leader and faithful servant of God, leaving behind his now famous quote, "To have been a criminal is not a disgrace, but to remain a criminal is the biggest disgrace of all." All of these people possessed a burning desire to make a difference in the world, in spite of their own calamities.

I really can't pinpoint when I started making my own change. Perhaps it came about when I went on my last bank heist on January 22, 1982. That would be my final crime. I had come to the end of my rope. Jack—my brother and best friend—had just OD'd on drugs a couple of months earlier. When he died, tears flowed from my soul for ten long years. And Brenda, after she was raped, got on drugs and ended up taking her own life.

Filled with bitterness and an emptiness so deep, I went on my last bank heist with the attitude of not caring whether I came out of it dead or alive. Most of my family was already dead, so I figured there wasn't much worth living for.

Three weeks before Christmas 1981, I met up with an old jail cell comrade named Sam. Together we ventured through southern Georgia until we came upon a little town called Oglethorpe, with a population of about five thousand. After casing it out for about two weeks, my partner and I decided to hit both of their banks. Sam would hit one and I would hit the other, which was the larger of the two.

On January 22, 1982, that's exactly what we did. On Friday morning at approximately nine thirty, I entered the Macon County C&S bank. No one noticed me as I came through the door wearing a red bandanna covering half my face, a blue skullcap, a navy blue coat, and navy blue slacks, with the .357 Smith and Wesson in a shoulder holster under my left arm, a .38 snub-nosed special in the waistband of my pants at the center of my back, and my Remington pump sawed-off shotgun hanging from a sling under my right armpit.

But it wasn't long before I got their attention, especially when I jacked a shell into the chamber of the shotgun and made my announcement loud and clear: "All right, you seen it in the movies! This time it's for real! On the damned floor! Now! Move it! *Move it!*"

After everyone dropped to the floor, I leaped over the counter and began filling my gym bag with money. All of a sudden, I heard a loud noise that sounded like a gunshot outside the bank. I thanked the people and bid them all a good day, then exited the bank with my body bent low. The shotgun was firmly in my hands with my index finger resting lightly on the trigger, ready for whatever fate had in store.

Outside, Sam was standing no more than seventy-five feet away, with his back pressed up against the side of a large brick building. I hollered to him, "This way, man. Come on, Bro'. Let's get the hell out of here!"

As we ran around to the back of the bank, a cop car cruised by. Suddenly Sam jumped up and started running. He pulled his pistol out and began shooting at the patrol car. I took off in the opposite direction, making it back to the getaway car we had hidden near some railroad tracks. I changed clothing as fast as I could, then got into the Ninety-Eight Olds and lit out of there. Sam would have to fend for himself. I'd be damned if I was going to wait around for him, especially after that foolish stunt he pulled. Patrol cars were moving in the opposite direction as I drove away from the small town of Oglethorpe.

Back in Atlanta that evening, I ditched the car, went shopping for some new clothes, and caught a flight to Detroit. Sam and I had made an agreement that if he got caught, I would give his half of the loot to his sister Mary, and if I were captured, he would give my share to my sister Evelyn, who lived in Atlanta.

Five days later, being true to my word, I boarded a Greyhound bus to Atlanta to give Sam's sister his share of the take. But, as happens to all wrongdoers, fate would eventually turn against me. When I phoned Mary from Detroit, she told me that Sam had been captured and that the cops had put some buckshots in his behind, but that he would be all right.

After leaving Mary's house, I took a taxi over to Evelyn's house to spend the night. The following day I would take a plane back to Detroit. But that day never came.

Around four the next morning, the GBI (Georgia Bureau of Investigation) and the FBI kicked in the door of my sister's house, and there I was, captured with nowhere to run. My partner Sam, whom I had trusted with my life, had turned on me like a dog with rabies. Sitting in the back seat of the squad car, handcuffed and shackled like a wild beast, I felt as though I had died and gone to hell.

In March I stood before the Honorable William Blanks, who sentenced me to life imprisonment for the crime of bank robbery. That day in court, I extended my sincere remorse for all the mistakes I had ever made in my life and vowed never to make them again. I had never said that in any other courtroom. I didn't know it then, but I think that was a major turning point in my life.

Fifteen years have passed since that cold winter morning when I robbed the Macon County Bank. Since I made the choice to rob it, I have only myself to blame. I take no pride in having been a criminal, but I do take pride in the fact that I have finally found peace in knowing that I don't have to live a life of violence and crime to make a difference and to be reckoned with in this world.

Whether a man resides in a castle or a ghetto shack, he is always free to use his internal powers of choice to paint his backdrop and arrange his background music. If he doesn't like the plan he has created for himself, he has only himself to blame. But even then, he still has a choice. He can get off the stage and produce a new play. In the words of George Jackson: "A man is still free to exercise his choices, even in the darkest dungeon."

I figure if a guy like me can make a change and start seeing things differently, then anybody can. I now live my life by a different set of codes and honor. As I continue to serve my time behind this steel, concrete, and thousands of feet of razor wire, I strive to maintain a progressive attitude. I shall always remember this prison Tophet as the birthplace of my repentance and redemption from a squandered past. Perhaps sharing my story will help someone see things a little differently. If I can do that, my living will not have been in vain.

One Hundred Soldiers

D. Michael Martin

Freeland, Michigan

Teenage boys, some with their bodies in the impossible positions only truly dead men can achieve, lay at all points of the compass. The hot, humid air was layered with the stench of burned gunpowder, coppery blood, and unrestrained fear. Orders were given and carried out, not by conscious decision, but by training and instinct. For the moment, the dead had ceased to exist for the living, not from hardness of heart, but out of emotional necessity and the need to care for the wounded. These were the cream of an entire generation of American males—adults by government decree and maybe in their own minds, but children in reality—fighting, killing, and dying in the jungle to protect each other because they could not fathom any other reason to be fighting.

With the wounded bandaged and medevacked out along with the dead, the remainder of the young marines established their night defense perimeter in the hostile jungle. There were one or two nervous jokes cracked, but most kept their thoughts to themselves. After all, they were United States Marines, the "baddest of the bad"—*Yea, though I walk through the valley of the shadow of death*, and all the other platitudes they had come to believe in. It just wouldn't do to be caught being emotional. Tears were something shed deep in a private place in the soul where even the individual sometimes didn't acknowledge their existence. C-rats were automatically eaten. Few slept; some stood guard. Life seemed to continue. Some of those who had died had not yet realized it, so they carried on and did not fall down.

It is said that we are born with one hundred soldiers whose job it is to protect us. As we grow and bad things happen to us, our soldiers, pieces of our heart, detach themselves from us to confront the traumatic event. They stay in that spot of our life and keep that memory from haunting us. If our life is particularly hard, we may run out of soldiers. When that happens we become emotionally dead. Our only protection then are the terrible walls we build that isolate us from other people and other feelings. The only way forward to life is to go back and re- trieve our protective soldiers.

We retrieve our soldiers by confronting the events and traumas that have affected us. We may need to forgive or be forgiven. We may need to grieve the loss of someone or something that was important to us. We may even need to express some deeply buried anger from long ago. Whatever we need to do, it is important that we not go it alone. We need the love and support of family and friends, and we need the strength of God.

When we retrieve our soldiers, we are able to resolve those things that have deadened us. Then we can break down our isolating walls. If we don't retrieve those soldiers, we can't reassemble our heart and we remain emotionally dead.

In Vietnam, whether you had one soldier or one hundred soldiers in your heart, the first sound and resulting tragedy of angry gunfire robbed you of all your humanity, all your heart. What was left were walking dead men.

I was one of the walking dead. Three days in Vietnam, eighteen years old, and in complete shock, I had no idea how so many men had died so quickly, and I certainly couldn't figure out why I wasn't one of them. I had been bloodied, I had seen the "elephant" and instinctively knew that I had changed, and I knew that the change wasn't for the good. I had been a sensitive, quiet, bookworm kind of kid, a loner. No one was more mystified than I when, shortly after graduation from high school, I joined the Marine Corps.

If there was one thing I had learned from the young faces on my grandparent's living room walls, it was that Martin sons went to war for their country. My father and uncles were all veterans, so it followed that I would be one also. But I really hadn't thought about any particular branch of service. I don't even recall thinking about enlisting at all. One day, I just did it.

A few days after surviving that ambush, we rotated to the rear to rest and pick up some replacements, both human and material. After cleaning up in the cold showers, I joined a bunch of marines. We drank beer and talked about the past few days. I had never drunk anything with alcohol because my father drank heavily when I was growing up and I had been emotionally hurt several times by his actions and words while he was intoxicated. Because of that, I swore I would never drink, but my horror from the ambush was so deep that it overrode my self-imposed abstinence. All I wanted was to be numb, so that night I began what turned out to be almost twenty-five years of self-medicating with booze and drugs. Reality was just too horrible, and I wanted nothing to do with it.

Over the years, I became a living example of the nursery rhyme:

> *Run, run, run,*
> *Fast as you can;*
> *You can't catch me,*
> *I'm the gingerbread man.*

Reality was just a distant, abstract concept for me as I ran from the contents of my mind. I talked to no one about what I had seen and done in the Nam. The war had split not only families but also the country. No one wanted to talk about it. The anger about the war was directed at those most easily reached—the Vietnam veterans—and it caused a lot of anger in our souls.

It seems that I was filled with anger for most of my life after that. I could not and would not love anyone. Nor would I allow anyone to love me, and if they tried, I would make sure that they soon saw the futility of it. I felt nothing—not joy, not happiness, not sorrow, not remorse, not love—only hate and anger. I could not admit why I was the way I was because then I would have to confront myself, and that I could not do.

I blamed others, especially God, for all of my problems. Back in the jungle, I had cursed God for the death I lived with every day. I decided that there wasn't a God, and if there was, I didn't want anything to do with one that would allow a hell like Vietnam. I was constantly in trouble. If you asked me, I would have sworn that I did not search out trouble, that it just seemed to follow me. The only things important to me were my drugs, my booze, and the money to buy them. Even sex was just a way of dulling my senses so I couldn't feel anything, and also to fool myself into thinking I had power over someone.

Eventually, I met a wonderful woman who had a daughter. Together we had a son. I should have been happy, but I was still in my private hell, unable to share my heart with anyone. I just could not bring myself to believe that I deserved to be happy. Through a succession of jobs, repossessed homes and cars, and myriad other debts, my wife stayed with me, trying to believe in me and trying to get me to believe in myself.

I was on a continual "search and destroy" mission, searching out anything that could make me happy, anything that could give me peace, and then destroying it. I would be hired for a great job, move up the ladder quickly, and then walk away. I would run up huge bills knowing that I couldn't pay them, knowing that I was driving my family into financial ruin. I would not befriend anyone who was remotely decent. I was only interested in people and things that could further my self-destruction. I believed that destruction was my fate.

Vivian, my wife, finally had to leave me to save herself and our children. Inside I was falling apart because they were the only good things in my life. I couldn't admit my anguish to myself or to anyone else, because my protective devices were just too finely tuned by then. Even with the collapse of my family, I could not seem to stop my life-shattering drinking and drugging.

I finally landed in county jail, and as I lay in my cell, I knew that I was going to prison. I was filled with rage against God and myself. I was angry one minute, plotting suicide the next. I finally called my parents, who told me that they still loved me. My mother told me that God loved me and that I needed him in my life. My parents' expression of love somehow opened a tiny crack in the carefully built shell in which I had encased myself. Tears began to run down my face, tears of grief that I had not allowed myself since I stood in the Nam jungle as that shell-shocked eighteen-year-old.

All the pain I thought I had protected myself against surged in through the holes in my crumbling fortress walls. I began to feel the agonizing loss of my wife and children, the death of so many friends and comrades, and the emotional distance I had put between myself and my parents and siblings. The pain was crippling and almost unendurable. I felt crushed by the loss of so many years, so many opportunities, and so much life. All the emotions that I had denied myself for twenty-five years tore at me until, unable to stand the pain any longer, I cried—no, I *begged* for the peace that would save my life. And God gave it to me.

I was stunned. I felt all the hate, rage, and pain rush out of me, and in its place flowed a peace so filling and so complete that I knew it could have come only from God. The release of my pain and anger gave me hope that I still had a future. It gave me a determination to make something out of the ripped fabric of a life that God had given me. My new heart gave me a curiosity for life and a fervent desire to be the best person I could possibly be. I realized that prison was not an end but a beginning.

I have tried to associate myself with people I can learn from, and I have shared my experiences with others in the hope that it will help them avoid the turns in the road that I traveled down. Today, with the support of God, my family, friends, and my new spirit, I have a fantastic life. I have a renewed relationship with my family. I have a highly satisfying job helping other men reach for an education, and I have pursued my own education as an addictions counselor. I have begun to use my talent for writing to reach out to others, to help them if I can. I have purpose and direction in my life, something I never had before. That all adds up to a satisfying life. The fact that there is a prison fence around me does not change the quality of my life one bit. It seemed impossible back in that death-laden jungle, but I am alive. Heart and soul, I am alive!

Was Vietnam worth the price paid? On a national level, I say that the price was too much. We lost too many doctors, lawyers, laborers, fathers, mothers, and maybe even a president or two. For what was achieved, the death of fifty-eight thousand men and women was fifty-eight thousand too steep. Was it worth it on a personal level? I don't know. That question is just too complex to be able to come up with a definitive answer. But I no longer burden myself with wondering. Am I proud of my service in the U.S. Marine Corps? Am I proud to call myself a Vietnam veteran? My answer is a resounding "Aye, aye, Sir!"

on both counts. After years of hiding our heritage, we have once again asserted ourselves as the cream of a generation. We are Vietnam veterans; we are winners. Our motive was to carry on the tradition of answering our country's call, our patriotism without question. We made our way back the same way we came through the horror of the Nam. We helped each other, and with that help and God's love, I am finally able to say I have come home.

A few years ago, I was given a quote that has meant much to me. It sums up the courage of the Vietnam veteran—the essence of our pride in our decision and ourselves. I quote it here as a more eloquent response than I could ever give to those who say we should be ashamed, or at least not proud:

> **It is not the critic who counts, not the one who points out how the strong man stumbled or how the doer of deeds might have done them better. The credit belongs to the man who is actually in the arena, whose face is marred with sweat and dust and blood; who strives valiantly; who errs and comes short again and again; who knows the great enthusiasms, the great devotions, and spends himself in a worthy cause; who, if he wins, knows the triumph of high achievement; and who, if he fails, at least fails while daring greatly, so that his place shall never be with those cold and timid souls who know neither victory nor defeat.**
>
> *Theodore Roosevelt*
> *speaking at the Sorbonne, 1910*

A Part of Me Set Free

Kevin James

Lorton, Virginia

I was a very confused and shy youth who was under the misconception that the only path toward acceptance was through deceit and violence. In my reckoning, power and status were achieved through material possessions and force. No one was to be trusted lest I allow myself to be taken advantage of.

Later in life I came to realize my grievous errors. But by then, many subconscious and habitual patterns were deeply ingrained. Today I am ever vigilant and striving to break the mold of these negative habits and subconscious triggers. Without a doubt, I have changed my values and way of thinking, and by the grace of God, consistency will eradicate many negative traits and habits from my life.

My earliest memories date back to around 1961, when I was four years old. One event in particular marked the beginning of many years of antisocial development and behavior for me. It was spawned from my curiosity concerning cigarettes. I felt that smoking was an adult pleasure denied me solely because I was a child. I could not understand why I should be denied something that was an icon of maturity and that others enjoyed so immensely. I began to pilfer cigarettes from my mother at every opportunity. In a sense, this was the beginning of my training as a thief. When my parents were at work, I would hide in concealed places around the house and light up. My aunt, who was responsible for the care of my brothers and me, never became the wiser until a tragic mishap occurred because of my covert activity.

One day in late 1961, I was off on one of my smoke breaks under the bed in my room when my mother arrived home early. When I heard her voice, I became panic stricken and threw the lit cigarette under my mattress. In a few hours, my mother said that she smelled smoke. Rather than coming clean, I tried to sneak off and handle the situation on my own. I tried to beat the smoldering mattress out. This only served to fan the embers into a full-fledged flame. Within minutes, the fire was out of hand. The result was that I burned my family out of house and home, and I never accepted responsibility for this atrocity.

By 1964 I was a regular juvenile delinquent. I would play hooky from school on a regular basis. While absenting myself from school, I spent my time stealing candy, bicycles, even dogs. My parents tried everything under the sun to bring my perpetrations to a halt. All their efforts were to no avail, and eventually their beatings became a standard, and lightly considered, part of my daily routine. They did little to correct my behavior because I was a very spiteful child.

There was one thrashing, however, that really got my attention. It was during the 1966 school year. I was hooking school and on my way to steal a bike around Wisconsin Avenue when my father saw me. He called me, and I took off running with the hope that he would think that it wasn't me. I was not so lucky. When I dragged myself home around seven o'clock that evening, he was waiting for me looking like the Grim Reaper. He had whittled down a collection of tree branches to the semblance of switches and with them proceeded to strip the skin from every inch of my body. He really laid it on thick! I could not sleep for two days because of the welts and lacerations. My mother fell completely out with my father after that because, in her view, it appeared as if he had been trying to kill me or damage me for life.

From then on, a hands-off policy went into effect for my father. I really went for it then. I started keeping late hours and began to drink beer and rum regularly with my friends. But being the youngest and smallest of our crew wasn't easy. I often had to prove myself by being the most aggressive initiator of trouble.

As I approached my eleventh birthday in 1967, I thought without a doubt that I was now grown. No one could tell me anything. I had developed a reputation as a fighter. My older brother and I were constant combatants; I had hit him with things and sent him to the hospital for stitches at least three times. Two or three days a week, he and I would be costars of the knock-down-drag-out neighborhood fight. I refused to let him think that he could dominate me. I had a fierce "little man" complex and was willing to meet any challenge if I thought someone was trying to slight me in any way.

During that year, I became an ace pocketbook snatcher and could break into vending machines, pay phones, pinball machines—anything. I also became a dope fiend. And for the first time, I started taking my first true interest in the opposite sex. Prior to this, I had played house and dry-humped with little girls, and I was forever grabbing girls by the butt. But I had never been infatuated and emotionally stimulated by one. The first girl I idolized was three or four years older than I. At fifteen, she was already a well-known hustler.

Although I was very much aware of the physical act of sex, I was still a virgin. I wanted to change my sexual status, yet I did not know how to approach this perplexing issue. This hustler and I became regular hangout and hustling partners. We started spending a lot of time together. In time, we became inseparable and shared a variety of experiences together. We fought together, robbed together, stole together, and used drugs together, but we never had sex. I never figured out how to approach her that way, although we had slept together many times. She never mentioned it and neither did I.

To this date, I am not sure whether she was attracted to me for any reason other than the immensity of my heart. When I say that I had a big heart, I mean that I would accept any dare and was always willing to initiate whatever action was necessary to get a dollar. I should add that she was an intravenous heroin addict. My association with her is how I was initiated into my first narcotic experience. I didn't want to make a bad impression by being intimidated, so I accepted drugs on the first offer. I adamantly refused to use a needle at that time, so I simply sniffed it. Over the next few years, I experienced a spectrum of criminal and addictive behaviors. I was sent to a psychologist at least twice, and in 1970 I made my debut at a receiving home.

My first trip to the receiving home was only overnight, and I eventually got one year of probation. During this probationary period, I began picking pockets, burglarizing homes, and committing strong-arm robberies. My female partner and I became separated because she had been arrested and sent to a women's detention facility.

In the summer of 1971, Cubby, one of my elementary school rivals, and I were riding our bikes with a couple of ounces of reefer on us when we decided to snatch a pocketbook. It happened by chance that we spied a hefty bankroll in this lady's purse while she was making a purchase at some store. Without hesitation, we decided to tear her off. At what we thought was the right moment, we executed the snatch on our bicycles. We didn't know that a park police officer was on our trail, and after we rode for maybe ten or twelve blocks, we stopped to count our loot and smoke a joint. Boom! From nowhere, the police appeared. My friend got away, but I was not so lucky. I was housed at Cedar Knoll, and after six or seven months, I was convicted.

In 1972 I was sentenced to juvenile life* for the offenses of robbery, burglary (stemming from my previous probation), and violations of the Uniform Narcotics Act. A caseworker who reviewed my case in 1973 knew my mother and persuaded the judge to give me a chance at redemption. I was faced with one of three options: enlist in the armed forces, sign up with the Job Corps, or remain incarcerated until my twenty-first birthday. I eluded the juvenile life sentence by entering the Job Corps at Harper's Ferry, West Virginia. However, I did not recognize the break afforded me by the juvenile court system. It is more ironic that rather than using this opportunity to my advantage and preparing myself for advancement, I used it to become a better criminal. Though I excelled in school and sports, I never let an opportunity pass when I could steal, shake someone down, loanshark, or outright take advantage. I was committed to being a hustler who could con or outslick anyone who thought he could intercede in my game. By sixteen, I was well on my way to becoming an archcriminal.

During my two-year experience in the Job Corps, I got away with everything from repeated AWOLs and loansharking to felonious assaults and burglary. In the summer of 1975, I left the Job Corps with the intent to wreak havoc on the world at large.

At the time, my chosen professions were burglary and shot-robbery. After succeeding at numerous petty local crimes, I decided to go on the road for what I considered the big sting. That summer, Cubby and I put into motion our plan to rob the Job Corps center that I had recently

---

* *Juvenile life:* until the age of majority; in some states, age twenty-one.

vacated. We armed ourselves with pistols. Our plan was to be executed by the stealth of night. Having been summoned repeatedly by my superiors in the administration to face either accusations or charges, I was able to acquire the combination to the safe in the administration building that contained the Job Corps' payroll. After stealing a neighbor's car, my partner and I were off to West Virginia.

We gained entry into the administration building easily and proceeded to open the safe. Either we could not work the six digits properly or the number had been changed, because we were unable to open the safe after several attempts. After an hour of trying to no avail, we heard someone approaching and discovered it was my former boxing instructor. I insisted that we leave. Even today, I am not sure why I was so eager to avoid a confrontation. I like to believe that it was out of respect to his mentorship, and not my fear that we would have to murder him if he saw us. We left frustrated but determined not to be denied.

On our way home, we stopped in Frederick, Maryland. After breaking a window, we committed snatch robbery on a jewelry store. This impromptu caper netted us about seventy rings valued at approximately three hundred to eight hundred dollars apiece. We were in the big time now!

We returned to Washington at about nine in the morning, only to be accosted by the police five blocks from our destination. A high-speed chase ensued, which resulted in my wrecking four cars, including the vehicle that I was driving. But we managed to escape on foot with our loot, leaving only a pistol behind in the stolen car.

Over the next nine months, my associate and I became popular in various drug circles. After selling most of our loot for bundles of heroin, we became ensnared in a cycle of supporting substantial habits by dealing in drugs. Once we had shot up all of our profit and the initial invest ment, we reverted to flat-footed hustling. By 1976 I was in Lorton's Youth Center with eight six-year sentences. I did eighteen months. During that time, I got my GED and learned offset printing and lithography. I also learned how to be a more sophisticated and vicious criminal.

In 1979 I got a job as a computer operator. The birth of my son that same year motivated me to stop using drugs for a while, but I persisted in picking pockets and creeping into office buildings on my way to and from work. About three months after my son's birth, the urge of my addiction overwhelmed me and slowly but surely I resumed my heroin habit.

In September 1979 I was arrested for burglary and a felony charge of receiving stolen property. I was sentenced to one to five years. For the first year, I abstained from using drugs and spent my time working out, boxing, and taking college courses. When I saw the board after a year, I was given a six-month set-off, although I had no disciplinary infractions and had participated in positive programs. Their justification was simply that they felt I was "institutionalized" and manipulating the system. I was furious and became bitter. I resorted to jailhouse robbery and theft to fulfill my mission of trying to stay high every day for the next six months. The next time I saw the parole board, I had several disciplinary infractions and no program participation under my belt. I was granted straight-out parole.

On April 5, 1982, I was jettisoned to the community forthwith. Every day I robbed to use drugs, because at that point in my life using had become the sole purpose of my existence. Within thirty days I was a fugitive from justice after escaping from police custody in both Maryland and D.C. For the next four months, I lived the life of a renegade.

By September 1982 I had been arrested and indicted for three armed robberies, assault with a deadly weapon, burglary, and carrying a pistol without a license. I was facing in excess of one hundred years in prison, not including a detainer in Maryland that would carry additional time.

Reality kicked in, and I began to feel regret, remorse, and sorrow. All I could think about was the pain I had caused and repercussions that my acts had on peoples' lives. I realized that I had become a worthless wreck. I was doomed to a fate befitting the dejected and antisocial creature I had become. By the grace of God, I ended up with eight to twenty-four years to serve.

In 1983 I was transferred to the federal prison system. I benefited by being in the federal system because it is far better equipped for self-improvement than is the D.C. Department of Corrections. For the duration of my term, I remained drug-free. I also maintained a full-time job that enabled me to support myself as well as make an honest attempt at contributing to the support of my son. In the federal system I acquired an updated GED and two college degrees, as well as insights into the workings of government and bureaucracies by functioning as a cochairperson within the structure of the NAACP. My tenure in the federal system gave me the opportunity to learn about goals and responsibility. I learned to make true assessments of my thoughts and feelings. Most importantly, I learned to deal with my feelings responsibly. I truly made giant steps toward self-improvement and change.

In 1990 I was returned to the D.C. prison system where I could only sit like a bump on a log, because the few opportunities available there are bogged down by a long waiting list. Eventually I was sent to a halfway house. In 1990 I secured full-time employment and went to business school at night. I did very well for a while until I made my first bad decision.

I was offered two federal employment opportunities. I elected not to go to work for the federal government because at the time I had been making eleven dollars and sixty-five cents per hour as a laborer/window installer. The federal jobs I was offered were paying only around nine dollars per hour. I never considered the benefits of job security and advancement potential, and I failed to consider that my present job had lay-off periods between every contract, and that I was constantly exposed to drug use.

In 1991 I took a long-term assignment in Syracuse, New York. For seven months I lived in a hotel with eight fellow employees. All eight were chronic cocaine users. Heroin had been my drug of choice, so I felt safe for a while. But my resistance was deteriorating fast, and old cravings began to resurface. After a year of frustrations with my job and an unhealthy sexual relationship, I found the self-justification to start using drugs again.

Finally, in 1993, I was arrested for distributing cocaine. Because of favorable recommendations and my efforts to be responsible prior to my relapse, the judge was lenient and sentenced me to a term of probation and a drug treatment program. I have yet to experience my probation because the board of parole did not see fit to be so lenient.

During this span of several years, I have been working again on something: me. I recently made parole, and currently I am awaiting my release. In my heart and mind, I know that I have one last opportunity to make amends and get on with the mission of putting my life in order.

I know that I have a tall order before me, and I know that it is going to be tough. And yet, with all things considered, I am confident that I have what it takes to strive toward maintaining my sobriety while functioning as a productive father and member of society.

In my anticipation of returning to society, I have prepared myself for the challenge by conditioning myself to keep in the forefront of my mind that Rome was not built in a day, and all sickness isn't death. I must exercise patience as well as the fortitude to remain consistent in the pursuit of my goals and endeavors, and in the event that things don't go according to plan, I must rewrite and execute a new plan. I recognize that now I have more weight of responsibility on my hands than ever before. I say and feel like this because I am a single parent approaching his fortieth birthday who must build a foundation from scratch. At this late date, I also must establish meaningful ties with a young man who is my offspring and who I really don't know but love beyond veneration. I no longer have a father upon whom I can lean, and I feel compelled to devote myself to becoming for my son a fraction of the man that my father was to me.

I am aware that it is easy for most people to pass judgment and condemn people for their past. People will say, "What happened the last time you had a chance?" It is difficult at best for anyone outside of this experience to understand that change comes gradually, and because similar mistakes occur, it doesn't always mean that the intent to do otherwise does not exist. In any form of relearning, structure and guidance are vital. If you know no better, you can do no better, and even when you know better, if you cannot gain insight into and access new patterns and activities, you will eventually revert to what you know best.

There is no excuse for recidivism, but I want to make it perfectly clear that there are concrete reasons why many individuals get caught in the same vicious cycles. On the institutional level, rehabilitation does not exist. Once institutionalization occurs, you are bombarded with stimuli that are contrary to self-improvement. Cosmetic applications of rehabilitation may be applied, but they often ignore, and in some cases may actually increase, an individual's problems. In the truest sense, rehabilitation is incumbent on the individual, but I believe that more tools should be made available to help people in their attempts to change their lives. Trial and error is a costly and time-consuming way to learn. But as the saying goes, "Learning occurs from the cradle to the grave," and as long as the individual strives and doesn't give up, a brighter future is possible and within reach.

My sense of responsibility is difficult to convey in words. I know without a doubt that I have squandered many opportunities and created many problems in my life as well as in the lives of others. Although I've endured the hardships of incarceration, I still have many debts to repay. I will never have the opportunity to begin repaying my parents, who are deceased, but I can honor their memory by striving to become accountable to my son and to society. Much remains to be seen, but even more remains to be done.

The Prison Pump

Jon Marc Taylor

Cameron, Missouri

Fifteen years ago, I was a raging, nihilistic young man, dangerously out of control. Not only did I deserve to be caged, but also I needed to be locked up for my own—as well as everyone else's—protection. In a strange sense, at least for a convict to admit, I was rescued from eventually killing someone and, in turn, being killed or executed by someone else during my criminal descent into hell.

A decade and a half later, I am no longer a dangerous man, at least not a physical threat. For a reasoning, thinking person is always a potential threat to the authorities. In the crucible of "the keep" I have evolved from the psychologically knuckle-dragging barbarian I once was into a concerned and compassionate individual.

The remarkable aspect of this metamorphosis is that it occurred in the modern American penitentiary—a milieu not noted for its positive, constructive atmosphere. Indeed, it is a purgatory better suited for quashing the spirit and putrefying the soul rather than reforming the character. It is a place where perpetually agitated and corrosive anger can eventually consume even the last vestiges of residual humanity, damning one to a cycle of committing crime, victimizing others, and being locked up again.

Yet the salvation I found, however rare in the gulag, is not impossible or unattainable. Many prisoners, after experiencing one or two forays through penitentiary gates, aspire to average middle-class values of steady employment, a stable, healthy family, and noncriminal lifestyles. They just don't know how to get there.

194

Under current correctional practices and overall operating philosophy, there is little encouragement to reach for this golden ring of normality. Any resurrection that does occur is almost wholly a result of personal choice and of what is typically a fierce, often demoralizing struggle against great systemic odds. However, this quest can be achieved if the prisoner desires it enough. At least until recently.

No correctional system can reform or rehabilitate a single inmate. Transformation is not a process that can be imposed upon a person; rather, it begins when the individual chooses, sometimes subconsciously at first, to change. All a penal operation can and must do is to provide opportunities and encouragement with which offenders can invest themselves once the motivation to change manifests itself in action. Involvement in these programs often starts a process of inevitable positive change.

My salvation came through physical fitness, education, and love. All of these areas overlap and reinforce one another, but all provided unique facets of my evolution.

The love of my family and friends, even after all that I had done, helped me to realize that if these good people found me worthy of their love, I too could find that worth within. From the flame of hope nurtured by the constant loving reinforcement, I found the spiritual drive to take each struggling step in self-discovery and growth.

With the partial assistance of Pell Higher Education Grants—eliminated by the 1994 crime bill and no longer available to prisoners—I began an odyssey through a humanities-based postsecondary education that illuminated vistas of vast reservoirs languishing within me. For eight years I persevered through one of the most difficult of all college curricula: one behind bars. I eventually earned a graduate degree—the first and, sadly, so far the only inmate to do so in the state where I was then incarcerated. During those eight enlightening years, I discovered many things about myself that allowed me to heal, to acknowledge my transgressions, and consciously redirect my energies to cultivation and expression.

As essential as this familial love and scholastic edification were, the underpinning of my imprisoned existence was my striving for and maintenance of physical fitness. From nearly the beginning of my incarceration, weight training has been an integral part of my survival strategy.

At first, the goal of my effort to "bulk up" was to present a more forbidding image. Being young, white, and lightweight makes one prime choice prey on the prison yard. But as time passed, I found myself enjoying the challenge of adding more size and strength. I also realized that the strenuous effort helped me to manage the tremendous psychological stress of incarceration—not so much the stress caused by other prisoners as the maddening tension imposed by a lockstep Kafkaesque regime, whose only goal was incarceration.

Through weight training I have discovered or cultivated several positive aspects of my personality from flexibility of organization, to reaching within to find the little extra drive to make things happen, to the patience to let things evolve in their own natural time. Of immediate importance, though, the image building of a hard waist, pumped chest, and buffed arms imparted self-confidence that merged with and enhanced other activities in my life. The stress-reduction effects of a sweaty hour strenuously "pounding iron," moving ever more weight as the years progressed, rechanneled my rage. Such exhausting effort helped to keep me from lashing out and hurting others, and ultimately myself, even more. There is no doubt in my mind that if I had not been able to expend considerable energy, frustration, and anger on the iron pile, somewhere along the way I would have assaulted one or more of the uniformed tormentors or numbered fools who afflict my daily existence.

In fact, my very best bench press (335 pounds) was the result of my choice between exercising and decapitating an all-too-often infuriating prison case manager. From a correctional management point of view, one of the prison's best provisions, using profits from the inmate canteen, was to provide access to weight-training equipment. At least it was for that particular maddeningly obtuse bureaucrat.

Congressional legislation, in the form of amendments to the 1994 crime bill, among other banishments, eliminated weight-training equipment from federal prisons and coerced states desiring or desperately needing prison construction dollars to eliminate such equipment as well to qualify for the federal largesse. Some states, such as Georgia, Mississippi, and Wisconsin, have already followed suit, and others are considering the policy.

Before Congress, the director of the Federal Bureau of Prisons opposed the legislation, citing research that prison weight lifters are involved in fewer violent incidents than the average inmate is. Other studies demonstrate a lower return rate to prison for such positively active offenders. Apparently, the research indicates, weight training provides prisoners with valuable therapy and the development of self-esteem previously missing in their lives. But against all this firm and persuasive evidence, most politicians are pushing their "Let's get tough on prisoners" agenda at the expense of reason and safety, and without having any true effect on the overall problem they are putatively trying to combat.

Even the argument that society should not provide prisoners luxuries at taxpayer expense is largely a moot point. In the majority of correctional systems, recreation equipment is purchased with profits from the inmate commissary and canteen operations. Thus, instead of costing the taxpayer money, prisoners themselves are funding a program that improves their self-esteem, reduces stress, encourages self-discipline, and results in immediate administrative as well as long-term societal benefits.

Closing the iron pile and making prisons "tougher" will neither deter crime nor make society safer. Prisons will only become starker, meaner, and more saturated with prisoners growing gradually angrier. Whether the anger is righteous or not is immaterial. With little to stimulate their minds or soothe their torments, those immersed in the violence of accumulated rage will one day discharge back onto our avenues, boulevards, and streets.

To make our correctional systems more effective and cost-efficient, we need several things. We need fewer laws that needlessly send nonviolent people up the river in the first place. We need more programs to educate, acculturate, and humanize those who do end up that river, not the virtual elimination of postsecondary opportunities or the closing of weight rooms. We need fewer inane, soundbite-motivated clarion calls of "Make prisons places for punishment, not palaces of luxury and relaxation" or "Stop building prisons like Holiday Inns." Most of all, we need substantive crime prevention programs that circumvent the supposed need for even more draconian prisons in the first place, and that address the roots of the social dysfunction we call crime in America.

Freedom from Within

Jennifer Howard

Rockville, Indiana

As I was placed, handcuffed, into the paddy wagon, I felt an indescribable tiredness envelope me, body and soul. I was numb with self-loathing. When would it end? When would I stop this insane lifestyle? Could I stop?

During the familiar routine of being taken to the Marion County lockup to be searched, printed, and processed, the numbness subsided and gave way to panic. I needed to get out. I still had cocaine at home! I desperately ran through a mental list of who I could call and con into bailing me out if I received a bond. I had to get out! I needed another shot. I was trapped, frantic for a way out.

I was booked on theft charges. Hours later, my bond was set at two thousand dollars. I was ecstatic. With the bond set so low, I decided the best course for me would be to wait until arraignment the following morning when I would try to get released on my own recognizance. In my distorted thinking, I thought, *Why waste money for bond when it could be used for more drugs?* Now that I had a bond, I could relax. Surely, I'd be home by morning.

The state of Indiana, however, had different plans for me. Several hours after the bond had been set, a guard called me out. He served me with a felony warrant that had been overlooked when bond had been set for the theft charge. The warrant, for forgery, was given a "no bond." I was devastated. Why hadn't I bailed out before they discovered the warrant? I needed to think. I had to find a way to convince the judge to give me a bond by morning!

By the time I appeared before the judge, my probation officer filed a violation of probation against me. The judge kept the no bond for the forgery and issued a thirty-thousand-dollar bond for the violation. It was over. There would be no getting out. All told, I had the theft charges, one forgery charge, and three probation violations. Thus began my incarceration.

I spent the next seven months at the county jail awaiting court dates and plea bargain offers. Eventually, I pled guilty to the forgery, a Class C felony. In return, the state dismissed three theft charges. I was sentenced to the Department of Corrections for four years on the forgery charge. I still faced the violation of probation charge. I was stunned by the sentence. Somehow, I just never believed I would go to prison.

Telling my beautiful nineteen-year-old daughter and precious seventeen-year-old son was the hardest thing I ever had to do. They were devastated. Their tears seared my heart. By the time I hung up the phone, I was in so much pain that I prayed for death.

Seven months after my arrest, I made my final appearance before the judge. Still reeling from the four-year sentence from the forgery, I was totally unprepared for the judge's decision—*another* four years at the Department of Corrections! This time I knew what to expect when I called home. The tears, hurt, and anger are etched forever on my heart.

How did I end up a convicted felon, a mother separated from her children, a wife leaving her husband behind to deal with the devastating aftermath, a person no longer in control of her life? The answers would come slowly, painfully over the following months.

I was born in Gary, Indiana, on December 25, 1954, the fourth of six children. My parents divorced when I was six. By then, I already knew there was something different about our family. My parents were alcoholics. I knew the fear, embarrassment, and chaos associated with alcoholism years before I took my first drink.

There is no stability in an alcoholic home. My mother, unable to care for her children because of her drinking, was forced to send us to live with my father on occasion. Moving back and forth between them was an ongoing event throughout my early childhood.

My mother was my heart. At a very young age, I recognized that she was sick and needed care. I never blamed her for her lifestyle. I knew that she was incapable of overcoming her behavior by herself. But I never doubted she loved us. Alcohol rendered her helpless to provide for us. In my child's mind, I saw her as a victim of a cruel and unloving man—my father.

My father was a strict, cold, and controlling man. He ruled with an iron fist. There was no communicating with him. It was always his way, or face the consequences. My father was a "functional" alcoholic who held the same job for as long as I can remember, until his retirement. He was consistent in providing food and shelter but knew nothing about being a loving, compassionate, or nurturing parent.

Behind the façade of being a hardworking man who provided a home for his six children, my father hid a dark secret. He began fondling me when I was about seven. He never used the "I-love-you-this-is-what-fathers-do" approach I've read so much about. He used a much simpler, very effective approach—fear. Each stage of his abuse, from fondling to intercourse, was enmeshed with terror. His favorite line was, "When you stop being a whore like your mother, I'll stop hurting you." Pretty powerful words to a child who didn't know what a whore was!

At the time, the closest I came to confiding in anyone was with my second grade teacher. I loved her with a child's love and thought she would help me figure out this "whore" business.

I vividly remember the day I decided I would ask her what a whore was. I inched up to her desk and whispered, "What is a whore?" Imagine the devastation when she told me, "Only bad girls say words like that." She then ordered me to the corner. I was awash with shame. Many years passed before I confided my secret to anyone again.

When I was thirteen, I left my father's house. For the next three years I was bounced between my mother, my sister, and various friends. It was about this time that I took my first drink. From the beginning, I drank with the gusto of an alcoholic. I even experienced a blackout the first time I drank.

My best friend and I had no trouble obtaining alcohol. We simply went to the various drug stores that carried alcohol and stole it. I had learned very early how to steal. Often, when living with my mother, money was scarce, so I became adept at stealing food.

Whenever I drank, I felt guilty. I had sworn I'd never become like my parents. Yet, despite the guilt, I craved the escape alcohol provided.

Alcohol took away my shyness, gave me confidence, and allowed me to forget my life—at least for a while.

Within a year of my drinking, I moved on to drugs. Like many, I started out smoking marijuana, then progressed to acid and pills. I enjoyed alcohol but rationalized that drugs were the safer route because they didn't make me act like my parents. For a year or two, my drug use was fun; however, that too would change when I discovered heroin. I fell in love with it the first time I used it.

Heroin quickly consumed my life. It evaporated all my loneliness, shame, and pain. It provided me with a world of peace and contentment. It filled the persistent, throbbing hole in my soul. I spent every waking moment using it or finding the money to buy it. It became my best friend and my worst enemy. With the increasing need for the drug came a surge of criminal activity. Driven by heroin, I stole, lied, and cheated. Eventually, my consuming need for the drug outweighed the risk of arrest.

I was first arrested at sixteen. I had been on my own for several months, living alone in a small town in Illinois. I was arrested for possession of a controlled substance and theft. In addition to the criminal charges, the judge had to address a custody issue, since I was too young to be living on my own.

I feared the custody issue far more than the criminal charges. The court did not consider my mother—who had allowed me to live alone—a viable option. They did, however, recommend my father as an option. I was petrified at the thought of having to return to him. The court was also considering my older, pregnant, sister. She and I met with court psychologists to establish whether living with her would be in my best interest.

I went to court on my seventeenth birthday. The psychologist recommended that my sister be awarded guardianship. The judge agreed, and I was released to her custody. I received probation for the criminal charges. As a part of my probation, I had to attend school and counseling sessions.

After returning to Indiana with my sister, I enrolled in an alternative school and began mental health counseling. Within a year, however, I quit both and returned to the only thing that I knew would ease my pain—heroin. Again I willingly allowed heroin to envelop my life.

Nothing else mattered. The hole in my soul grew large, and I attempted to fill it with drugs.

It wasn't long before I was arrested again. I was busted in the act of shooting heroin. This time I was tried as an adult and was given a choice: a rehabilitation center in Virginia or jail. I stayed at the center for thirteen months. While there, I met a man and convinced myself I was in love. Taking an eight-hour pass together resulted in my first pregnancy.

Released from the center two months pregnant, I was alone and scared. At the time, my younger sister was living in Virginia and graciously let me stay with her. Everyone was advising me to put my baby up for adoption. Few people had anything positive to say about my upcoming motherhood, as I was carrying an interracial child.

While I understood some of the advice, I refused to give up my baby. I convinced myself that a baby was just what I needed to fill that ever present hole within. A baby meant someone to love and someone to love me. I felt I now had a reason to live.

For several months after she was born, Tina fulfilled my every need. She became the balm to heal my scars. She needed me and I needed her. Despite all my love for her, however, the pain gradually returned, and her presence no longer was sufficient to fill the void. The emptiness inside returned.

I hated myself for my weakness. I put my precious daughter's welfare second to my addiction, believing my love for her would cure me. Instead, the hole in my soul grew bigger. Strung out on heroin and alone with a seven-month-old baby, I decided to return to Indiana, where my mother was living. Perhaps I could succeed with a "geographic cure."

As soon as I arrived, I found a job and a drug connection. The only difference was that I had my mother taking care of my daughter while I worked and lived for my next shot. I lived to use and used to live. I took advantage of anyone and everyone who could help feed my addiction. I was miserable and could see no way out of my private hell. I no longer wanted to live, but I was too scared to die. I continued to self-destruct.

Then, at the point where I felt no hope, I met Robert. At the time, I was a waitress, and he was a steady customer. I saw him daily. When he asked me out, I immediately assessed whether or not he could aid in my quest for heroin. Deciding he could be used, I went out with him.

I never lied to Robert. He knew from the start that I was an addict. He also knew about my child and asked for nothing more than a chance to take care of us. His feelings scared me, and I attempted to discourage him by telling him I was no good. I told him things I believed would cause him to run in the opposite direction. Instead, he pledged his love for me. He saw things in me I couldn't see. He believed in me and refused to give up on me despite my obvious problems. I was confused. What could he possibly see in me?

Robert and I began to live together. He worked and took care of Tina and me, while I worked and used my drug. Finally, Robert had enough. He gave me an ultimatum: him or heroin. He gathered all my needles and other drug paraphernalia, held my arms to see the needle tracks, and said, "I love you too much to watch you die." I'll never forget those words. No one had ever said they loved me except for my mother, and I knew he meant it.

Robert took a week off from work to care for me while I went through withdrawal. He held me as my entire body trembled. He changed my gowns as they became soaked with cold sweats. He bathed me and spoon-fed broth into my weakened body. He never once left my side.

On September 15, 1977, I became Robert's wife. He adopted Tina, and I became pregnant with our son, Robert, Jr. I had never been so happy, content, and secure. At last I felt loved and needed. We moved to a house on Robert's parents' farm in Tennessee. We had very little in terms of material wealth and few friends. Yet we were rich beyond my dreams with love.

In 1985 Robert complained of persistent back pain. He was treated with pain pills and muscle relaxants for several months. One day, when it became apparent that his back was getting worse, he went to the VA hospital in Memphis. That day, my world began to end.

My Robert had lung cancer, which had spread to his spine, brain, ribs, and collarbone. The doctors estimated that he had six months to live. He stayed in Memphis for forty-four days. They gave him radiation and chemotherapy, which proved ineffective, so they sent him home to die.

I was numb. Not my Robert! God couldn't be so cruel. I went to doctor after doctor with his records, hoping that someone, anyone, would tell me he wouldn't die. I couldn't lose him. He was my world.

Two days before Thanksgiving, Robert caught pneumonia and his left lung collapsed. He labored for every breath. I would have gladly given him my breath if only I could. He was admitted to the local hospital, where I was told the end was near. There was no more to be done.

Robert begged me to take him home. He didn't want to die in the hospital. I took him home on December 2, 1985. On December 4, 1985, my Robert died at home. With him, the biggest part of me died too.

I was barely functional after Robert's death. The pain was excruciating. I was thirty years old with two young children and no hope. After years of sobriety, I again searched for that quick cure, a drug, to fill the hole that emptied into Robert's grave. Anything to numb the pain. This time, my drug of choice was cocaine. And so a new cycle in my life began: addiction, treatment, relapse, and jail.

From Robert's death to my current incarceration, my life reads like a drug-a-log. I have been through three treatment centers and arrested numerous times. I managed a fifteen-month and a nineteen-month period of sobriety in the last ten years. I remarried, but that too I threw away for drugs.

When I was incarcerated sixteen months ago, I thought it was the darkest day of my life. Little did I realize at the time that my incarceration was to become my first step to true freedom.

My biggest regret is the pain and suffering I caused my children. It has been devastating for them. I left them alone, confused and angry. People have asked me how I could love my children yet willingly lead a lifestyle that jeopardized them and our lives together. I have no answer.

While both Tina and Robert, Jr., have suffered immensely, their coping skills differ, as does the status of my relationship with them. Tina has always been extremely close to me. She always knew when I was using. However, like me with my mother, she always tried to protect me. She rarely showed her anger with me. When I was sentenced, her anger boiled over. Even then, she tried to hide it from me. As the months went by, we communicated less and less. Finally, we became honest with one another and slowly, very slowly, began rebuilding our relationship.

It was so selfish of me to confide in her as though she were my "friend" instead of my daughter. Unwittingly, I forced her into the same role of caretaker that I played with my mother.

Tina attended college and attempted to hide the secret that her mother was in prison. The stress affected her grades, as well as her health. Eventually, she confided in her boyfriend that I was an addict, but not that I was in prison. Recently, she took the final step and told him I was in prison. She is well on her way to healing.

My relationship with my son has been more complicated. We have also been very close; however, unlike Tina, Robert has never had a problem expressing his anger with me. His anger has been extremely hard to overcome. I have seen my son four times since I've been incarcerated. I talk to him regularly. For fourteen months, every conversation and visit was excruciating. He felt betrayed by me, and justifiably so.

Robert, Jr., bless his heart, is a grown man trapped in a young body. He is the most responsible, level-headed eighteen-year-old I know. He just graduated high school (another precious moment I sacrificed). He begins college next month with a four-year ROTC scholarship. He has concrete goals. He writes me his goals and underneath he writes mine. I will do anything and everything in my power to live up to his faith that I can achieve the goals I set for myself and perhaps some of those he sets for me!

For the past three months, he and I have finally been able to have positive conversations. He is starting to forgive, but he demands proof of my change. I understand that. I put him through hell and will have to earn his trust and respect.

I am so thankful to God that my children still love me and want to remain a part of my life. There have been many bitter tears for all of us. But through time, prayer, and hard work, we are finally beginning to heal.

Prison has not been easy. There are hundreds of personalities and twice as many rules. The homosexuality was hard for me at first, as were many other aspects of prison life. It took many months and thousands of tears before I became accepting of my incarceration.

I have gained a tremendous amount of control over my life, even in prison. I have attended a variety of groups—groups dealing with self-esteem, anger management, incest, codependency, domestic violence, substance abuse, and relapse. In each, there was a wealth of knowledge for the taking. I've gone through stages of pain, denial, and guilt as well as acceptance, hope, and change. But attending groups doesn't mean much if you are unwilling to look at yourself. I started out by blaming everyone except myself for my incarceration. Slowly and painfully, I began to place the responsibility for my actions where it belonged: on myself. I was the victimizer, not the victim. That has not been an easy truth for me to face.

Yes, I suffered abuse, incest, the deaths of loved ones, and many disappointments in my life. So what! My situation is not unique. My past does not justify my present. I made many bad choices. My father didn't force me to use drugs, drink, lie, cheat, and steal. He's been dead for twenty years. It's time to stop using him as an excuse for my actions.

Once I began taking responsibility for my actions, my journey of recovery began. Not merely recovery from drugs and alcohol but also recovery from self. I've learned through my trusted psychologist that I am not what I feel. I am not dirty or stupid. I am not a whore who deserved what my father did to me. Yes, I've done wrong. I've been selfish and have hurt many innocent people along the way. But despite the guilt, I am beginning to believe that I'm not a bad person trying to get good. I'm a sick person trying to get well.

It would be remiss of me if I did not share with you the vital role God has played in my recovery. I am not a product of jailhouse religion. I have known God for years. He was my favorite scapegoat. Today, he is my savior. He never gave up on me. I gave up on him. But there is no way I could have faced my past, present, or future without him. He has given me the strength to overcome.

I can't undo any of the things I've done. I can't erase the fact that I am a convicted felon. Nor can I gain back one day of the time I've lost with my children. But I can change my future.

It will take time to regain the lost trust and to prove myself to my children. But I am ready to move forward and to put my ghosts to rest. I know without a doubt that through my children, my friends, and with God's help, I will succeed.

Hired at the Last Hour

John Beasley

Bushnell, Florida

I had been in and out of prison most of my life, so when I found myself staring through bars again in October 1991, it was nothing new. But one thing was different. This time I wouldn't be leaving. Prison would be home for the rest of my life. I became very depressed and began to think, "Why go on living and put yourself through all this?"

In the next few days, I was moved to the new Polk County Jail in central Florida to an area called the Annex, where I went into an even deeper depression. There were several other prisoners there who had been involved in the same circle of drug dealers as I had been. This was the second time I had been arrested for trafficking. As a habitual felony offender, the Polk County Sheriff's Department was not about to give me a second chance.

Word was out on the streets and even in jail to watch out for J.B.: *He's facing too much time, and he'll "roll over"* (snitch). I was furious and all I could think about was how I could stop this talk. But it only grew worse. There were now rumors on the street that I wasn't in jail but was working undercover for the MATF (Methamphetamine Task Force) and living in motel rooms. Fortunately, at least the other inmates knew those were lies. But I had never before been treated like a snitch, and this was what nearly drove me over the edge, to want to end a life of misery.

The Annex is a new type of facility. The day room in one of the wings is two stories high. I lived on the second floor and often looked out over the TV area, with its cold steel tables and the hard, gray concrete floor where I wanted to land when I dove off, headfirst.

An inner voice kept taunting me, reminding me of the lowlife I'd always been and asking me, "What do you have to lose? Get it over with." I started to think, "Really, what do I have to lose?" I realized I'd be in prison for the rest of my life. If it was at all like it used to be, maybe I could handle it somehow. But now, all these guys who once looked up to me now looked down on me. I used to be the life of the party and everyone respected ol' J.B. Now things were different. Everything I'd owned outside was gone: my tools, gold, stereos, TVs. They even sold my motorcycle, truck, and car. My so-called girlfriend had left me, and after getting my bond money back, she moved in with a new drug dealer. I couldn't handle life any longer. I was ready to end all this misery and jump. Each time I felt I had the courage to jump, however, someone interrupted me.

One night, as I stood against the rail, a young black guy walked up to me and started a conversation. He said, "You look very familiar. Don't I know you?" Well, I wasn't in any mood to talk and even tried to break the guy off, but he wouldn't leave. He then recognized the tattoo on my arm and said, "Now I remember you. You're John Beasley."

"Who are you?" I asked. He told me he was Phillip Woods. The name didn't ring a bell, and I told him so.

"Of course not. I was just a kid," he said. "You used to hang out with the blacks back in the '70s. You supplied all the weed in town."

I must say it was a bit of a relief, at last, for someone to remember the old J.B. Our conversation about drugs, however, was short-lived. Phil asked me if I had anything to eat, so we went back to my cell to get a snack. When we got there, he saw a Bible and asked if it was mine. I told him it wasn't, that it had been on the bunk when I arrived. "Do you ever read the Bible?" he asked.

"I have," I replied. "But it really never made any sense to me."

At this point, Phil opened the book and turned to Matthew, chapter 20. He encouraged me to read with him the story about the man who had a vineyard, who sent his servants out to work. Several times during the day, the man went to the marketplace and hired more people to work. Some were hired as late as 5 P.M. Yet when the day ended, they all received the same pay. After we read the story, Phil asked if I understood it. "Well, I know that the people who went to work at 5 P.M. got a good deal," I said.

"You can get the same deal," he replied. He went on to explain that the story was about God, who owned the vineyard, and that we are the hired hands, and that the pay is eternal life. He said God calls people at different times in their lives. Some are very young and are able to serve God all their lives. "And some are like you, J.B.," he said. "Older, with messed-up lives. But he can still use you."

That night, I did a lot of thinking. I asked a lot of questions and did a lot of talking. I remember saying, "God, if you're up there, you know the situation I'm in, and you know I've wanted to end my life. I know I'm going to hell when I die, but I'm going anyway. I've wasted my life living it just the way I wanted, and now I'm old and all alone. Everyone I cared about is gone, and I'm facing two life sentences. I have no reason to want to live anymore. No one loves me, and there is no one for me to love."

Mail call was always something I wished they never had. It only made me more aware that there was no one out there for me. Then one day, to my surprise, an officer called my name. As the officer handed me the envelope, I noticed it looked official in nature. The return address was some kind of drug rehab center, and the handwriting looked familiar. The letter was from Kim Eubanks, an old girlfriend I had lived with for several years before I went to prison in 1989. Kim had come to see me a couple of times back then, and she had brought another girl with her on one of her visits. Her name was Pat, and she was on my visiting list as an aunt, though all she really was to me was a drug connection. I tried to explain this to Kim, but she left and never came back.

After my release in 1991, Kim came back to town. We saw each other a few times, but I was too busy trafficking dope to have a girlfriend. So Kim was the last person I would expect to receive a letter from.

Though I never really felt responsible for Kim's addiction, I certainly knew I was responsible for her being strung out, and for some reason I had compassion for this girl who, when we'd first met, had been very beautiful. Yet the last time I'd seen her, she had the unmistakable look of a junkie, and it made me sad to think about her.

As I read her letter, these things raced through my mind. She wrote that she was hoping to get her life straightened out and wanted to know if she could come see me.

The following weekend, I heard them call my name for a visit. I was spit shined and ready. When I got inside the visiting room, I saw Kim and her mom. But there was something different about Kim. At first, I couldn't tell what it was. Then I saw how big she was, and I realized she was pregnant. I was surprised. Kim had always wanted children, but she'd never had any. Yet here she was, nearly forty, about to have her first one.

During the hour we had for the visit, we tried to out-talk each other. I missed her and wondered if she missed me. At one point during our conversation, she said, "J.B., I'm still your friend, and I love you." I remembered how I felt that no one loved me. Yet she just said she did. I told her of the jam I was in and the awful time I was facing. I don't know how the conversation got to me being "Daddy," but when I left the visiting room, we had agreed that this precious child, whom we'd call Kirinda, would bear my last name.

Kim and I wrote each other every day. On August 5, 1992, the jury came back with another guilty verdict on my second trafficking charge. I remember the date well, as it was also the day Kirinda Beasley came into the world. I received a card announcing her birth a couple of days later and remember thinking how small she was at four pounds, thirteen ounces.

I was so excited and couldn't wait to see her. On October 14, 1992, the visit finally came. What a day! As I nervously walked into the visiting room, Kim was standing there with our little bundle. Before I knew it, she handed me the little child and said, "There she is, Dad. She's all yours." Nothing else seemed to matter. I knew I was holding someone who would truly love me, and I was falling in love with her. She was so tiny and beautiful. As I held her, I started thinking about my son, John Austin Beasley.

Johnny was born in December 1968 and died in January 1984 at the tender age of fifteen, of cystic fibrosis. He went through fifteen years of terrible suffering. After I found out how sick he was, life was never quite the same. I met Priscilla, Johnny's mother, before I ever went to prison. Our relationship began in 1967, when she pulled me off a guy I was fighting at a local bar. I moved into her house, where she lived with her three kids. The next year, Johnny was born.

At the time, I tried to do all the right things. I had a job. I went to church occasionally. But I realize now how far I was from being a good father. Priscilla became Johnny's nurse, his maid, his playmate, his friend, his mother, his father, and at times, his teacher. Johnny didn't make it to school very often, as he was in and out of hospitals all across Florida. Priscilla was the best thing for Johnny, and I'm sure God picked her for the job.

I left Priscilla and Johnny in the early 1970s. I had no idea how much I had missed until just before Johnny died. At times, I'd go by and visit for a day or two; occasionally, I stayed longer. But the road and another hustle were always calling, and I'd be gone again.

During one of my brief stays, Johnny caught me with a needle in my arm. He knew I was a dealer and always suspected I was a junkie. Now he knew for sure. I'm sad to say I wasn't very ashamed.

Priscilla had already lost all respect for me. I later heard some of the things she said about me, and I'm sure Johnny heard them, too. I never loved her, or she me, yet Johnny was our bond.

One Sunday afternoon in January 1984, I'd spent my weekend as usual, shooting up and drinking. At the time, I was married to a girl named Jane, and we lived in a house her family owned. It was a place where junkies bought their dope, so when I heard a car drive up, I figured it was someone looking for a buy. I dragged myself to the window and saw Ricky, Priscilla's oldest boy, getting out of the car. Right away, I sensed something was wrong. I shuffled to the door, and Ricky told me I needed to get to Lakeland. Johnny was in the hospital again, and in bad shape. If I wanted to see him one last time, I'd better hurry.

As we traveled to Lakeland, Ricky explained to me that Johnny had been asking for me. That's why Ricky had come for me. When we arrived, we headed straight to Johnny's room. As soon as I saw him, I knew he was bad off, yet his smile was still there. He never let me know about his pain, physical or emotional. I hugged him and told him that I loved him and would never leave him again. My heart broke for him.

In the lobby, Priscilla and I talked. She told me the doctors didn't expect Johnny to make it this time, that he was ready to go. She said the doctors had told her the cysts caused his lungs to swell so badly that there was hardly any room to breathe. Johnny was slowly dying from lack of oxygen and was in a lot of pain.

When we went back to Johnny's room, he called me over to his bed, hugged me, kissed me, and asked me if, when he went to sleep, I would stay with him. He said he was tired but didn't want me to leave. I promised him I wouldn't.

At some point, I heard Johnny make an awful noise. His sister, Marilyn, went over to look at him inside the oxygen tent. "He's not breathing!" she cried out. I ran over to the window and started talking to God. I told him I needed some time to show Johnny how much I loved him before he took him away. I asked God to please help me. I knew I hadn't been a good father and hadn't shown Johnny the love he deserved. I couldn't stand to see him go knowing these things.

I don't remember everything I said, but clear as a bell, I heard Johnny say, "Daddy, what's wrong?" Though my tough-guy image had not allowed me to cry openly, by now I could not contain myself, and the tears flowed freely. As I turned around, I saw that they had the tent off him and he was almost sitting up. The back of the bed was raised up, and from that point on, he never allowed them to let it back down. I said, "Johnny, I'm crying because I love you."

For the next few days, Johnny was tired a lot. But I wouldn't leave. I'd be talking to him and his eyes would begin to close, but the minute I'd quit talking, his eyes would pop open. He'd always smile and say, "Daddy, I hear you," and so I'd go on telling him stories about trucking and any other story he wanted to hear. His greatest desire was to be able one day to go out with me on the truck, and his favorite stories were always about when we were a family.

I told Johnny of how, when he wasn't even big enough to walk, I'd take two belts, strap him to my chest, and take him for rides on my motorcycle. He loved to hear about those times and laughed when I would recall them. He'd always been a happy little boy, never complaining, although he knew how seriously ill he was and that he wouldn't live long. In spite of it all, he loved life.

In the early days, I used to blame God for cheating me out of a healthy son. I never realized the blessing I had, and even in those last days with him, I didn't yet understand what Johnny would one day mean to me. I loved my son all right, but I wasn't the one who'd been cheated. I'd cheated Johnny.

Another Sunday rolled around. Priscilla asked if I would ask the doctor to increase Johnny's medication. When I did, the doctor informed me that he was aware of Johnny's pain, but that there was really nothing more he could do. He said that perhaps I could do something. This puzzled me. He went on to say that Johnny shouldn't be going through all this suffering, that he belonged to God, yet was holding on to something here—me. This doctor had known Johnny all his life. He said that I needed to talk to Johnny and set his mind at ease so he could go on home to God. When I left the doctor, I had no idea what to do.

Later, alone with my son, I began to talk. I told him that I knew I'd never been a good daddy, and that I'd been even less of a man. I told him I'd been straight all week—no dope or booze—and that I was going to stay that way. I let him know I knew he was going to heaven and that I wanted to go with him. I wanted to be with him forever. I said, "Johnny, you're the best son a man could ever ask for. All these years you've never complained, though I did. You've been more of a man than I have. I was never there for you, and now I realize how I've missed out. And, son, I've asked God for this extra time to spend with you, but you've had to suffer. Please don't be afraid to leave me—I'll be all right." Johnny just smiled and never said a word. However, as he stared off into space, I saw the look in his eyes that said it all.

That was the last night I spent with Johnny. Before he went to sleep, we hugged and he kissed me and said, "I love you." He didn't ask if I'd be there when he woke up, and he never woke up again. God had given me a full week with my wonderful son.

I ran out of the hospital when they told me he'd died, and within days, I was back to my old life. I did my best to forget our last talk, and for the next seven years, I stayed wasted, in and out of prison. During this time, I OD'd many times, but could never take myself out.

On August 14, 1992, as I held little Kirinda in my arms, I thought how much she looked like Johnny when I had held him in my arms the day he was born. I also remembered the passage in Matthew that Philip Woods had shown me.

I realized then that I had been hired at 5:00 P.M.

213

When Student Teaches Teacher

Larry Bratt

Jessup, Maryland

"People call me dumb. I don't like that. Call me dumb and I'll kick your ass!"

Kevin spit out these words in the hope he could intimidate. This embittered man, big as an NFL middle linebacker and hard as wood-pecker lips, almost had me convinced.

As a follower of a spiritual path of love and compassion, and after fourteen years of battles with my own demons, I knew better, though. Buddhism and yoga have transformed me, an abnormality for someone serving a life sentence for homicide. I believe I am now able to sense the inner fears of fellow prisoners. That is one reason why I accepted a job offer from prison authorities to become a reading tutor. After partici-pating in a fifteen-hour workshop, I was deemed competent enough to tutor functionally illiterate men the basic skills necessary for them to learn how to read and write on an intermediate school level. Thirty-eight-year-old Kevin was my first student. He resented that the authori-ties had drafted him into this newly formed tutoring program.

"Kevin, can you read at all?"

"Very little."

"Can you write?"

"No."

"Do you know the alphabet?"

"What's that?"

"The ABCs."

"No, I don't know them."

"Well, that's why you're here—to learn." I patted his shoulder. "I can teach you to read and write. Just be honest whenever I ask you questions concerning the lessons, OK?"

"I'll be straight. Just do what you said!"

We started with the level 1 book. It uses simple words accompanied by pictures, such as *bird, cup, dish, fish,* and *girl.* Through repetition and constant reinforcement for doing a good job whenever he read a word correctly, Kevin quickly gained confidence.

At the end of the session he couldn't believe he was able to read words and relate them to their pictures. He left smiling like a kid with straight A's on his report card.

For the next five weeks Kevin worked hard. Within days he had memorized his ABCs. I taught him how to recognize the vowels and their sounds, both short and long. He quickly learned to recognize the sound *-er* as in *sister* and *-ng* as in *ring.* I taught him how to print his letters; then he learned cursive well enough to write loving letters to his wife and daughter.

We also read short stories designed for beginners. I usually read a page, then Kevin would reread it. He never became frustrated. I would have him point out certain words in specific paragraphs and spell them. Then together we would look up the word in the dictionary and read its definition.

One day, we began a new mystery story when magic occurred. Kevin read an entire three pages of the story before he asked me to help him with the word *fledgling.* Before I could respond, that beautiful lightning bolt struck. His face illuminated with joy. Then, just as suddenly, he was wiping his eyes, but he couldn't stop the flood.

I reached for his shoulder to calm him. "Larry, I don't care about the tears. I'm actually reading. You kept your word and taught me. You're OK. Thanks."

I was shocked. Overt displays of emotion are unheard of in prison. Frankly, they still make me uneasy and, yes, somewhat resentful. Yet I embraced this titan in the spirit of brotherhood. For we were two men, losers in life, who had finally achieved something noble and beautiful together—freedom. And I realized to my amazement the ability to recover our individual humanity that we had once lost in crime.

Prison as Monastery

Ronnie Turner

Nashville, Tennessee

Have you ever read a book that changed your whole outlook on life? That happened to me after reading Thomas Merton's *Contemplation at the Garden of Gethsemane*. Merton said that a monastery could be like a prison for a monk who thought he had to be there. It occurred to me that if a monastery could be like a prison, then a prison could be like a monastery. The only difference Thomas Merton's monks displayed was the difference in their attitude. I reasoned that I could change my prison into a monastery by changing my attitude about where I was and why I was there.

Thinking of a prison as a monastery is not such an unusual idea when you consider that throughout history great thinkers have regarded the body as a prison. Others have regarded the world as a prison. In the Book of Genesis the confinement of Joseph by an Egyptian king can be seen as a metaphor for transcending life's confining circumstance. Joseph worked his way up to being a supervisor of the other prisoners. He eventually became an adviser to the king.

Confinement comes in many forms. It can be in a monastery, a jail, or a household. It can be in the form of an addiction, a compulsion, or a fear. These prisons of the mind can be as restrictive as a physical prison. Ultimately, prison is any force that confines us and keeps us from being free.

The mind makes the prison. As Bo Lozoff says in his book *We're All Doing Time*, "Prison is completely beside the point . . . we're all doing hard time until we find freedom inside ourselves." The physical prison is confinement in its most extreme manifestation. If it is in the mind where we find the real prison, then it is in the mind where we find real freedom.

If I had kept the attitude that I was in a prison, I may have begun to model my behavior after what I saw others in my situation doing. With a paradigm shift to the monastery model, however, I was able to make personal decisions such as what books to read and whether time should be spent in church or watching TV. Based on the monastery archetype, my decisions were of a much better quality than they would have been based on anything else in prison.

The idea of prison as a monastery is not original with me. Although the idea first came to me after reading *Contemplation at the Garden of Gethsemane*, I have read of others who have come up with the same or a similar concept. Bo Lozoff's Prison Ashram Project is designed to encourage prisoners to turn their prison cells into monastic cells. Although he uses the term *ashram*, it is saying the same thing in a different language. Charles Colson's Prison Fellowship also promotes the prison-as-monastery idea.

Quakers were responsible for early prison reform. According to *The Oxford History of Prison*, "Quaker penal thought was distinguished by a belief in reformation as the only real task of punishment." Two people involved in prison reform around 1812—about the time America started forming its prison system—promoted a system that essentially was "prison as monastery," even if they did not use the term. Elizabeth Frye and Michael Hoare, both Quakers, saw that prison produced a hardened, rather than a penitent, criminal. Through a series of prison visits, lectures, and Bible study, they believed their example would be a positive influence on prisoners.

The word *penitentiary* comes from the idea that a prisoner would be penitent while incarcerated. In the beginning, a prisoner was placed in a solitary cell to be alone with the Bible and his thoughts, much like a monk. The notion of a solitary cell was not based on punitive desires. The purpose of solitary confinement was not only reflection and penitence but also to protect against the mutually polluting influence of other offenders. The system was scrapped not because it did not work but because it was expensive and interfered with prison industry. The present system isolates prisoners from society and those who would be a positive influence and totally immerses them in a criminal society.

Monks, too, were considered to have withdrawn from society. Sometimes the cloistering was voluntary; at other times it was punitive. In the Middle Ages, each monastery was expected to have a place for the process of *detrusio in monasterium*, or confinement in a monastery. This system was used to punish secular clergy. Over the centuries, monasteries have been used as prisons and prisons have been used as monasteries. The two ideas are mutually inclusive, commonly held, and even interchangeable.

Once deciding to turn my own experience in prison to that patterned after a monastery, I had to develop a routine congruous with the monastery model. Since there was little information available to me about what goes on in a monastery, I was free to develop my monastery the way I thought it should be.

I wanted my routine to be well rounded—that is, covering the mental and the physical as well as the spiritual. So I divided my study time between spiritual literature and academic subjects. I spent at least an hour a day in Bible study and about two hours daily studying academics. I also went to the yard to exercise for about an hour, three or four days a week. Of course, I had a prison job and meal and shower time to consider, but most of the rest of my time was spent in programs provided by volunteer groups. My schedule varied over the years depending on what was available to me or what I was concentrating on at the time. Whatever I could find to do that was positive, healthy, and contributed to my spiritual, mental, and physical well-being, I included in my schedule.

Because of my regimen, my time in prison has been mostly productive. I have remained relatively free from the extremes of emotions I see displayed in others. I have had little time to experience the boredom I hear others talk about. And I have developed self-esteem from having met goals I set for myself, such as obtaining an associate's degree.

Prison life is filled with endless hours of TV, hanging out in the yard, card games, or, worst of all, drugs and the inevitable violence, theft, and sickness that accompany the drug lifestyle. In my five years in prison, I have observed the lifestyles of hundreds of prisoners. With the exception of two or three others and myself, mostly what I see is men wasting their lives.

As already noted, Elizabeth Frye in 1812 saw that being hard on convicts produced a hardened convict. Alexander Paterson, the innovative English prison commissioner of the 1930s, said, "Men are sent to prison *as* a punishment, not *for* punishment." Today powerful politicians win elections by promising to "get tough" on the most disenfranchised group in the state. Throughout the history of American prison reform, the pendulum has swung back and forth between retribution and rehabilitation. Sometimes, in a blind attempt at economy, programs that work are discarded. At other times, vindictiveness motivates people to campaign for "tougher" laws. Well-meaning reformists fail to consider politics, organization, or funding, and their programs deteriorate and are abandoned. The history of the American prison experience seems to prove the German philosopher Georg Hegel's observation: "What experience and history teach is this—that peoples and governments have never learned anything from history, or acted on principles deduced from it."

There are those who would reject the idea of a prison monastery as "coddling criminals." For them, there is a danger of looking at the prison monastery and forgetting that most monasteries are very austere places. The spirit of transcendence does not have to be abandoned because of a desire to punish. The two principles can work together within the same organization.

Whatever the nature of the organization that contains the criminal, a government does not do a service to its community unless the service it provides helps to change the mind of the criminal. If government will allow into prison volunteers and information necessary for prisoners to transform themselves, they will have made a start in a healthy direction.

Although the keepers of prison play a significant role, eventually it is the prisoner's responsibility to precipitate change. The prisoner must educate himself. The best university in the world, ultimately, is but a pile of books. It is up to the individual to study and apply this information. Government, society, and the prisoner can each work toward the goal. Winston Churchill said, "The mood and temper of the public in regard to the treatment of crime and criminals is one of the most unfailing tests of the civilization of any country." It is commonly held that our civilization is in decline. To turn this around, right-thinking people have to let go of a lot of anger and allow healing to begin.

Jaye's Story

Jaye Bookhart

Marcy, New York

Every day of my lengthy incarceration in New York State prisons, I have longed for my freedom. I have dreamed about it day and night. Like a child, I have wished upon a star and secretly hoped that someone would hear my pain, give me the key, and release me from this torture chamber.

But I soon learned that my freedom, like the key, cannot be given to me. It is something I have to obtain on my own. But damn if that dream of freedom didn't seem unreachable for this adamantly proud African American.

Like most inmates, I associated freedom with going home, a release from physical confinement. But a few years ago, when I arrived home from a previous incarceration, there were no hurrahs, no fanfare, and no one to listen to me recite my victory speech. There wasn't even anyone to greet me. There was just a nothingness—the same depressing familiarities I had been running from all my life: broken windows, boarded-up houses, streets cluttered with garbage, men sitting in door-ways with bottles and getting drunk because they have given up, kids begging for money for food, women with heavy hearts and tears in their eyes, wondering what had happened to their families. In the streets I once called home, I saw only pitiful eyes that gleamed with despair.

As I looked across the bleak landscape, I longed for the small comforts of my childhood: Moms tucking me into bed with her homemade quilt that always felt so heavy, so warm, so secure; Sunday morning breakfasts; the smell of my sister's hair being straightened as the boys bathed themselves squeaky clean before church. But I also remembered going to bed cold and hungry because it was someone else's turn to use the quilt and there wasn't enough to eat at dinner. In my prayers I would ask God what we had done to suffer like this.

Something was frightening the hell out of me. It felt as if it might catch and devour me if I stood still too long. So off I went again, running to somewhere I did not know.

My reactions to the pain were to try to numb it with alcohol and drugs—anything I could find—and to inflict pain on others, even the very ones who loved me, although at times I felt as if no one did. But this only continued the cycle of self-destructiveness and eventually led me back to prison.

This time around, prison was a refuge. I looked at the man-child in the mirror and I didn't know who he was or how he should live. I had spent at least half my life trying to control the pain and fear by will-power alone. But I finally realized that the demon I feared most was myself. I had become humble enough to know that something was definitely wrong and that I needed help. I was still in pain and a lot of it. But asking for help went against everything I had been taught about being a man, being strong, and being independent.

Fortunately, I was able to find the help I needed through the Alternatives to Violence Project (AVP), an international Quaker-sponsored effort that stresses community building, problem-solving and communication skills, and something called "transforming power" to counter violence.

Through AVP, I recognized the violence in my life and its disastrous consequences, for which I was now paying. I learned how overwhelming fear can be and how negative feelings lose their power when shared with someone I trust. I learned that I had to trust myself first, and to be honest enough with my feelings in order to have anyone else trust me. AVP provided a safe arena where I could practice being open and honest. I learned how to react to stressful conditions and, in violent situations, how not to respond to feelings. The program's constancy was what I needed. The volunteers provided love, affirmation, and community.

Eventually, my efforts were recognized and I was asked to become an AVP facilitator. This simple token acknowledging the work that I was doing in my own life, from people I respected and admired, helped me to see some light at the end of the tunnel. AVP was, and continues to be, the place where confined men like myself, and occasionally a few women and men from the outside, felt comfortable and trusting and courageous enough to talk about the past, our futures, love, anger, fear, hate, and any other feelings we wanted to share. From it, I learned that I no longer have to hide behind a mask of "I know it all"—a mask I once used to keep the world from getting too close. I now understand that the amount of fear and pain hidden deep within me, and the "know it all" attitude to cover it, is not unusual. I'm not alone.

In my personal search for freedom, it feels great to know that the key I have been looking for I've always had within myself. Thanks to some very special people that I consider my family and an excellent AVP program that enables people to be touched in their hearts and souls, I am no longer self-destructive and am fully committed to living a nonviolent life. Permanent and substantial change is possible. I'm living proof. Although still incarcerated, I am freer than I have ever been in my life.

Before, I was on a suicide mission. Now I am on a mission to live and to help others live by giving to them what was given to me in my time of need. This time, going "home" will be different.

Salvation

Juan Shamsul Alam

Malone, New York

I made my way to the mosque, removing my shoes at the entrance. I walked in, right foot first, and passed through the crowd. Muslims were milling around waiting for the *adhan* (call to prayer). I placed my state boots and state green coat on a rack filled to capacity with state boots, city boots, Reeboks, Filas, and army-issue greens. I found a spot to say my prayers. I felt out of place. It had been four years since I had entered a mosque. I had lost my faith in God and anything dealing with religion.

On January 22, 1993, I was arrested for a homicide that took place in 1987. It took the police nearly seven years to apprehend me. I was arrested as I walked out of my building. Five homicide detectives approached me with their Glock 9-mms drawn. One pointed his gun at my head; another dug a shotgun into my ribs. A burly Irish cop with graying hair calmly asked me my name.

"He's our man," the cop told the others. They immediately handcuffed me and carefully placed me in the back of a blue Dodge four-door.

I took one last glance at the building and window of the apartment I had lived in for the past thirteen years. My wife, Sandy, and my children, Wesley, Anthony, Shamsul, Hakim, Yaasmynn, Alia, and Rafael came to mind. Would I ever see them again? My life, my career as an actor and playwright, flashed through my head.

This essay was originally entitled "Keeping It Real," under which it won a PEN Award.

Before I knew it, I was at the Forty-Eighth Precinct, hustled up a side entrance, and placed in a cell. I was still handcuffed. As I sat in the cell, I scanned the "wanted" pictures on the bulletin board. Right there on the top and middle was a picture of me, a small version of an eight-by-ten photo I used for acting work.

An officer came by, motioned me over, and removed the cuffs. He disappeared. Beers, the burly officer, approached me with some documents. He looked me over.

"Juan, we have you here for questioning. I'm sure you know what this is all about," he said.

He led me into a room, gave me paper and a pen, and told me to write down in my words what had happened seven years ago. I had waived my right to counsel; I wanted to get this over with. I was here to tell the truth. I wrote my confession, then was given my Miranda rights, two hours after my arrest. I was placed back in the cell and told a DA would come down to hear my confession and that it would be videotaped.

At 9 P.M. Beers was back, this time assuring me that everything would be fine.

"Juan, I was reading your résumé. You actually worked with Sylvester Stallone?" he asked, surprised.

I was thrown off when he asked me that. How did he get my résumé, I wondered.

"Yes, sir," I said.

"What role?" he asked.

"I was the mugger who got hit in the mouth. *Night Hawks*—that's the name of the film."

"I'm gonna rent it as soon as I can," he said proudly. "Your sister gave us your photo and résumé. She was trying to help you. So, what else have you done in films?" he continued.

I told him about the bit parts I'd had in *Rage of Angels*, *Easy Money* with Rodney Dangerfield, *Moscow on the Hudson*, and *The Equalizer*, and that I'd done a lot of commercials.

Beers cut me off. "Listen, the guy you killed was a scumbag, a low life. You did us a favor," he said, then walked away.

By 11:30 P.M. the DA had me in the interrogation room. In front of a video camera, I told him, as truthfully as I could, how it all had happened. "I was on my way home from work. Three men approached me. I had a pocketknife, which I always carry late at night. Words were exchanged. The guy was pulling something out of his pocket, and I stabbed him and ran off."

"Words were exchanged?" the DA asked.

"Yes, sir. The guy called me a stupid motherfucker three times while pulling out what appeared to be a small gun," I said. He jotted down something and excused me with, "Thank you, Mr. Alam, for your cooperation."

I was led back to my cell. I sat there, thinking of my life.

I was born on August 20, 1946, in Bellevue Hospital in Manhattan. For seven years I lived in East Harlem, where I learned how to fight and steal. After that, to Chelsea I moved with my mother and brother. There I applied my crafts as a street fighter, shoplifter, street hustler, burglar, and gang leader of the Young Assassins of West Twenty-Seventh Street. I went to P.S. 33, where I spent most of my time in the principal's office. One time, the police caught me stealing at Macy's and brought me to school. Another time, I stabbed a bully with a penknife. I hated fighting but was always in a fight. Once, my gang robbed a truck and stole its delivery. One of the guys got busted and snitched on me. I got busted. They placed me in Spofford Juvenile Center. After going to court, I was placed on probation.

But that didn't stop my life of crime. One day, we made plans to go over to Jersey and rob the home of a rich person we had met early that morning. I was a school monitor with a white belt and triple-A tin badge. We all snuck on the train and made our way over the George Washington Bridge. In Paramus, New Jersey, we found our target—a big gray house. I was the lookout, but not for long.

A state trooper spotted me hanging on the corner of a neighborhood that had no Latinos or blacks. I happened to be Latino with black, white, Indian, and East Indian blood in me, and I stuck out like a penis on a dance floor. Shots rang out and the state trooper arrested me on the spot. One of my boys, George, was shot in the leg. Freddy and June Bug, who was black, went with me to Paramus State Hospital. I stayed there for five months, and when they set me free, they told me never to come back to New Jersey. Six months later, a kid got mugged and we all got arrested. I was sent back to Spofford and sentenced to three and a half years at Highland State Training School. It was 1958. I was a stone rebel at twelve.

At Highland I learned how to read and write. My drama teacher, Mrs. Geer, always had me in a play. I even recited the Gettysburg Address with a stovepipe hat.

After three years at Highland, I was paroled to my mother. She had moved to the Upper West Side of Manhattan. There I joined a gang called the Vampires and earned the nickname "Johnny Baby Face." I also got into shooting dope, stickups, and pimping. I got shot a few times, once with a shotgun and another time with a .357 Magnum. I tried changing my life by getting into politics as a Young Lord and Black Panther sympathizer. But I was always getting high and screwing the girls. I almost died a few times from liver problems.

By 1975 I decided it was no more drugs, no more alcohol. I wanted to write, to create. So I joined a theater group of ex-inmates called the Family. They were getting noticed from a play, *Short Eyes*, by Mickey Piñero. At the Family, I studied the crafts of acting and writing. My first play, *Bullpen*, was produced off-Broadway at the South Street Theatre in 1980. It received five Villager Awards.

In 1982 my play, *Benpires* (The Vampires), about a street gang, was performed at St. John the Divine. It was nominated for a Pulitzer Prize. I was guaranteed a part in a movie called *Weeds* with Robert DeNiro, and even did some ghostwriting for Al Pacino in *Scarface*. By 1985 the name Juan Shamsul Alam was ringing bells in the theater world. I started teaching theater communication in prisons and schools. I was flying naturally high.

But by 1986 I was exhausted and just plain out of it. Many of my friends were succumbing to the silent monster, AIDS. I needed a break from theater. I decided to take a year's hiatus.

I found myself working part-time, renovating a theater space and combating crackheads and drug dealers who were trying to forcibly sell their wares in my sister's apartment building. A week before I caught the body,* this Latino man was beating his wife and child. I heard the woman's screams and ran to her aid. The man had broken a statue over

---

* *Catch a body:* to be charged with manslaughter or murder.

her head. She looked grotesque. Her head was lumped to twice its size and blood was dripping from her eyes.

"¿Que pasa?" I asked.

"¡Carlos me dio!"* she cried.

When she told me what her husband had done, I went looking for him. I caught up with him in the lobby. He was a thin, wiry man. As soon as he saw me, he pulled out a knife. I sidestepped it and gave him a left hook to his jaw. He went flying out the door and dropped. My nephew, Mike, was nearby. He stepped on Carlos's hand and removed the knife. He then smacked him, which woke him up. Carlos was a druggie. His head had gone from white to black. I didn't know I had hit him that hard.

"¡Te voy a matar!"† he uttered, trying to clear his head.

"Get the fuck outta here before you become a body bag!" I warned him. He staggered off down the dimly lit street.

About an hour later, a squad of cops was knocking at my office door. Mike answered and let them in.

"We have a complaint that a Johnny assaulted a man by the name of Carlos," the Latin cop stated, looking around.

"I'm the guy who hit him," I said. "The creep pulled a knife on me. He was beating up his wife and kids." Carlos's wife forced her way through the army of cops and pointed at her head. She spoke in Spanish. The cop shook his head, then took Carlos's wife aside. After hearing what she had to say, he apologized to me, then left with the other cops.

The following week, I kept a low profile. I had been speaking with a film producer who wanted to buy my play *Impact*. We had discussed options and where and when they would shoot the film.

Meanwhile, I got a call from my ex-wife, Liz, that my son, Hakim, was in the hospital with pneumonia. I had to get to the hospital. I exited the building and got halfway down the street when I was approached by the deceased and two others.

"Juan. Juan, we're taking you to the Bronx Central Booking," Officer Beers said. "I hope you beat this. I hope one day to see you receive an

---

* "Carlos hit me!"
† "I'm going to kill you!"

Academy Award." He let me out of the holding cell, this time gently cuffing me.

Three days later, I met with my court-appointed lawyer, a balding, middle-aged man named Appacella.

"This is very serious, Mr. Alam," he said. "The DA has indicted you on murder in the first degree and possession of a deadly weapon, two counts. I can get you fifteen to twenty-five. You take it to trial, you'll get twenty-five to life. You want to put in a plea, cop to a lesser charge and take the fifteen?" he asked, as if it were no big deal. I sat there, shocked. Shit, fifteen years, I thought. I'm forty-eight. This shit is crazy for self-defense.

"*You* do the fuckin' time!" I shot back.

"All right, then. If that's how you feel," he said, irritated by my response.

"Listen, I know I look like shit to you, the way I'm dressed. But I am somebody, and this somebody reacted out of self-defense. *That's* my plea. I'm not guilty of murder."

Finally, I got in front of the judge. It was all over in five minutes.

I had been to Rikers Island—the House of Blood*—back in 1969, when every man stood his own ground. Word on the bus was that the Bloods, Crips, Latin Kings, and Ñetas were at war. "It's a butcher shop," someone said.

The process was long and tedious. Six hours later, I got to my cell at 8-Upper. I checked out the way things were running, who was who. I called my wife, Sandy. She said that she had given my lawyer all my press clips and awards and published plays. She assured me that things were under control and that the kids were fine.

I was in Rikers Three Building for two months and on my way to court. Always the DA wasn't ready and my bail was too high—seventy-five thousand dollars—so there really was no chance of my getting out. I had to make the best of it.

At Rikers my nickname was Santo, a name given to me by a friend, Lee. He couldn't pronounce Shamsul, so he would say "Santo." The name blew up when I got into a fight and beat up this young guy who

---

* *House of Blood* refers to the Bloods street gang.

had a reputation. Santo was now ringing in the Three Building. My case went to the Bronx Supreme Court. All Supreme Court cases were placed on the Hunts Point Barge, also called MTF. One night, I was sent packing to MTF 3. There I befriended a guy named Indio. He had heard about me and wanted me as part of his Ñeta team of prisoners for inmate rights. Sounded good. I was all for inmates' rights. The Ñetas put me on probation. Those with rank wore a white, black, and red bead.

Meanwhile, I had found a case in the law library similar to mine. It was under the justification law and the person was acquitted of manslaughter. Another person served two to four years. I jotted down this information, and the next time I saw my lawyer, I told him to present my case as justification.

Ever since I caught the body in 1987, my wife and I slowly drifted apart. I knew we would come to an end after that incident. A few times, I'd been caught in shootouts right on my block. One night, Sandy witnessed over a hundred rounds of ammo flying all around me. She thought I was dead. But God was with me. Those around me weren't so lucky.

I knew fifteen or twenty-five years would be too much for her. At forty-six, she was still young. I didn't blame her when she packed up and moved, taking everything with her except my plays and clothes.

By November I was a strung-out junkie and the head leader of the Ñetas. On December 6 I went to Bronx Supreme Court. The ride from Rikers was long and bumpy. It didn't matter. I was getting an offer for my homicide. I prayed on the bus for the first time in a year or so.

My lawyer, Frank, met with me briefly. He was all smiles. "Hi, Juan. How are you feeling these days?" he asked.

"Like shit," I said.

"Well, be thankful you're alive," he replied. "The DA wants to make a deal. He's offering two to six. You want it?"

"Shit, yeah! Where do I sign?" I said.

"We'll go through the formalities inside. We won, Juan. Even though you are doing time, it's better than five to fifteen or twenty-five to life. I'm happy for you. You'll be out in two, you keep your nose clean. You may CR,"* he said.

---

* *CR:* to get out on conditional release.

"I'm just glad it's over, Frank. Now I can start my life again," I told him.

Judge Goldbloom was a stocky, bearded, middle-aged judge with a receding hairline. I entered his courtroom and my cuffs were removed. I waited for the judge to look in my direction. When he glanced my way, I brought my right arm over across to my left and down in a sweeping motion to let him know I was a Mason, or had knowledge of Masonry. (My grandmother was a Mason; her name was Electa, after the eastern star.) Judge Goldbloom had all my press clippings and letters of support from the community. He said something to my lawyer in layman's terms. I pleaded guilty to reckless endangerment and second-degree manslaughter, and the judge handed me a sentence of two to six.

In late January 1995 I let the multitude of brothers at Rikers know that on February 1 we would strike for better conditions there. Sick call was a disgrace, the food they served, nasty. Our visitors were being harassed, and the random abuse by officers among inmates was getting out of hand.

It was 9:00 A.M. when I got back to my dorm. By twelve, I was escorted out of C-73 to HDM 8 block. It seems that informers were working for the captain.

C-74, my next stop, was the House of Pain. Alarms were going off all the time. The Ninja Turtles were always marching in the hallways. The Ninjas were an elite team of special officers. I was in 2-Main House of Pain and placed in a cell where a Ñeta had been blown up (stabbed) by the Bloods. Word came fast that I was in C-74. Pure heroin came my way as a gift, and I made it last all the time I was there. I had a few close calls, as far as war and being attacked, but I always managed to stay afloat.

I had called Maura, a friend I'd met at Rikers. We spoke about my life. She felt she knew the right someone for me and gave me the name of Gloria Rivera and told me to write to her.

By February 14 I was out of Rikers and shipped to Downstate Reception. Here I was stripped of clothes and hair, dressed in greens, and locked in a cell for twenty-one hours a day. It was cold. I've been cold in my life, but this was the worst. I prayed to kick my dope habit. I slept in two pairs of everything and my coat. I couldn't do anything. I lay around Downstate for a week for medical testing, IQ testing, test on top of test. Coming back from chow one day, I was told I was on a draft (being transferred).

Loaded onto a bus and chained down, we were taken on a six-hour ride to Clinton Dannemora, a scary-looking place near the Canadian border that resembles a fort. I adjusted quickly and identified myself to the Ñetas there. They had heard of "Santo 13." (The "13" was for my cell number at HDM's box, and a code.) I was given a position as First of the House.

Before the week was out, we had an incident in the shower where I had to subdue a bully who was trying to rape a white kid. I stuck a shiv right up the guy's rectum and gave him a warning. Another time this black kid was being extorted and I stepped to the individuals—a Puerto Rican named Scarface and a black guy named Star. I lifted my shirt and showed them that if they extorted the kid, I'd put the shiv I was exposing through their hearts. They got the message and packed to another dorm. About the same time, I started received mail from Gloria Rivera. She wrote that she wasn't looking for a man but for a friend, and that she wanted to write me.

After my final testing and placement evaluation, I was sent packing to Franklin. There I was given a position as head security. One night, a group of corrupt Ñetas were kicking, stomping, and beating an old man with rocks. I jumped in and snatched the old man away. "You touch this man again, you're gonna have to hit me too!" I barked at them. All but a guy named Sida retreated like scolded dogs. Sida was fuming.

"Who the fuck you think you are? Huh? That's a violation!" he grumbled.

"Santo 13, that's who!" I said, as I walked the old man over to the gate.

"Thank you. God bless you," the old man whimpered.

The following day, while on my way back from my computer class, I was approached by some Ñetas. They thanked me for saving the old man. They told me he was dying of cancer. "They should have left him be," some said. My popularity was growing, not only among Ñetas but also among Five Percenters,* Muslims, and Kings. Sida had other plans.

---

* *Five Percenters:* members of the Five Percent Nation, a loose-knit black supremacist organization with Nation of Islam roots, considered a gang by some Departments of Correction and law enforcement agencies.

One August night, a brother by the name of Dog provoked a black guy I knew whose name was Rick. I stepped to Rick. He was very apologetic.

"Santo, you know how we pump. We keep it real, son," Rick said. "Dog threw his hands up, so I defended myself. I hit him once and he ran." Rick was a Blood who had been down seven years. He always gave me respect and never lied. I had the incident investigated. Everyone corroborated what Rick had said. So the issue was dead as far as I was concerned.

But the following day, news got to the Annex that Dog was jumped by five blacks. Sida had a field day taking every opportunity to discredit me as president. Things got so out of hand that the Ñetas at the Annex were attacking those at the Main, and vice versa. Civil war among the Ñetas brought on by an insect—Sida.

Some idiot decided to end this fighting. Rick would have to be hit up (stabbed). So that's what it came down to. At a vote, the Ñetas from E-2 decided to blast Rick. Lubio, a black Puerto Rican, and Old Man Attica were now running the show. My body of government was frozen; in other words, there was a coup.

On August 20 at 9 P.M., the Main yard was jam-packed with Five Percenters and Ñetas, along with scattered naturals.* War was declared. The battle would begin at the first sign of darkness. Rick was leaning up against the handrail wall. We looked at each other with disgust and disbelief at what was about to happen. Everyone on the court was dressed in green, including our people. We were armed to the tee. *If I get through this alive, I'm leaving the Ñetas*, I thought to myself.

Darkness was now falling into the yard. The dim lights were the only light we had. Then someone yelled, "¡De corazon!," and all hell broke loose. The two groups met in the open field. We were like wild savages, swinging bar bells and baseball bats at each other. Some guy swung an object at me, catching me on the arm. I countered with a punch to his jaw and a kick to his groin area and dashed off, attacking the enemy. The thuds were loud and the yelling and moaning were just as bad. When a whistle blew and two blasts from a twelve-gauge had everyone on the ground, the yard was transformed into a sea of green—and red,

---

* *Naturals*: inmates who don't belong to any group or gang.

from the blood. Bodies lay everywhere, hurt and banged up. We were rounded up and sent back to our housing units. The next day, there was an exodus to other prisons. I was sent to the Box.

The Box turned out to be a salvation for me. For the first week and a half, locked in for twenty-four hours a day without talking to anyone, I prayed and began to write poetry. I started with *Take the Seed*. I wrote it for Gloria. I felt a true change come over me; the bitterness was leaving, the anger was no more. Gloria helped me a great deal, sending me a letter every other day, so I wouldn't feel alone. I spent thirty-three days in the Box without taking a shower or taking my hour rec. I had lost a lot of weight because the food stunk and was always cold.

Bare Hill, across the street, was my final stop. Here I was warned about my gang activities and sent to Dorm No. 1. I joined Alternatives to Violence and Compadre Helpers and received alcohol and substance abuse training.

My life started to change. I no longer wanted to be part of something that had no foundation. I was tired of the phonies who came stating they were leaders when they were not. One day I told Flaco, a manito, that I was tired and wanted out, that I wanted God back in my life. "I'm devoting my life to Allah," I said.

I went to the parole board and they hit me with two years because of my disciplinary record. I wasn't bitter. I expected that, and besides, maybe God had other plans for me. My counselor spoke briefly with me. He explained why I had been hit. A guy had said I was going to kill him, but it was untrue.

On January 3 I did my *shahada*—pledged myself to God. A week later, I began Ramadan.

Here it is 1997. I'm in a mosque learning how to pray again. God, what I have gone through in three and a half years. Rabana, Lakal, Hamal, my Lord, to thee is due all praise. Since going back to the way God intended, I am different—humble and quiet. I won an award for my poem *Take the Seed*. My play *Midnight Blues* was recently produced in New York, and my film *Purple Paradise* is going into production.

My life is better these days. And I have God on my side.

Reunion

Christopher J. Rodriguez

Stormville, New York

> Spanky,
> This is someone from your past. I've been looking for you
> since '88, kiddo. Please come to the yard Saturday morning
> and I'll tell you all about it. I'll be with "Gotti."
> 50 Lincoln

Thus read the anonymous note I found on my bed late one Friday
evening after returning to my cell from working overtime at my job
with Corcraft. Corcraft is the state agency within the New York State
Department of Correctional Services that uses inmate labor to manufacture everything from office furniture to clothing, bath soap, and automobile license plates. For someone to address me as "Spanky," my
childhood nickname, and know me from "50 Lincoln," the address of
the tenement building I once lived in during my youth in the East New
York section of Brooklyn, he undoubtedly had to be from my past—my
very distant past.

The last time anyone has addressed me as "Spanky" was over fifteen
years ago, during a period in my life when I was an ultradelinquent
Puerto Rican kid from Brooklyn who gave the term *juvenile delinquency*
new meaning. I knew it could be only one person who wrote the note,
and that he was white, for I have never heard a Hispanic or black person, especially from New York City, use the term *kiddo* before.

In spite of my educated guess that it could be none other than Anthony Livieri, my childhood friend and former partner in crime, I arranged to have several men I know arm and position themselves around

the recreation yard to watch my back, in the event that I guessed wrong and was being set up for a surprise attack by an unknown enemy. All night Friday I wrestled with the fact that I had to go out to the yard the following day armed ready to kill someone who may be out to get me. Paradoxically, I found that I had to revert to who I was in order to protect and preserve who I am today. Survival was the only thing that mattered, so I decided to "strap up" (arm myself) and steel myself for battle—or possible death.

I slept fitfully all night. I awoke Saturday morning filled with anxiety, not knowing what kind of situation I was going to confront in the yard in less than an hour. Over the years, I had witnessed countless men stabbed, sliced, hit over the head with free weights, and extorted to no end, and here I was about to go out into the very same yard I so despised, possibly to stab someone.

I found myself becoming angry because I was in an unpredictable situation I did not wish to be in. I, who often reproached other prisoners for acting savagely toward one another, was now thinking of resorting to that very same savagery myself. I cursed myself, my situation, the prison system—the whole damn world for being so cruel and unpredictable. Sure, I could easily not go out to the yard. But then what would I do? There is no place to hide in prison. And what would others think of me?

I couldn't report the perceived threat. In the world of prison, with its own ethics and code of conduct, to report anything to a correction officer that can potentially bring a new criminal court or interdepartmental charge to a fellow prisoner is equivalent to committing social and physical suicide.

I didn't want to sign myself into protective custody (PC). Life in PC is tantamount to solitary confinement: no contact with the general prison population, no sports activities, religious services, academic or vocational classes, or rehabilitative programs that are essential to release on parole. Prisoners in PC are often confined to their cells for up to twenty-three hours a day and allowed out only for visits, showers (three per week), clinic appointments, and the court-mandated one-hour daily recreation period, which consists of walking around a small, isolated yard. In essence, for doing the "right" thing, prisoners in PC are punished. Now, just imagine a prisoner who has twenty years to serve doing his time in this manner. As you can see, I was in a catch-22.

I walked down the corridor that leads to the yard. With each passing step, a moment of my life flashed through my mind—my friends and family, my accomplishments since coming to prison, the changes that had taken place inside me, the maturity that had set in. I thought of my past and of all the wrong I had done to people. How I wished I could somehow apologize to them all and repay them in some way. In the back of my mind, I had always harbored the thought that perhaps one day someone would sneak up behind me and repay me for some previous wrong. I could not believe that these things were going through my mind all because of a little damn note I found on my bed! As I pushed open the door that leads into the yard, a blast of cold air hit me square in the face, as if to remind me that sometimes life is just like that: cold and unforgiving.

Most of the prisoners were walking about the yard. Others were lifting weights. Several men were standing near the wall, talking. All looked calm. Among a small group of blacks waiting on line for the phone were two white men talking. I immediately recognized the taller of the two: he slightly resembled Anthony. Only the man I was looking at was around five feet, ten inches tall and close to 250 pounds. The Anthony Livieri I remembered was five foot two. Before approaching him, I decided to walk around the yard with my Haitian friend, Chinoire, to see if my other friends were posted and ready to go. I was moved when Chinoire, after learning of my situation and its inherent danger, volunteered on the spot to accompany me and, in essence, place his life on the line. Chinoire, a normally humorous but subdued dead ringer for a black Woody Allen, surprised me when he said that he, too, was strapped up and ready to help me combat whatever attack came my way. His gesture made me realize that, for a long time, I had underestimated his courage and loyalty to me as a friend.

Walking the yard allowed me to observe if "Anthony" made any motions or signals to anyone. Only after an hour of watching the man I believed to be my former friend, and the people with whom he spoke, did I approach him.

With fifteen men positioned around the yard watching my back and Chinoire standing five feet behind me with his hand on his weapon, I walked right up to "Anthony" with my hands at the ready and asked, "Excuse me, is your name Anthony?"

He looked me squarely in the face, gently raised his hand and brushed my left cheek. I did not budge or flinch. We merely stared at each other, seemingly in shock, as though trying to figure out where the fifteen years or so of our separation had gone. "Yeah. What's up, Spanky? I saw you come out but didn't recognize you. I said to myself, 'Damn, if that's him, the nigger looks smoked out.' "

By "smoked out" I knew he meant that I resembled an emaciated person addicted to crack cocaine, which made no sense to me, considering that I weigh two hundred pounds and am actually overweight for my height of five-ten. Perhaps he meant that, in comparison to his own weight, I looked smoked out. As for "nigger," he used the normally racially derogatory term in the context that many blacks and inner-city Hispanics—who grow up alongside blacks—do to refer to themselves and others, regardless of racial or ethnic identity. Unfortunately, since the mid- to late-1980s and with the growing popularity of rap and hip-hop, even white kids now find it hip to refer to themselves and others as niggers. I say "unfortunately" because I do not believe anyone should refer to himself or anyone else as a "nigger," just as I do not believe anyone should refer to a woman as a "bitch," "hooker," or "ho." Dr. Martin Luther King, Jr., fought and died for the dream of one day seeing us all come together as brothers and sisters, not as niggers and bitches.

"I can't believe it's you," I said. "What's it been, fifteen years?"

"Something like that. I had you looked up on the computer and found two Christopher Rodriguezes in the system: one had an '88 number and the other a '91 number. I wrote the one with the '88 number, thinking it was you, and he responded with a crazy letter to my mother's house. I figured you'd lost your mind or something."

The mention of his mother brought my own to mind: "You know, my mother died. She died of AIDS-related complications in '03," I said.

"Yeah, her ex, Percy, told me. My mother died too. She had cancer."

"I'm sorry to hear that," I sympathized.

There was a momentary silence between us. I found it sad that we both lost our mothers to terminal illnesses while in prison, unable to be with them during their final moments. I remembered how it tore at my heart when my aunt had revealed to me that one of my mother's last wishes was for me to be by her side in Florida. But my being imprisoned in New York made her wish simply impossible. Remarkably, though, even before knowing of my mother's wish and on the very same day of her passing, I had a profound dream. I dreamed that I was in my mother's hospital room kneeling beside her and holding her hand as I watched her spirit rise above her body and make its way to a world that I can only hope offers greater peace than this one does. Perhaps her wish did come true after all, in a realm that we have yet to fully understand, a realm in which the state is powerless to control the final wishes and dreams of others.

Anthony told me that his older brother, Jimmy Boy, as we called him, was in prison, and that his aunt, Mona, had been sent to Bedford Hills for murder. During my early youth, I had a secret crush on Mona, who is a few years older than I. As Anthony continued talking, I thought of how sad it was that instead of going to college and paving our way to success and a better life, everyone I knew from my past was either dead or in prison.

Through the years, I had made a conscious effort to distance myself as much as possible from my past, to forget it. Now it was standing before me in the person of Anthony Livieri. To think of my past meant to be reminded of the alcohol and drug abuse I had witnessed in my family, the poverty, dysfunction, pain, and loneliness I had often experienced as a child. It took many years of psychotherapy and introspection to overcome the psychological and emotional damage my past had caused me, and now I was standing before a person who represented a part of that past I so wanted to forget.

"Attention in the yards! The yards are now closed! All inmates return to your blocks!" The disembodied voice blasted over the loudspeaker like some omnipotent god.

"Anthony, are you coming out this afternoon?" I asked.

"Yeah, are you? Come out and I'll bring out some pictures. Wait until you see my daughter. She's four years old."

"OK," I agreed. "I'll come out, but I want you to know that I don't normally come out. I can't stand the yard. There's nothing out here but trouble. Besides, it's cold out, and I don't play the 'Let's-stand-in-the-cold-and-shiver' game."

Awaiting the count to clear and the chow run to be called, I kept going over my meeting with Anthony. I found it difficult to believe that I had actually reunited with him after so many years. So much had taken place in my life since the last time we were together. The whole thing seemed surreal, like a dream from which you cannot awaken.

"On the chow!"

I snapped out of my reverie and discovered that I had lost my appetite. I did not join the others in the mess hall. Before I knew it, it was one o'clock and the yard was called.

Anthony was sitting at one of the many picnic tables that dot the yard. He had a big, white, bulging envelope in his hand.

"Yo, Spanky, over here!" he yelled out.

I immediately became self-conscious when he summoned me by my former nickname. "Listen," I said. "Call me Chris. I don't want anyone else calling me Spanky."

"OK, Spanky," he persisted. "Check these pictures out, this is my daughter, Taylor-Marie. Isn't she beautiful?"

I was dumbfounded. The child I was looking at in the picture looked like a veritable angel, and the brute sitting adjacent to me, her father, looked like Satan. "How the hell did you make such a beautiful baby?!" I exclaimed.

"Well, it all started with a hard-on—"

"You know what I mean," I interrupted.

"It's in the genes," he said with a sly grin. "Look at this one . . ."

In picture after picture, I looked at the beautiful little angel he took part in conceiving. I wondered what kind of father Anthony would be to this bundle of innocence, and what kind of future would be hers when she grew up? As he shared the pictures with me, he told me all about Taylor-Marie's mother and of the strong relationship he had with her.

"Anthony, you have to get yourself out there and be a father to this beautiful child," I said. "The game is over. She needs you."

"Believe me, I know, Spanky. This is it for me, kid. I'm not coming back. This is my second time upstate. If I get out and commit another crime and get busted for it, they're going to shut my lights out." He said these words while looking at his daughter's picture.

"Anthony, you have a child now and, from what you've told me, you're married and your wife is solidly by your side. Nothing is worth losing them. It's time to take life seriously. Look around you. I mean *really* take a good look around you. Many of these men here will never again know what freedom is, much less have what you have in your life. Appreciate the people in your life, and yourself, and you will not come back. I would give my left leg to have a woman in my life who sincerely cares for me, and a beautiful child like Taylor-Marie."

We spent the remainder of the afternoon going over the many pictures he had. He showed me photos of everyone I knew from my childhood, and I shared my pictures with him as well. He told me his youngest sister, Farrah, was heavily into rap and hip-hop, and that she once even dated a black guy. I had to laugh when I heard that. Farrah once lived in Woodhaven, a previously white section in our former stomping grounds in Queens, New York, that used to be so racist that if you so much as had too much of a suntan you got chased out of the neighborhood. The only thing that saved me was that Spanish blood runs deep in my family and, unlike many of my darker-hued Puerto Rican brethren, I have fair skin and obvious southern European features. However, not even that saved me from being called a "spic" every now and then.

Anthony lasted less than four months in Green Haven before being transferred to another prison farther north. During those few months, it became apparent to us both that we were no longer compatible. Our characters and personalities were diametrically opposed to each other, and we clearly no longer had anything in common. Whereas I had made every effort in my being to change, Anthony had not and essentially remained the same. Talking with him brought me back to the old neighborhood, an old way of thinking, and I did not want to go back. Eventually, our conversations grew shorter and shorter, to the point that we merely greeted each other. I tried to get him involved in positive programs, even lent him a book, *Houses of Healing: A Prisoner's Inner Guide to Power and Freedom*, all to no avail. He proved too adamant in his ways, and I had to move on.

My time with Anthony allowed me to see myself clearly. Despite where I came from, despite my current circumstances, I had changed. I had become a better person—a more intelligent, articulate, caring, and conscious human being—because I made the decision to do so. I did not allow my humble origins, dysfunctional family background, lack of a formal education, ethnicity, low self-esteem, or imprisonment to hinder me from progressing and educating myself. In prison I had be-friended historians, philosophers, mathematicians, scientists, poets, lit-erary giants, artists, and composers. They became my new friends and guided me along the right path through their words and wonderful, lasting works of art and music. Over time, I felt less and less like a common thief, a murderer, a spic even, and more and more like a man, a whole, conscious, thinking, living, feeling human being with poten-tial—that wonderful possibility that we all possess inside. My new friends made me realize the wonders of the world, the human mind, and my own capacities, and one day forced me to look in the mirror, with tears streaming down my face, and utter to myself in a sotto voce voice, "You can."

The Tale of a Kite

Larry Bratt

Jessup, Maryland

It is spring. In the spring, I fly kites. I do it the way I did as a Boy Scout. I begin by drawing a diamond pattern on newspaper. A tabloid does not provide enough surface area; you need a broadsheet. Through trial and error I have discovered that the *Washington Post* is aerodynamically the best. The pages are thin enough to catch a breeze and billow, but have enough tensile strength to withstand the gusts of air at high altitudes. Next, I cut thin strips of cardboard to be used for the kite's crossbars. When these are secured I affix them to the skin and have my kite. Cardboard has surprising skeletal integrity. For the string I use waxed dental floss. I braid it from three 100-yard tubes of this wonderfully tough, durable, lightweight tether. The wax helps, cushioning the friction against your skin as you let the string out between your fingers. Last, the tail. The stabilizer. I fashion this from old, worn-out bandannas and handkerchiefs that earned their retirement from cold and flu season. I knot them together in a riot of faded color.

Mingling with friends, who provide a protective cocoon, I enter the yard. Suddenly, they disperse and I take off, my round body running as straight a line as the crowds allow. In the first fifty yards, the kite usually rises thirty feet. After two trips, it is eighty feet in the air.

Now I tug on the spool in my hand and the air spits the paper bird higher. I try to do dives and loops. Sometimes, I can coax it to two hundred feet. I can tell by the dental floss, by how much is left. Sometimes I almost run out of string.

I let friends take turns. A thrilling lucidity overwhelms me. I realize that this fine spring day lets me breathe more purely. I imagine the air is as fresh and clean as pre-Columbian air. We are free as children in a playground. And we are momentarily at peace.

In this exuberant melee someone spots a phalanx of guards rapidly approaching. To avoid any unnecessary hassle in case my stealth kite is considered contraband, I cast it adrift and walk away with the crowd. All eyes are cast upward, including the guards'. Murmurs of awe ripple through the grounds as the men make their way back to their cells for count.

I take one last glimpse skyward and swear I see a bright patch of pink. It is spring. In the spring, I fly kites.

Afterword

The semiologist Roland Barthes has written about the terrible and terrifying prospect of "being judged by a power which wants to hear only the language it lends us," and he observed wisely that "to rob a man of his language in the very name of language: this is the first step in all legal murders."* Our legal system still too often robs people of their identity and enables them to be reconstructed in images that better suit the media, or politicians, or the law itself, by taking away their language and voice, by speaking for them or about them, as though they had no claim over the discourse used to represent them and no agency with which to properly produce it.

There are now some two million people in the United States who have traveled the painful path from suspect to defendant to prisoner and currently sit confined in one of the thousands of prisons and jails that our society has constructed for the explicit purpose of punishing them. In addition to the painful places in which they are physically kept, these unprecedented numbers of prisoners are all consigned to a kind of narrative netherworld. Originally the presumed subjects of jargon-filled police reports, then "processed" by the legalese that dominates the criminal court system handling their cases, and finally sent off to prison, where they are reconfigured by the concepts and lingo of incarcerative social control, they have been judged by a power that hears only the language it lends them.

---

* Roland Barthes, "Dominici, or The Triumph of Literature," in *Mythologies* (New York: Hill and Wang, 1972), 46.

245

Indeed, prisoners find their identities denatured at each step along the legal pathway to a prison cell. Their unique history, individuality, complexity, and internal contradictions become increasingly unimportant as they move through this process. They are redefined, flattened, rendered simple and simply scary—a suspect, a defendant, and in the end, a convict. In this way, and only this way, the public is allowed to "know" them, the better to know what to do with and to them, and the easier to do it.

When Jeff Evans solicited this collection of autobiographical writings from prisoners, he asked them to do something people rarely allow them to do in prison—tell honest stories, free of contrivance, and to an audience that would not judge, analyze, label, punish, or condemn them for who they were and what they thought. Evans reports that many prisoners wrote him expressing gratitude for the opportunity to express themselves. I am not surprised. This is one thing among many that nearly all prisoners lack, and many find that it is more painful than most of their other deprivations: an avenue of genuine self-expression.

In fact, most prisoners have been denied a legitimate voice—the opportunity to engage in the process of choosing the words and concepts with which to understand and describe and explain themselves—long before they were ever incarcerated. The economic and social marginality to which many prisoners were consigned early in the troubled lives that eventually led them into prison typically also meant that among the many things that were denied them was legitimate narrative power, or what the linguist Robin Lakoff termed "language rights." And especially once they and their crimes had become the occasion for others to study, comment on, characterize, and pass judgment upon, prisoners had surely lost the "language war."* Whatever the role of thwarted self-expression in the etiology of crime itself—and I concede that we do not yet know a great deal about this—the opportunity and ability to find and use one's own voice seems central to the process of healing and growing and moving beyond.

As anyone who takes the time to listen to them immediately learns, many prisoners take quickly to the task of telling their own stories. But

---

* See Robin Lakoff, *The Language War* (Berkeley and Los Angeles: University of California Press, 2000).

it is not because—as the media would often have us believe—they are particularly skilled verbal manipulators and excuse makers. Some are, to be sure, but most are too unpracticed at exercising language rights to use them as a weapon or even as a defense. Their versions of events and experiences have been rarely solicited and even more rarely believed. Once in prison, however, they find their lives slowed down, and they have few familiar avenues or outlets left with which to channel their frustration—opportunities for constant activity and stimulation are limited, for example, and access to pain-numbing drugs made more difficult.

For the first time in their lives many prisoners find that they have the time and space to think and reflect. Eventually, they want to talk about the sense they have made of what has happened to them and the things they have done, but there are few people around to listen. Prison is not a safe place to share feelings, reveal vulnerabilities, or engage publicly in honest self-reflection. Sometimes they talk openly to people like myself, hopefully patient listeners who spend time writing their social histories and analyzing their experiences. But even knowledgeable social scientists who interview prisoners still write *about* them, and the words and concepts that are finally used are often ours, not theirs. Of course, some prisoners are lucky enough to find people like Jeff Evans who extend a rare invitation for them to write their own histories in their own words. And they tell powerful stories, in part because the pent-up frustration of having so little voice in their own lives can now be released.

There is more to this than catharsis. Whatever else the process of autobiographical writing accomplishes, it forces storytellers to make decisions and choices about the words that they believe best characterize motives and feelings, and to describe accurately events, sequences, connections, and consequences. In this genre, especially, honest writing rings true and powerful, self-delusional writing false and hollow—not just to the reader but to the writer as well. It is a mechanism that allows and even obligates one to a kind of self-awareness and insight that, for many prisoners, their earlier life denied them. This kind of writing is also full of the knowledge and understanding that people badly need in order to appreciate the complex origins of criminal behavior, the motives and desires and hopes and expectations of people whose actions have simultaneously become a mass obsession in our society and a topic about which the general public knows almost nothing that is accurate and true.

Ironically, but perhaps not surprisingly, as the numbers of people placed in our prisons has swelled to astronomical proportions over the last several decades, the amount of accurate information disseminated in our society about crime and punishment has dwindled. Part of this stems no doubt from our increasing dependence on the mass media for "knowledge" about the criminal justice system. The messages have too often been distorted by profit motives (the sensational sells, whether it is accurate or not), political expediency (the use of extremist law-and-order rhetoric has become de rigueur in American politics and threatens to remain so for many years to come), and the recent rise of a powerful prison industrial complex (whose motivation to create widespread crime-related fear and anger is truly substantial and largely without precedent).* These are forces of misinformation and truth distortion, the enemies of honest understanding and wisdom about crime and punishment, and they have been hard at work over the last several decades.

They have been aided and abetted by two developments in law and penology. The first is a legislatively imposed de-emphasis on the exercise of discretion in sentencing criminal defendants, so that their background and character, surrounding circumstances, and reasons for their actions have become increasingly irrelevant in the legal discourse and decision making that will determine their fate. The distinguished Norwegian criminologist Nils Christie put it best:

> A political decision to eliminate concern for the social background of the defendant [as reflected in sentencing guidelines] involves much more than making these characteristics inappropriate for decisions on pain. By the same token, the offender is to a large extent excluded as a person. There is no point in exposing a social background, childhood, dreams, defeats—perhaps mixed with some glimmer from happy days—social life, all those small things

---

* See, for example, Katherine Beckett, *Making Crime Pay: Law and Order in Contemporary American Society* (New York: Oxford University Press, 1997); Nils Christie, *Crime Control as Industry: Towards Gulags, Western Style?* (London: Routledge, 1993); and Craig Haney, "Riding the Punishment Wave: On the Origins of Our Devolving Standards of Decency," *Hastings Women's Law Review* 2 (1998): 27–78.

> which are essential to a perception of the other as a full human
> being.*

In addition to these developments in law that removed any remaining incentive to perceive prisoners as "full human beings" in the courtroom, American correctional policy shifted to a more dehumanizing framework of its own. Under the "new penology" first described by Malcolm Feeley and Jonathan Simon, there was a change in focus away from examining the individual characteristics of prisoners and designing correctional policies and programs to address them (not to say that this had ever been done in an entirely humane or meaningful way), and an explicit and unapologetic move instead not just to punish rather than rehabilitate prisoners but also to what was termed the "actuarial consideration of aggregates."† That is, rather than considering the individual needs of criminal offenders, prison systems and correctional decision makers began to think much like insurance actuaries, predicting risks, probabilities, and likely outcomes for huge populations. Prisoners were no longer seen as people, but rather as masses of raw material to move and manage effectively.

The shifts in legal and correctional policies further constricted prisoners' language rights and rendered their stories irrelevant in most official domains, inconvenient and troublesome in others. As a result, prisoners have been pushed further to the margins of the discourses that are used to manage and control them. To be sure, these changes have facilitated the "processing" and "containment" of large numbers of people, but as masses rather than as individuals. Whatever other information the legal system collects in the course of making decisions about defendants, and whatever data the prison system manages to accumulate in the course of monitoring prisoners during their terms of incarceration, little real knowledge is acquired or retained or disseminated about prisoners as people, about the lives that brought them to these places, or about what kinds of changes would be needed in the society at large if we ever undertook the task of developing a crime control strategy that was not only effective but humane and fair. The

---

* Christie, *Crime Control as Industry*, 138.
† Malcom M. Feeley and Jonathan Simon, "The New Penology: Notes on the Emerging Strategy of Corrections and Its Implications," *Criminology* 30 (1992): 449.

public has increasingly few places to look—and books like this one are among them—for important and honest lessons about crime and punishment.

So, what *do* we learn from the powerful stories Jeff Evans has assembled in this remarkable book? We learn, in a different and in many ways more convincing sense, exactly what many social scientists have been learning over the last several decades about the roots of criminality in our society, lessons that members of the public and political and legal establishment still too often ignore. That is, that social history is in many ways destiny, that people who commit crimes are often victims long before they become victimizers, that extreme deprivation and trauma experienced early in life leave psychic scars that can shape and influence adult behavior, that the places where people are sent to be helped for the problems they develop often do more to make things worse than better, and that structural barriers such as poverty and racism, along with untreated addictions, poor education, and little or no vocational training, sometimes make criminality almost inevitable.*

Distinctive social, historical, or biographical patterns are reflected in the stories that have been collected in this book, and they tell us a great deal about what a humane yet truly effective system of crime control would look like if we ever wanted to construct one. Who are the people who populate our vast prison system, and what do the things they have

---

* The literature on these issues has grown vast over the last several decades. For representative examples, see D. Dutton and S. Hart, "Evidence for Long-term, Specific Effects of Childhood Abuse and Neglect on Criminal Behavior in Men," *International Journal of Offender Therapy and Comparative Criminology* 36 (1992): 129–37; Craig Haney, "The Social Context of Capital Murder: Social Histories and the Logic of Capital Mitigation," *Santa Clara Law Review* 35 (1995): 547–609; Craig Haney, "Psychological Secrecy and the Death Penalty: Observations on 'the Mere Extinguishment of Life,' " *Studies in Law, Politics, and Society* 16 (1997): 3–69; Craig Haney, "Mitigation and the Study of Lives: The Roots of Violent Criminality and the Nature of Capital Justice," in *America's Experiment with Capital Punishment: Reflections on the Past, Present, and Future of the Ultimate Penal Sanction,* ed. James Acker, Robert Bohm, and Charles Lanier (Durham, N.C.: Carolina Academic Press, 1997), 343–77; L. Huff-Corzine, J. Corzine, and D. Moore, "Deadly Connections: Culture, Poverty, and the Direction of Lethal Violence," *Social Forces* 69 (1991): 715–32; A. Masten and N. Garmezy, "Risk, Vulnerability, and Protective Factors in Developmental Psychopathology," in *Advances in Clinical Child Psychology,* ed. F. Lahey and A. Kazdin (New York: Plenum Press, 1985), 1–52; J. McCord, "The Cycle of Crime and Socialization Practices," *Journal of Criminal Law and Criminology* 82 (1991): 211–28; R. Sampson and J. Laub, *Crime in the Making: Pathways and Turning Points through Life* (Cambridge, Mass.: Harvard University Press, 1993); and C. Widom, "The Cycles of Violence," *Science* 244 (1989): 160–66.

in common tell us about crime? Jeff Evans's stories tell us that many of them were poor: "We had no money. We lived on food stamps, welfare, and handouts" ("Where I Come From"). Many of them were "misplaced children, discards from [one] different demented situation" or another ("Turned Out"). But the demented situations that produced them typically had a pattern or destructive logic to them.

These stories remind us that the roots of criminality are long and deep, extending back into prisoners' lives and the traumatic, life-altering experiences to which they were subjected as children. Many of the authors of these stories were raised in families that often abused them. Some were mistreated by fathers or by stepfathers or other relatives who were "physically and sexually abusive to all of my mother's children" ("Where I Come From"). Sometimes the abuse was chronic and enduring and extreme.

Indeed, a number of the authors of these stories were mistreated in one way or another, and their terse descriptions convey a sense of profound, inescapable pain: "Each stage of [my father's] abuse, from fondling to intercourse, was enmeshed with terror. His favorite line was, 'When you stop being a whore like your mother, I'll stop hurting you'" ("Freedom from Within"). When the abuse was not physical or sexual in nature, it was emotional: "No one ever told me why I was taken from foster care. . . . Never mind that I was scared and confused. Never mind that I didn't understand why I was being separated from my brother and sister. It didn't seem to matter to the powers that be that a family was being broken up and that irreparable damage was being done to all of us" ("Turned Out"). And some of them witnessed others—typically their mothers—being victimized as well: "The ensuing times were hectic days of threats, beatings, and police involvement, until one day my mother took a couple of shots at [my stepfather] with a .357 Magnum. . . . He didn't come around after that" ("Where I Come From").

In addition to the abuse, many of them were neglected as well. Some lived in the shadow of an absent father they never knew, one whose "absence played a larger role in my life than his presence ever could have" ("Where I Come From").

Some of the stories seem to glorify a model of choice and agency that conforms to the rhetoric of our times: "Whether a man resides in a castle or a ghetto shack, he is always free to use his internal powers of choice to paint his backdrop and arrange his background music. If he doesn't like the plan he has created for himself, he has only himself to blame" ("The Ice Man Speaks"). But read closer, and you will hear tales of people surviving dire circumstances and unexpected tragedies rather than creating life plans or background music.

Thus, many of the stories also chronicle abusive, unjust treatment at the hands of a larger, uncaring society to which they have been exposed. These were often children to whom nothing was explained, to whom no explanation was owed: "No one said anything. They left it to me to figure out. But I had no time to. My main concern was to overcome my fear." Too often, some felt, the course of their young lives were determined by faceless others: "I was afraid of those who were in control of my life. Those unknown and mysterious people who made decisions about where I lived and who would take me scared me to death" ("Turned Out").

Sometimes they ended up in juvenile institutions, places that assumed control over lives spinning hopelessly out of control, but also places where they might as easily encounter "a world of competitive, misplaced, evil, confused, and angry children" as one filled with stability. They were raised in juvenile institutions that forced them to develop intimidating façades, skilled in the art of confrontation and intimidation: "I taught myself how to be what I wasn't." The stigma of mistreatment runs deep, and early in life many people become convinced they will never be rid of it. Juvenile institutions sometimes provide a sense of belonging—among others who have had similar experiences and share the stigma—but at the price of alienating them even further from the larger society: "I'd never fit in anywhere but in an institution. I just couldn't relate to what everyone else was about. They all had family, friends they grew up with, memories of a childhood, and all that normal stuff. I stayed outside the perimeter of that inner social circle. I had nothing to offer them" ("Turned Out").

There is a starkness to much of the writing here that shocks readers out of a sense of complacency and forces them to question the conventional assumption that people who have done bad things have just made bad choices out of their own sense of selfishness or entitlement or superiority. There are harsh, raw sentences that most people do not expect to find in autobiographical sketches: "Shortly after I turned eleven, I witnessed my mother kill a man" ("Where I Come From"). And there are honest admissions about twisted motivations, looking back and thinking about a victim who "didn't realize that I was getting ready to take his life because I wasn't satisfied with my own" ("Turned Out").

Evans has included revealing accounts about how much of the pain gets numbed with drugs and alcohol, by people who turn to the only things they know or have been taught about how to cope. One drug addict "allowed heroin to envelop my life. Nothing else mattered. The hole in my soul grew large, and I attempted to fill it with drugs" ("Freedom from Within"). Another has a brief moment of self-awareness before he shoots up again and drifts off into another drug-induced reverie: "I catch a glimpse of myself in the mirror. I see big eyes, full of fear, a body shaking terribly, sweat running down my face. I stand there, gazing in the mirror. I can't move. I'm frozen, staring at myself in the mirror. I feel shock. How did my life get like this?" ("A Shot in the Dark").

These stories sugarcoat very little and leave you with little doubt about where failing to address these issues will lead us. There is as chilling a story as you will ever read about gangbanging, the matter-of-factness with which young kids with nothing else to look forward to or invest in turn to violence at the slightest provocation, out of some misguided sense of gaining "power" and "respect" in a world that virtually guarantees they will be given neither. But even someone as deeply committed to this lifestyle as Lalo Gomez also confesses that

> when I was gangbanging and drug dealing, I never really got to enjoy true peace or happiness, because I was always looking over my shoulder, never trusting anyone, and always wondering if someone was lurking in the shadows waiting to put a bullet in me. No matter how hard I tried to do good, the bad would always surface and prevent me from achieving that. I wanted to have my cake and eat it too. But no gang member can serve two masters. I tried and fell flat on my face, hard. ("Back in the Dayz")

But these are also stories written by prisoners, not just by people who have committed crimes. As such, they reveal important insights about the conditions to which criminal offenders are exposed in our society once they have been incarcerated. They raise important questions about what we can expect once people have paid their debt to society and return to live among us again, as the overwhelming majority of prisoners eventually do. Here, then, are the descriptions of the places we put people our society finds inconvenient, now that we have decided our mandate is to do little more than "contain" and punish them. Since they are there for punishment, we concern ourselves little with the "containers" we provide:

> **Three hundred of us were packed into a room that could safely and comfortably hold fifty. Men lay on the cold brick floor, end to end and side to side. Once in place, one could scarcely move without touching his neighbor intimately. We were sardines in a can. The scene, almost ghostly in the dim yellow light of the exit signs, showed men moving and writhing to get comfortable on the cold stone floor, not as men, but as some great undulating worm, squirming and struggling to get free of something. ("Martha")**

The voices in these stories come out of places where we send people to be "quarantined behind concrete and steel, encircled by silhouettes of faceless men in uniform and armed guard towers" ("Notes from Life and Death"). The experience takes its toll on those who endure it: "Prison is a world of unending sorrow. . . . When the steel gates are slammed closed and the lights are extinguished at the end of yet another day of pain and irrelevancy, the true nightmares begin" ("Christmas: Present"). And they tell us, in words we are naïve to try to ignore, that "truth now told, I am a creature inextricably tied, in both failures and accomplishments, to what has happened to me in prison" ("Notes from Life and Death").

For those folks in the larger society who still harbor illusions about prison being pleasant places, or worlds in which it is easy to do and pass time, the voices of these prisoners will disabuse them: "The 'hard time' [is] when you want out so bad it's hard to breathe and your heart beats fast and your temperature rises. Then you have to get hold of yourself and calm down and try to put your mind at ease. You have to pretty much forget what is out there, and what your place in it was" ("1937").

The futility of a warehouse prison system that holds prisoners for unprecedented lengths of time but does little or nothing to address the problems that brought them there is not lost on them either, and it should not be lost on us:

> Many prisoners who only need a drug or alcohol program become more institutionalized with each mandatory return. If one is caught having a beer while on parole, he is considered in violation and is usually returned to this same programless environment. No help. No rehabilitation. Only warehousing. You become accustomed to being returned. It is no longer a deterrent but rather a way of life. You begin to look for ways to beat the system instead of cooperating with it. ("Revolving Door")

In short, these are some of the most riveting first-person accounts of what it feels like to be caught so completely in the cycle of addiction that you literally cannot think from one moment to the next about anything except the rush, the high, the craving; or what it's like to be so immersed in a gang culture that you cannot comprehend the arbitrariness of your cause and the callousness with which you have come to pursue it; or trying to decide whether the prospect of escaping from the place where you are being held is more frightening than what will happen to you if you don't; or the thought process by which a prisoner prepares to engage in what he knows is senseless but unavoidable violence because he has been threatened (or thought he had been) and is trapped by the fact that "there is no place to hide in prison" ("Reunion").

Yet, although these prisoners tell tragic tales of horrible, soul-destroying abuse, they do not use their lives as the basis on which to make crass excuses: "I committed crimes for money because I was lazy, self-destructive, and felt rules were for other people" ("Where I Come From"). These are people who take responsibility for what they have done and who they have become. "I have just recently become aware of who and what I am. There is no sad story or tragedy to blame. I made myself into the person I am" ("End of the Game"). Indeed, despite having had too little agency in the making of self when they were young, they worry that they are forever doomed by the labels society has attached to them and the permanence of the prison system's view, despite having achieved maturity and purpose at a time in life where the opportunity to use them is running out: "When I think of my upcoming parole board appearance, I think about who I was and who I am. I would like to be seen in the present, not in the past. I don't want the thirty-five-year-old to be judged again for what the sixteen-year-old did. I don't want the man to be punished for what the teenager did. They're two different people" ("Upon Completing Twenty Years").

Moreover, through all the tragic tales of abject deprivation and abuse, and of mistreatment at the hands of a larger society and its institutions, a fundamental humanity can be heard and seen here. Perhaps the most important lesson of stories like these is that the people who tell them share so many of the same emotional reactions, fears, and reflections as those who read them, including crime victims who have learned to hate and despise them, legal decision makers who have undertaken to judge and condemn them, and members of the public who have embraced the media's demonic imagery of prisoners so fully that they have lost sight of who our prisoners are and whence they came.

These stories are uncooked and unfiltered. They come without the baggage of social science analysis, and in many instances they have not been processed through the conventions that more practiced, stylized writing imposes. Instead they are raw and real, and they speak about a variety of experiences inside and outside the walls of the prisons in which they were written. They are basic, honest stories, unalloyed and unsettling. Despite their simplicity, many of these stories are haunting; they will stay with you for a long time. They pose more questions than they answer. But they represent the opening up of a long overdue dialogue between the free citizens of this society and the two million people we have chosen to lock away. These are the voices of people who are denied voice in our society. And there are increasing numbers of them. Books like this help to give them voice and personhood, both things that are effectively denied them. It is in our interest and theirs to try hard to hear them.

Craig Haney
University of California, Santa Cruz

Editor and Contributors

Jeff Evans was raised in western Massachusetts and attended Middlebury College and New York University. His writing has appeared in the *Los Angeles Times, USA Today, Spotlight, Europa Times*, and *Gist*. An accomplished musician and ear training coach, he lives in New York City.

Jimmy Santiago Baca is the author of several books of poetry including *Immigrants in Our Own Land, Martin & Meditations on the South Valley*, and *Set This Book on Fire*. His screenwriting and film production credits include *Bound by Honor* (a.k.a. *Blood In Blood Out*), *Mexican Roots, The Pancho Gonzales Story*, and *El Chamaco*. He lives with his two children in Albuquerque, New Mexico.

Craig Haney is a professor of psychology at the University of California, Santa Cruz. Trained as a lawyer as well as a psychologist, Haney writes widely about social justice and civil rights, the psychological effects of incarceration, capital punishment, and the social histories of persons accused and convicted of violent crime.

Steven King Ainsworth has served over a quarter of a century behind bars, the past twenty years on San Quentin's death row.

Juan Shamsul Alam was nominated for a Pulitzer Prize in 1982 for his play *Benpires*. He is the recipient of the PEN American Award, the Bronx Brio

Award, and the McDonald Award, and received five Villager Awards for his play *Bullpen*. Ollanty Press published his play *God's Children* in 1993. Mr. Alam was released from prison in October 1997.

John Beasley is serving an eighty-year habitual sentence at Sumter Correctional Institution in Bushnell, Florida. An arts and crafts enthusiast, he has two children. He enjoys working out and studying the Bible.

Lamont Bolder is serving a three-year sentence at D. Ray James Correctional Institution in Folkston, Georgia. Before his incarceration, he was a machinist. He plans to attend college and become a counselor for troubled youths when he is released.

Jaye Bookhart was a ward of New York State for eighteen of his forty-five years. While behind bars, he was a teacher in the pre-GED program and a counselor/facilitator for men's self-empowerment groups. He was released from prison in 1999 and is a newly reconnected father to his beloved daughter.

Larry Bratt originally was serving two consecutive life sentences for homicide at the Maryland Correctional Institution in Jessup. Recently he won a sentence modification and was given twenty-five years time served. Once a hedonist, he is now a yoga practitioner and a literacy tutor and works with the originators of the Touchstones Discussion Project, which uses great works of literature to encourage open discussion among prisoners nationwide. He was a second-place winner in the nonfiction category of the 1998 PEN Writing Award for Prisoners and has 135 national and international bylines, twenty-eight with the *Washington Post*. He married in December 1998 and plans to move to London with his wife after he is released.

Robert Chambers writes: "Somewhere in Manhattan. A cool, summer night. Many years ago. There's nothing to mark the spot, no signs for a person to read. But somewhere, somehow, just down the street from my front door, I entered someone's nightmare. I'm thirty-one years old and I've spent ten years looking for a way out. I've grown, I've learned, and I believe on certain nights, when the sky is full of stars and the winds are just right, I can hear the faint sounds of civilization. I can't eat. I can't sleep. I've got a pack of cigarettes, but no matches. Still, I go on."

Oscar Chandler is now serving his sentence at a minimum-security facility at Vienna Correctional Center in southern Illinois. An avid reader, he reached his eighty-second birthday in May 2000. He is scheduled to be released from prison in December 2000.

Barry Conn began his prison term in 1981. A Michigan court convicted him of burglary and sentenced him to twenty-five to fifty years in prison. His earliest release date falls in 2001. He attends college through correspondence with Ohio University's college degree program and remains focused on maintaining good health and improving his chances for success once the system finally releases its grasp of him.

C. Kaye Ferguson is serving a life sentence for killing her physically abusive boyfriend. Her hobbies include making toys for underprivileged children, horticulture, and being a jailhouse lawyer. When not in legal mode, she enjoys painting watercolors and writing poetry and short stories.

Christopher Lynn Garner writes: "After crying out for help, I turned myself in and confessed to my crimes. My confession was used against me and I was sentenced to three fifteen-year prison terms. Since my incarceration five years ago, I have earned numerous certificates, several in theology, from a university that offers correspondence courses. My objective is to reach others who are suffering and to share with them the simplicity in accepting deliverance from the shackles of hell."

Ronald Gearles served ten years for armed robbery. He is currently working for a commercial collections firm in New Hampshire. He plans to continue taking courses in an undergraduate college program he began in prison.

Lalo Gomez was born in 1963 and raised in Chicago. He joined a gang at twelve, started selling drugs at fourteen, had a son at eighteen, and was arrested for a gang-related murder at nineteen. He has been in prison ever since. His interests include writing and business, and he says he would like to start his own communications company when he is released. He holds an associate's degree in general education and is scheduled to be released in 2008.

Richard Hinger is a fine art painter who, since his conviction, has turned to writing short stories as well. He hopes one day to see justice fairly administered in his case, which he stands by as self-defense.

Jennifer Howard was released from Rockville Correctional Facility after serving two years and nine months. She currently resides in Indianapolis, where she plans to attend Indiana University–Purdue University for journalism.

Michael Wayne Hunter was arrested for homicide in 1982 at age twenty-three. He was convicted and sent to San Quentin's death row two years later. His first story, "Mother Teresa on Death Row" was published by *Catholic Digest* in 1993 and reprinted in *Prison Life* a year later. "Another Day" won the 1995 William James Award for prose, the first of three consecutive William James Awards for the author. Mr. Hunter is presently engaged in a new trial.

Kevin James has been serving time for a parole violation at the D.C. Department of Corrections since 1993. He will graduate from the University of the District of Columbia with the class of 2000, having earned a bachelor of arts degree in urban studies. He hopes to further his education upon his release.

Robert L. Johnson is serving a sentence for grand theft at San Quentin State Prison. Before his incarceration, he was a computer analyst.

Tonya Star Jones is presently incarcerated in the Illinois Department of Corrections for aggravated battery and murder—crimes, he maintains, he didn't commit. He currently heads a support group called UPLIFT (Using Persuasive Language in Fighting Terrorism), dedicated to ending gangbanging in America. A civil rights activist and a drum major for justice, his motto is "Change your mind and you'll change the world."

Benjamin La Guer is a writer at the Norfolk State Penitentiary. A magna cum laude graduate of Boston University, his writing has appeared in *Boston* magazine, *Boston Poet*, *Worcester* magazine, and the *Columbia Review*. In 1998 he won a PEN Award for his memoir "A Man Who Loves His Mother Loves Women."

Kevin Lee served time in the California prison system. Prior to his conviction, he was a supervisor at a cannery in the San Francisco Bay area. He was released in 1999 and plans to attend college. His first child was due in April 2000.

Mike McLane was released from prison in 1997 and currently lives in Oregon.

Charles C. Mallos (a.k.a. Frankie Lee Bass) is serving multiple life sentences for numerous robberies and escapes. His hobbies include ink and pencil drawings, writing fiction, and reading. He has no parole date, but he keeps the dream of freedom alive. He hopes one day to publish some of his fiction. "That would be the next best thing to getting out of prison."

D. Michael Martin was the winner of the memoir category of the 1996 PEN Writing Award for Prisoners. He is currently serving a ten-year sentence at the Saginaw Correctional Facility in lower Michigan. He plans to pursue a career as a paralegal after his release.

Darlene Nall is serving time for involuntary manslaughter at the Ohio Reformatory for Women in Marysville, Ohio. She holds an associate's degree in liberal arts from Urbana University. Her greatest education and motivation have been her constant prison fellowship and ministry. After her release, she hopes to start a youth program on 110th Street with her son.

Jeff Parnell has been serving a life sentence since 1986 for first-degree murder. He is presently residing at the James Crabtree Correctional Center in Helena, Oklahoma. Prior to his arrest, he owned two pizza delivery shops located in Pryor and Nowata, Oklahoma. He is scheduled for a parole hearing in 2001. If released, he plans to reopen his delivery business.

Christopher J. Rodriguez is currently serving time at Green Haven Correctional Facility in Stormville, New York. In addition to teaching classes in business, history, and human potential, he facilitates workshops for the Alternatives to Violence Project, Inc. He is also a member of the Project for a Calculated Transition, a self-empowerment inmate organization that holds biweekly discussions with students and professors from Yale Law School. His future plans include earning a college degree and pursuing a career in business.

Michael Ross's death sentences were thrown out after the Connecticut Supreme Court ruled that the state had withheld crucial psychiatric information from the jury. After the court ordered that a new penalty phase take place, Ross fired his public defenders and, wishing to spare the families of his victims further emotional distress, entered into an agreement with the state to accept the death penalty. In May 2000 Mr. Ross was resentenced to death after a jury handed down six verdicts of death in the murders of four of his eight victims.

Phillip Santiago was released from New York State's Camp Gabriels Correctional Facility in September 1998. He enjoys writing, Latin dancing, fishing, and tennis, and plans to pursue a Ph.D. in behavioral science. He is currently a substance abuse counselor in New York City.

William Skeans, Jr., is serving part of his eight-and-a-half-year sentence at Marcy Correctional Facility in upstate New York. His interests include reading, writing letters, and awaiting the day when he becomes a free man, a condition he hopes to attain permanently.

Jon Marc Taylor spent over thirteen years in the Indiana prison system and is now serving a consecutive forty-year term in Missouri. Widely published in academic journals, magazines, and newspapers, he has received both the I. F. Stone and Robert F. Kennedy Awards in journalism.

Lou Torok entered San Quentin Prison in 1948 at age twenty and is in prison again in Kentucky, at age seventy-three. He writes, "I feel that my own life—abandoned at birth, raised in foster homes and orphanages—might show that others' struggles are not unique. Perhaps they can learn from mine."

Ronnie Turner is serving fifteen years for rape. Prior to going to prison, he was a police officer. He earned an associate's degree in paralegal studies while in prison and is currently working as an inmate legal helper at Southeastern Tennessee Regional Correction Facility in Pikeville.

Nemo Valentine, a.k.a. "K-9" and "Butch the Butcher," is originally from New Orleans. He completed two tours of duty in Vietnam and received two Silver Stars. About those years he says, "I bagged twenty-six ears. It was just madness. But I was never ambushed." He attended Wayne State and Marquette Universities. In his spare time, he reads the dictionary. He is serving a life sentence.

Easy Waters was sentenced to twenty years to life for felony murder as a nonkilling accomplice. He has won seven PEN Writing Awards and four Honorable Mentions in nonfiction, drama, and poetry. He also won the 1998 Mellen Poetry Prize for his epic poem *Black Shadows and Through the White Looking Glass*.

Cheyenne Valentino Yakima (a.k.a. "Ice Man") is serving a life sentence in Georgia for a January 1982 bank heist. A native of Detroit, Michigan, he grew up in Atlanta, Georgia, and earned a Ph.D. in theology from the American College of Metaphysical Theology. He writes, "I hope my story will prevent young people from making the same mistakes I made as a youth. Learn from the mistakes of others; you won't live long enough to make them all yourself."